IN DEFENSE OF THE GOSPEL:

BIBLICAL ANSWERS TO LORDSHIP SALVATION

[Revised & Expanded Edition]

LOU MARTUNEAC

Copyright © 2006, 2010 by Lou Martuneac

In Defense of the Gospel [Revised & Expanded Edition]
by Lou Martuneac

Printed in the United States of America

ISBN 9781597818674

Library of Congress Cataloging-in-Publication Data
Martuneac, Lou, 1955 - In defense of the gospel: biblical answers to lordship salvation / Lou Martuneac.p.cm. Includes bibliographical references.

All rights reserved solely by the author. The author guarantees all contents are original and do not infringe upon the legal rights of any other person or work. No part of this publication may be reproduced, stored in a retrieval system, or transmitted in any form or by any means-electronic, mechanical, photocopy, recording, or otherwise-without the prior written permission of the author or the publisher, with the exception of brief excerpts in magazine articles and/or reviews. The views expressed in this book are not necessarily those of the publisher.

Unless otherwise indicated, Bible quotations are taken from the King James Version of the Bible. Copyright © 1981 by Thomas Nelson, Inc.

www.xulonpress.com

TABLE OF CONTENTS

FOREWORDS xi

A NOTE FROM THE AUTHOR xiii

ACKNOWLEDGEMENTS xix

WHY THIS BOOK? 21
    HISTORY AND BACKGROUND 21
    WHY NOW? 22
    WHY DID I PUBLISH? 24
    LETTING THEM SPEAK FOR THEMSELVES 25
    MILK AND MEAT 27
    HOT LEAD 27
    CALVINISM 28
    HOW DOES THIS BOOK COMPARE? 29
    ZANE HODGES, BOB WILKIN & THE GRACE
        EVANGELICAL SOCIETY 31

INTRODUCTION 37

IS UNDERSTANDING THE GOSPEL ESSENTIAL? 43

WHAT IS LORDSHIP SALVATION? 47
    WHY IS IT CALLED "LORDSHIP
        SALVATION?" 50
    WHAT IS THE MOTIVE FOR LORDSHIP
        SALVATION? 52

WHAT ARE SOME OF THE RED FLAGS? 53
HOW SHOULD YOU RESPOND WHEN YOU
   HEAR THE LORDSHIP GOSPEL? 55

WHAT IS THE CALVINISM CONNECTION? 60
   LORDSHIP IS ROOTED IN CALVINISM...............60
   DOES REGENERATION PRECEDE FAITH? 63
   IMPOSSIBLE DECISION! 67
   WHICH CONCEPT OF GOD IS GREATER? 68

SALVATION AND DISCIPLESHIP: IS THERE A
   BIBLICAL DIFFERENCE? 72
   WHAT IS A DISCIPLE? 72
   A STRANGE PARADOX INDEED! 73
   WHO REALLY PAYS? 76
   THERE IS A COST, BUT WHERE IS IT? 81
   HOW ARE SALVATION AND
      DISCIPLESHIP DISTINGUISHED? 85

CAN THERE BE A CHRISTIAN WHO IS CARNAL? 101
   WHAT IS THE MEANING OF THE WORD,
      "CARNAL?" 101
   CAN THERE BE BOTH CARNAL AND
      SPIRITUAL CHRISTIANS? 102
   DO CARNAL CHRISTIANS APPEAR IN
      THE BIBLE? 109
   STATEMENTS FROM NOTABLE
      COMMENTATORS. 117

WHAT IS BIBLICAL REPENTANCE? 123
   PREFACE. 123
   WHAT BIBLICAL REPENTANCE IS NOT 124
   HOW DOES THE LORDSHIP ADVOCATE
      DEFINE REPENTANCE? 125

- WHAT IS THE MEANING OF THE WORD "REPENTANCE?" 129
- I THESSALONIANS 1:9-10 133
- DISCUSSING THREE ASPECTS OF REPENTANCE 139
- CAN REPENTANCE AND FAITH BE SEPARATED? 142
- FURTHER EXPLANATION OF REPENTANCE. 143

WHAT IS BIBLICAL SAVING FAITH? 150
- WHAT IS THE MEANING OF THE WORD, "FAITH?" 150
- WHY DOES LORDSHIP FOCUS ON THE "KIND" OF FAITH? 151
- IS LORDSHIP'S "SAVING FAITH" A BARTER SYSTEM? 154
- DID THE APOSTLES PREACH LORDSHIP'S "SAVING FAITH?" 155
- WHY IS THE "OBJECT" OF OUR FAITH ESSENTIAL? 158
- EXAMPLES OF SAVING FAITH 160

THE RICH YOUNG RULER 169
- ETERNAL LIFE AND SALVATION. 170
- THE YOUNG MAN'S APPROACH. 170
- A SINCERE QUESTION: OR IS IT? 172
- THE FIRST SET OF COMMANDS AND THE MAN'S RESPONSE. 172
- THE LORD'S CONVICTING WORDS. 176
- NOT OF WORKS! 178
- DOES CHARITABLE GIVING LEAD TO SALVATION? 182
- CONCLUSION. 185

ROMANS CHAPTER TEN 188
    WHAT IS CONFESSION AND WHAT ARE
        WE TO CONFESS? 188
    HOW DOES THE BIBLE DEFINE
        "BELIEVE?" 190
    IN THE CONTEXT OF ROMANS 10:9-
        WHAT IS THE MEANING OF THE
        WORD, "LORD?" 195
    WHAT DO NOTABLE MEN SAY ABOUT
        ROMANS 10:9? 200

ACTS 16:30-31 205
    HOW DOES LORDSHIP CONFUSE
        "BELIEVE" WITH SUBMISSION? 206
    WHAT IS THE BIBLICAL ORDER? 209

IS IT THE CHRISTIANS DUTY TO FIGHT FOR
THE FAITH? 212
    IS CONTENDING A BIBLICAL
        MANDATE? 216
    IS CONTENDING ALSO FOR TODAY? 218
    IS IT RIGHT TO JUDGE? 220
    CONTENDING: WHAT IF I DO, WHAT IF
        I DON'T? 222
    RECOMMENDED BOOKS. 227

A HEART TO HEART WITH PASTORS AND
CHRISTIAN LEADERS 228
    WHY LEARN ABOUT LORDSHIP? 228
    HOW DO I RESPOND TO LORDSHIP? 232
    WHAT ABOUT SPURGEON'S STAND FOR
        DOCTRINAL PURITY? 243
    SHOULD DOCTRINAL DEVIATIONS BE
        DISMISSED? 247

A FINAL WORD 249
    THE DISCONNECT 250
    POWERFUL & PENETRATING SUMMARY 253
    ERRORS IN OFFSETTING PAIRS 256
    BLOGGING IN DEFENSE OF THE GOSPEL 256
    WHAT IF YOU HAVE BEEN WRONG? 257
    WHAT IS MY HOPE FOR YOU? 258

APPENDIX A- WHAT ABOUT CALVINISM? 261

APPENDIX B- DOES REGENERATION
PRECEDE FAITH? 280

APPENDIX C- SUMMARY OF LORDSHIP
SALVATION FROM A SINGLE PAGE 284

APPENDIX D- THE RELATIONSHIP BETWEEN
GOD'S GRACE AND LORDSHIP LEGALISM 287

APPENDIX E- THE "NO LORDSHIP"
COUNTER-CLAIM 290

APPENDIX F- A REVIEW OF
WALTER J. CHANTRY'S *TODAY'S GOSPEL:*
    AUTHENTIC OR SYNTHETIC? 294

APPENDIX G- "UNLESS THE LORD JESUS IS
LORD OF ALL HE IS NOT LORD AT ALL." 298

APPENDIX H- DOES "FINAL SALVATION" SERVE
AS A COVER FOR WORKS-SALVATION? 303

SELECTED BIBLIOGRAPHY 307

FOREWORDS

The church purchased by Jesus Christ must have a clear understanding of salvation by grace through faith. It is the very heart of the gospel message. Some have turned the grace of our God into lasciviousness or unbridled lust (Jude 4), thinking that since they are saved and going to heaven they can live any way they please. Others, rightly concerned about rampant carnality in the church, have distorted the simple gospel message and have burdened the sinner with additional requirements that extend well beyond simple faith in the crucified and risen One. The unsaved person is told that if he does not turn from sin, surrender, have a willingness to obey, fulfill the demands of discipleship, etc., then he cannot be saved. Sadly, the focus is turned away from the all sufficient, finished work of Christ which is the sinner's only resting place. Lou Martuneac has presented the biblical balance between these two erroneous and extreme positions. In this confused theological climate, his book is like a breath of fresh air and deserves a wide reading.

George Zeller
Middletown Bible Church

Lou Martuneac's book *In Defense of the Gospel* is urgently needed because many pulpits today are inundated with erroneous teaching concerning the Gospel of Jesus Christ—the Lordship Salvation advocates have perverted the Gospel by issuing requirements for salvation that God never issued! Yet the Gospel is the major theme of all of Holy Scripture; it must be preached from the pulpit in order for any church to say or claim it is a gospel-preaching church. "What is the Gospel?" and "What must one do to be saved?" are two questions every born again believer in our churches should be able to answer *doctrinally from the Scripture* without hesitation. If you are concerned lest our churches lose the Gospel of Jesus Christ and leave the only message that can save a lost sinner, then this fair-minded, objective, and biblical book must be read with prayerful consideration!

Dr. Chris Shepler, Pastor
Victory Bible Baptist Church, Irmo, SC

A NOTE FROM THE AUTHOR

What is more important than a proper understanding of the gospel of Jesus Christ? Serious-minded Christians understand that the stewardship of the gospel is a great responsibility, and that the presentation of the gospel to the unsaved man must be based on a precise understanding of the biblical doctrine of salvation. History repeatedly demonstrates the tendency of well-intentioned men and women to react to false doctrine by embracing an equally heretical belief at the opposite end of the theological pendulum swing. First year Bible college students are taught to keep a balance in their theology, because once they lose their balance they will go off into extremes.

This is not a question of a weak gospel verses a strong gospel, but of the one true gospel standing apart from all other false gospels. If the weak gospel erred by omission, the strong gospel equally errs by addition. All witnesses for Christ desire true conversions. In my zeal to secure more genuine conversions, however, I do not have the liberty to alter the terms of the gospel. Any alteration of the gospel either by omission or addition must be rejected. In the evangelical community there are two polar opposites in the debate over what constitutes the gospel message that leads to eternal salvation. These extremes are commonly known or referred to as "Easy-Believism" and "Lordship Salvation."

Many have been alarmed at the increasingly meaningless presentation of a gospel that seems to ignore the person of Christ, the sinfulness of man, the finished work of Christ and the pending judgment of God. This gospel calls men to salvation when they have been given only a vague idea of just what they need to be saved from, who Christ is and what He did to provide salvation. This is a reductionist interpretation of the gospel, i.e. the content of saving faith with which I strongly disagree. This is the so-called "Easy-Believism" gospel, which in one of its most extreme forms is propagated by the Grace Evangelical Society (GES) Dr. Bob Wilkin, Executive Director. The GES gospel is commonly known as the *"Crossless"* or *"Promise-ONLY"* gospel, which was originated by Prof. Zane Hodges (1932-2008). Later we will take a closer look at the teaching of Zane Hodges and Bob Wilkin.

While I do not hold to any reductionist approach to evangelism and would admonish those who seek quick uninformed decisions for Christ to repent of their error, this document has been produced to address the opposite extreme, Lordship Salvation.

Dr. John MacArthur is arguably Lordship Salvation's best-known advocate. Dr. MacArthur defines the core of Lordship theology with statements such as, "Salvation is for those who are willing to forsake everything."[1] Beginning by speaking in a paraphrase on behalf of Jesus Christ, in what he believes is the Lord's offer of eternal life MacArthur said,

> "I will save you from eternal Hell. I will give you spiritual blessings all of them right now and forever if you will abandon yourself, all your hopes, all your dreams, all your ambitions...."
> Would you give up your life here to have eternal life.... Is your salvation important enough? Would you give up your life if that is what it takes?[2]

Those statements may at first glance appear balanced and orthodox, but instead they define a gospel that is foreign to the Scriptures.

Many who hold to Lordship Salvation label the views that are antithetical to their own as "Easy-Believism," "No Lordship" or "Cheap Grace." They leave no room for the possibility of a balanced position. In recent years I have heard men preach evangelistic sermons in which the words, "faith," "repent," and "believe" were rarely or not used at all. The emphasis was on behavior in the form of commitment and submission of one's life to Christ's lordship. For many Lordship advocates committing one's life to Jesus, for Him to rule and reign, is the way an unsaved man receives the gift of eternal life and begins a relationship with God.

> The relationship with God starts always by acknowledging His supremacy, His Lordship. And this morning there is someone in here that needs to give God the throne and let Him rule. And when you do you will have from God exactly what you need to have, a relationship with Him.... You've got to have innocent hands and a heart empty of sin, and the only way is to have the righteousness of Christ, and that is a gift from God, when you admit, 'God you rule in my life. The man who is willing to make an entrance for God is the man into whom Christ will come and rule.[3]

> Christ went to the cross, our sins were transferred to Christ and He bore them for us. He paid in full the entirety of our sin debt and there is nothing we can contribute to our eternal salvation. But you need to understand the terms for receiving this gift. If you want to receive this gift it will cost you the total committment (*sic*) of all that you are to the Lord Jesus Christ. "There are many here who think they are saved, but are not; they have never really done business with God.... I want to single you out in the midst of this crowd. Have you taken up a cross in

order to follow after Christ? Have you recognized your own sinfulness, acknowledged that God's judgment is true, have you acknowledged Christ's right to rule your life? Have you submitted to the lordship of Christ? Have you really come to the end of self? Because Jesus does not begin until you end." Lawson's message was as convicting an evangelistic appeal as I've heard in a long time.[4]

When a man teaches that the lost must come to Christ for salvation with anything in addition to faith, believing and repentance, he has adopted a "works" philosophy and has departed from the "faith which was once delivered" (Jude 3). If you hear a man condition the reception of eternal salvation upon a commitment to self-denial, cross bearing, following, obedience, allegiance and/or submission, mark it down: he is teaching works salvation, he is teaching Lordship Salvation.

As you read through the pages of this book please bear in mind that the Lordship Salvation controversy primarily revolves around **the requirements for salvation, NOT the results of salvation**. A genuine conversion should evidence itself in genuine results. New believers will vary in levels of growth, but growth should be evident to some degree. The primary focal point of controversy, however, is Lordship's requirements for the reception of eternal life, i.e. how to become a Christian.

This revised and expanded edition of *In Defense of the Gospel* is my best effort to compose a comprehensive and balanced biblical answer to Lordship Salvation. I have succinctly defined the key issues, terms and positions, while avoiding the temptation to get bogged down in heavy theological discussions. Another primary motive for the production of this book has been to educate and equip the pastor in our pulpits, the congregation in the pews, professors and their students in Bible college classrooms so they all can first recognize and then effectively resist the teaching and spread of Lordship Salvation.

Throughout this work I have avoided the frothy rhetoric that sometimes enters into the debate to provide objective and balanced scriptural answers. I have presented and defended the historic position on the gospel that has been held throughout church history.[5] I have sought to bring clarity to the issue. It is my hope and prayer that this book will become a helpful resource for pastors, the Bible college classroom and concerned Christians across the broad spectrum of evangelical Christianity.

None of my work should be taken as a personal attack on any advocate of Lordship Salvation. I have treated the Lordship advocates charitably and with respect. I have no axe to grind, no grudge to settle and harbor no personal animosity toward any advocate of Lordship Salvation. My remarks will not be about the character of those who teach Lordship Salvation, they will instead be about what the advocates of Lordship Salvation are teaching. Personality is not the issue! The debate is focused solely on the doctrine of the gospel.

In the pages to follow we will consider many things both doctrinally and practically. My final authority, however, is the Word of God.

Among Christians, there is plenty of room for diversity over a relatively broad spectrum of theological positions. There is, however, no room for diversity when we come to the major doctrines of the Bible. The gospel is one of those major doctrines. The eternal destiny of every human soul is dependent upon a clear understanding and presentation of the gospel. I have written *In Defense of the Gospel* to provide the biblical answers to Lordship Salvation.

Lou Martuneac

ENDNOTES:

1. John MacArthur, *The Gospel According to Jesus*, p. 78.
2. YouTube, "Kirk Cameron Interviews John MacArthur," http://www.youtube.com/watch?v=M_YYNuMN5II&NR=1, (accessed January 10, 2010).
3. Evangelist Mark Kittrell, *The Salvation of a Seeker*, a sermon recorded at Marquette Manor Baptist Church, Sept. 2004.
4. Steve Lawson, *The Cost of Discipleship: It Will Cost You Everything*. A sermon recorded Feb. 18, 2007 at the Resolved Conference. Commentary and sermon transcription by Tim Challies. Challies: Informing the Reforming, http://www.challies.com/archives/liveblogging/resolved-2007/resolved-confer-3.php, (accessed February 20, 2007; January 20, 2010.)
5. For an extended treatment of Lordship Salvation's teaching as it relates to church history see Thomas G. Lewellen: *Has Lordship Salvation Been Taught throughout Church History*? Bibliotheca Sacra, Vol. 147, #585, Jan-March 1990.

ACKNOWLEDGEMENTS

The author wishes to extend a special thanks to Pastor Kevin Brosnan, Dr. John C. Whitcomb, Pastor Tom Stegall and Dr. Charlie Bing.

Pastor Kevin Brosnan and I served as missionaries together in Johannesburg, South Africa. He and I were President and Vice President respectively of the Calvary Baptist Theological College. Because Lordship Salvation was introduced through subtlety in the college class rooms Pastor Brosnan asked me to write an official position paper for the college on the issue. He encouraged me to undertake this project and gave me the encouragement to see it through. Several times, I felt the job was done or I just got weary of writing. It was at those times that the Lord prompted Kevin to encourage me to continue. He also added valuable research and composition to several sections that provide technical information about the theological significance of Greek words and syntax. I owe a debt of gratitude and thanks to Kevin Brosnan for completion of the original manuscript in 1998.

Dr. John C. Whitcomb reviewed the original edition's manuscript and made several contributions. Dr. Whitcomb has also enthusiastically endorsed my work on this subject.

Pastor Tom Stegall provided various contributions to the new sections on Zane Hodges, Bob Wilkin and the Grace Evangelical Society. Pastor Stegall also made some valuable suggestions toward the chapter *What is Biblical Repentance*.

Having written the initial version of this book in South Africa, I found it very difficult to find much in the way of resources for either side of the Lordship Salvation debate. Through e-mail with an acquaintance, I was put in touch with Dr. Charlie Bing (GraceLife Ministries) who had written a doctrinal dissertation entitled *Lordship Salvation: A Biblical Evaluation and Response*.

Dr. Bing and I corresponded several times via e-mail. Briefly I shared with him how Lordship Salvation had been introduced into our Bible college, and that I was writing an official position paper to redress the matter. I also related my frustration in not being able to find many resources in South Africa on the subject. To assist me in my research, Dr. Bing sent to me a copy of his dissertation in book form. His dissertation has been a valuable resource in the writing of this book. A number of the quotations from the Lordship advocates are drawn from the pages of Dr. Bing's dissertation.

My wife exhibited great patience, for many times she heard me say, "I am done writing," but later hear me retract that statement. There were occasions when she was awakened in the wee hours because I was up clacking away at the keyboard. A new thought had taken shape, and I dared not commit it to memory awaiting sunrise over the Dark Continent. Liz, thank you for your patience and understanding as I labored through this project.

WHY THIS BOOK?
History and Background

My first contact with the interpretation of the gospel commonly known as Lordship Salvation came in 1988. During the months of June, July, and August, I worked at a Christian radio station (WPCS) on the campus of Pensacola Christian College. At that time, Dr. John MacArthur's radio program *Grace to You* was part of the programming schedule. The doctrinal position on the gospel presented in his book *The Gospel According to Jesus* resulted in the station's management deciding to drop *Grace to You* from the broadcast schedule. I was asked to handle all contacts to the station in regard to its having dropped Dr. MacArthur's program. This required my having to become familiar with the book and its doctrinal ramifications, which lead to the programming change.

Prior to my arrival in South Africa for missionary service in October 1996, it had not occurred to me that I would encounter the Lordship position there. Very shortly after my arrival, however, during the doctrinal exam of a candidate for graduation from our Bible college, I learned that fellow American missionaries had taught Lordship Salvation through subtlety in the college. We also learned that the Lordship position was beginning to gain ground in South African Bible believing churches. As a result the college president, Pastor Kevin Brosnan, and I decided that this issue needed a biblical response.

Pastor Brosnan asked me to draft two documents that would state the "official" position in two areas of doctrine for the college. The first was to address Calvinism, the second Lordship Salvation. What I initially thought would be documents of about four to five pages each quickly became major works on the subjects. The Calvinism document ended up being approximately sixty pages; the Lordship position paper became this book.

Why Now?

The Lordship debate was raised to a level previously unseen when Dr. John MacArthur published *The Gospel According To Jesus* in 1988. While the Lordship Salvation position was not new in 1988, its promotion by such a prominent personality provided for the position a new credibility and unprecedented influence across a broad spectrum of evangelical Christianity. Five years later MacArthur wrote, "I expressed a desire that the book would be a catalyst for discussion and ultimate resolution of the issues."[1] Shortly after the release of *The Gospel According To Jesus* several men wrote in response to it, and the "discussion" was on.

Since the initial response, however, there has been very little published from those who reject Lordship theology that comprehensively addresses the on-going Lordship controversy. The pro-lordship advocates, on the other hand, have remained resolute in their propagation of the Lordship interpretation of the Gospel. In the introduction to his book *The Gospel According to the Apostles*, released in 1993 and again in 2000 John MacArthur wrote,

> But there's no denying that these matters pertaining to the gospel are fundamental and therefore our disagreement on them is a serious matter. Surely everyone involved will agree that we cannot simply act as if nothing of importance is at stake.
>
> Ultimately, the best forum in which to air this kind of doctrinal dispute is through careful, biblically reasoned dialogue, preferably in written form.[2]

MacArthur is right: this is serious, there is much at stake, and the written forum is the best place to deal with "this kind of doctrinal dispute." John MacArthur has published five major works on the Lordship position beginning in 1988 with his first edition of *The Gospel According to Jesus*. The fifth and most recent (May 2008) is the *20th Anniversary* edition of *The Gospel According to Jesus*. Walter Chantry and Kenneth Gentry, both long time Lordship advocates, have had their works on the subject reprinted and are on Christian bookstore shelves today. There has not been an "ultimate resolution of the issues." John MacArthur recognizes that this issue has not gone away, and for Lordship theology to be promulgated and defended it must be done in the written forum. MacArthur, Piper, Chantry, Gentry, Boice, Horton and other pro-lordship men such as Pastor Steve Lawson are keeping the issue alive, and thereby capturing the minds of Christians across a broad spectrum of evangelical and fundamental Christianity. Regrettably, a comprehensive, balanced biblical answer to Lordship teaching has been, for the most part, missing from the written forum for years. Lordship advocates, therefore, have dominated the discussion on this issue. There is a danger of surrendering the issue and allowing the pro-lordship advocates to achieve an "ultimate resolution" in their favor by default.

My personal experience has been to find that many pastors and Christian leaders have not studied the issue and consequently do not fully understand what the Lordship interpretation of the gospel is. Others have not yet recognized the issue as, "a serious matter," with much "at stake." Consequently, many pastors often do not recognize Lordship preaching, and subsequently do not know how to respond when confronted with Lordship Salvation. My desire is to equip Christians in the pulpit and in the pews to recognize and understand Lordship Salvation, and how to respond from the Scriptures.

Why Did I Publish?

This book was never initially intended for broad publication. We had a doctrinal problem at the Calvary Baptist Theological College in 1996 and I was asked to write a paper to convey the official position of the college. Once my writing was complete we distributed copies to our faculty, staff and students. Over the years more people heard of my manuscript and I received requests for copies and was asked by some who read it to consider making it available to the Christian community at large.

For years I did not want to pursue publication because I was questioning my own motive. Never did I want to allow for pride or ego to enter into the decision to release this project for a wide audience. The calls for and interest in my book continued to flow in. Upon the release of the original edition of this book the number of contacts increased significantly from people who wanted to discuss the issue because they encountered Lordship Salvation and were not sure of how to deal with it.

Two incidents convinced me to publish the original edition. First, in September 2004 a preacher I had known for years spoke in my home church's pulpit on a Sunday morning. He brought an evangelistic message, which was purely the Lordship interpretation of the gospel. I was shocked because I had heard him preach the gospel on several occasions over the years, and always heard him preach a solid grace oriented gospel message. The 2004 sermon was far askew from the gospel of grace I once heard him preach. Within minutes I realized he had been drawn toward and adopted the Lordship position.

The second incident is, in my opinion, more serious with far reaching implications. Many young people are raised in homes and churches that reject Lordship Salvation. After high school graduation some of these young people head off to Bible college. Some of these students come home after their freshman year having been introduced to and indoctrinated into the Lordship position. The parents and pastors of these young people are shocked and saddened when this occurs. There are families I know of personally who have suffered this experience. Imagine the distress you might experience if after 18 years of training in your home and local church to balance your child's theology to then have those years of training unwound in just one semester at Bible college. It is irrefutable that professors and their graduate assistants at some of our Bible colleges are teaching Lordship Salvation to unsuspecting young people with impunity. When teachers and their assistants work at turning the hearts and minds of young people toward Lordship Salvation that is a line crossed that demands a response. This book, *In Defense of the Gospel*, is my response!

Letting Them Speak for Themselves

Whenever you engage the theology of Lordship Salvation you can count on mantra like cries of "misrepresentation" from many of its advocates. You can quote verbatim and in context Lordship's advocates letting the stark truth of their message unfold in their own terms without commentary and still you are going to hear cries of misrepresenting what they teach and/or believe. Throughout this book I quote liberally from some of Lordship Salvation's best-known advocates. I quote them for a simple reason: I want them to speak for themselves. This way there is no possibility for misrepresenting what they believe. You can read from their own books and sermons what they believe, how they articulate what they believe and how they arrive at their conclusions. Through this approach any charges of "misrepresentation" or creating a "straw man" have no merit.

As I define and answer Lordship Salvation I will be drawing primarily from the teaching of Dr. John MacArthur because he is this generation's most prolific apologist for the position. To date MacArthur has published five major works on Lordship Salvation, plus numerous articles and sermons in audio, print and online formats. Please understand that Dr. MacArthur's character is not under scrutiny or being called into question, MacArthur's teaching, however, is. As far as I know John MacArthur's character is above reproach in both Christian and secular circles. Although I am grieved over his interpretation of the gospel I am grateful for his personal testimony especially since so many preachers have lost theirs and in so doing have harmed the cause of Christ.

You will also find that I often quote from well-known commentators who reject Lordship theology. This I have done because I am not well known and I want my readers to realize there are many godly, highly trained and recognizable preachers who have for decades taken a stand against the doctrinal errors in Lordship's theology.

Milk and Meat

Since I began writing the first draft of this book I asked myself: Do I write for those with theological training or for those with little to none? One of my editors questioned me in regard to which group I was writing for. My answer now is quite direct. I want any readers, regardless of their level of theological training to receive a blessing and instruction from what I have written. When I began composing the manuscript I knew I was going to address an audience from first year Bible college students to men with advanced theological training. It, therefore, seemed appropriate to incorporate materials for both groups.

To be sure there is "meat" for the pastor and theologian. If I had not written to some degree for those with theological training I felt their attention might drift. The one drawback is that there will be some technical areas that may leave those without formal Bible training a little overwhelmed. Even in those areas, however, I did try to present the meatier material in such a way that all might benefit to one degree or another.

Much of what I have written is along the order of "milk" for the relatively new or untrained believer. Peter wrote, "As newborn babes, desire the sincere milk of the word, that ye may grow thereby," (1 Peter 2:2). It is this group that I had primarily on my mind because it is this group that is most at risk for falling into the trap of Lordship Salvation.

Hot Lead

I was not so naïve to think that I was going to be well thought of by the advocates of Lordship Salvation once my book was published. One Evangelist told me, "Once you release this book the hot-lead is going to be flying in from every direction." When the first edition of this book was released (Feb. 2006) I found out that the Evangelist was right in his prediction. The same thing happened to my missionary co-worker and me in South Africa when years before in 1998-99 we were forced to take a stand on this issue there. If you take a stand in the defense of doctrinal purity you will not win a popularity contest. Your motives will be called into question, and you are likely in for a spiritualized tar and feathering.

I also suspected and found that some who were in agreement with what I have written did not appreciate that this work raised the level of awareness and debate. I know of several preachers who instead of contending for the faith (Jude 3) prefer to ignore this issue and would like to see it go away. If Lordship Salvation would just go away like a passing trend I would not have spent countless hours on this project. The Lordship position has steadily gained ground, its spread insidious and it must be met head on to counter the damage it is doing among the ranks of Bible believing Christians, their churches, Bible colleges and fellowships.

Calvinism

Calvinistic theology appears and is addressed in the pages of this book because Lordship Salvation is rooted in Calvinism. It is not my desire or intention to needlessly enflame Calvinistic brethren and thereby create a distraction from the main thrust of this book. I do, however, want to be very clear at the outset that I reject all five points of Calvinism as I understand them. In the few instances where Calvinism is referenced, I made a sincere attempt to be fair. Men who are Calvinistic in their theology will not agree with my remarks on Calvinism, I do not expect them to. My primary desire is that they will carefully examine and prayerfully consider this polemic on Lordship Salvation.

If you are unfamiliar with Calvinistic theology or know little about it, it may be helpful for you to read Appendix 'A' *What About Calvinism?* You will find it beneficial to have a basic understanding of Calvinism because it will help you understand the interrelationship with Lordship Salvation.

How Does this Book Compare?

With the release of Dr. John MacArthur's *The Gospel According to Jesus* (1988) debate and controversy broke out across a broad spectrum of evangelical Christianity over the definition and terms of the gospel. Prior to the release of MacArthur's book the debate over Lordship Salvation was conducted under the general radar, and essentially limited to pastors, commentators, theologians and Bible College dorm rooms. Because John MacArthur was such a well known and respected pastor/teacher *The Gospel According to Jesus* generated a ground swell of interest among believers who were hitherto unaware of the controversy over the Lordship interpretation of the gospel.

Men in evangelical and fundamental circles, who rejected MacArthur's Lordship interpretation the gospel, began to respond. In Fundamentalist circles for example, Dr. Ernest Pickering wrote, *Lordship Salvation: An Examination of John MacArthur's Book, The Gospel According to Jesus.* Although brief, it is, in my opinion, a must read and a very helpful critique of MacArthur's book. Dr. Pickering's review is available through Baptist World Mission, Decatur, AL.

Men from a segment of evangelical Christianity known as the *Free Grace* movement also began writing in response to the Lordship interpretation of the gospel. In

1986 the Grace Evangelical Society (GES) was founded. The GES was initially made up of men who would identify themselves as part of the Free Grace (FG) community. Among them would be notables, such as Zane Hodges, Michael Cocoris, Charles Ryrie as well as the founder and current Executive Director of the GES, Bob Wilkin. Upon the release of MacArthur's *The Gospel According to Jesus*, the GES became the most vocal and prolific opposing voice. The *Journal of the Grace Evangelical Society* began in 1988 and has since published dozens of theological articles, many in response to Lordship Salvation. Hodges, Wilkin, Cocoris, and to a lesser extent, Charles Ryrie, were among FG men writing from an opposing position. Dr. Ryrie's book *So Great Salvation* is arguably the most reliable refutation of Lordship Salvation from that period, and I cite it a number of times in the pages of this book. Many on the Lordship side of the debate, while disagreeing with Ryrie's view consider him more balanced than others in the Free Grace camp, especially Hodges and Wilkin.

Dr. Charlie Bing wrote extensively on the Lordship issue in his Ph. D. dissertation titled: *Lordship Salvation: A Biblical Evaluation and Response*. Dr. Bing did some excellent work in his dissertation and I frequently cite from it in the following pages.

Other helpful volumes on the gospel in general exist such as Dr. Robert Lightner's *Sin, the Savior, and Salvation*. Lightner's book, however, dedicates only a brief single chapter to the Lordship issue. A recent contribution (2008) to the Lordship debate was written by Dr. J. B. Hixson. Hixson's *Getting the Gospel Wrong* dedicates a significant chapter titled *The Performance Gospel* to the discussion and refutation of Lordship Salvation.

Zane Hodges, Bob Wilkin & the Grace Evangelical Society

Zane Hodges was a major figure in the Lordship Salvation debate. It is not my desire to take anything away from the few helpful contributions Zane Hodges made to the Lordship debate. There are, however, grave concerns among many, even in the Free Grace community, over the extreme and polarizing positions Hodges articulated in various books and publications. These extreme views that follow are positions that have been adopted and propagated by Bob Wilkin and the Grace Evangelical Society (GES).

Zane Hodges totally eliminated the necessity of repentance from the conversion experience. In his book, *Harmony With God* Hodges took the position that the process of repentance may be a preparatory step in coming to salvation, and should be evident in the life of a believer, but a lost man can be born again apart from repentance by any definition.[3] Hodges also said he no longer held to the "change of mind" view of repentance. Hodges said there is only one answer to the question, "What must I do to be saved?" Hodges emphatically stated that repentance is not part of the answer.

Bob Wilkin does not believe sin separates the lost from everlasting life. In his opinion, no one will be condemned because of their sins. They will be condemned because their names are not in the Book of Life.[4] At the GES website you will find their official interpretation of the gospel. The article is titled, *How Can I Be Saved?* In that article this statement appears,

> Jesus died on the cross for the sins of the whole world (John 1:29). He has removed the sin barrier which separated us from God. However, we still lack spiritual life, eternal life. To get that life, we must simply believe Jesus for it.[5]

The specific details of the GES statement have not been fleshed out by Wilkin. One can, however, see the connection GES is making. Since sin is not an issue anymore, the only problem is life, thus all we need to believe is who can give that life.[6] Knowledge of our sin and/or believing in Christ's payment for it is logically unnecessary in their system. They appear to think Christ's death merely removed sin as a barrier between God and men, but that (for some reason) men still need forgiveness from God. In the blogs one of the most theologically extreme members of the GES wrote, "One needs eternal and temporal forgiveness of sins even though Christ died to remove the barrier." This, of course, makes no sense.

That teaching on sin leads to the area of most serious concern with Hodges, which is his unique interpretation of the gospel that has come to be known as the *"Crossless"* or *Promise-ONLY* gospel.

The *Crossless* gospel can be summarized as follows: The lost man simply needs to believe a man named Jesus guarantees eternal life, and by believing in nothing more than the promise of eternal life he (the lost man) is born again. According to GES the lost man does not need to know, understand or believe that he is a sinner under the wrath of God. The lost man does not need to know, understand or believe in the Person (deity) of Jesus and what He did to provide salvation. The GES insists the Lord's titles; "the Christ" and "Son of God" do not mean or infer His deity. The GES defines "the Christ" in purely functional terms, such as "the Guarantor of everlasting life." Furthermore, *Crossless* gospel advocates believe a lost man can openly reject the Lord's deity, but still be born again. They consider any one can be saved including the Jehovah's Witness, Mormon and Hindu "no matter what misconceptions" and heretical beliefs they hold about the Lord Jesus Christ. In an evangelistic setting any misconception the lost man has about Jesus, including open rejection of His deity, is to be "put on the back burner" and left there.

The *Crossless* gospel is the most egregious form of reductionist soteriology ever introduced to the New Testament church by one of its own; namely the late Zane Hodges. Examples of *Crossless* gospel teaching can be found in sources from various GES members including a two part series by Hodges available through the *Journal of the Grace Evangelical Society*. The series is titled, *How to Lead People to Christ*. The most comprehensive answer to the *Crossless* gospel is Pastor Tom Stegall's *The Gospel of the Christ: A Biblical Response to the Crossless Gospel Regarding the Contents of Saving Faith*.

Finally, Hodges believed a large number from the Church will be cast into outer darkness where there will be weeping and gnashing of teeth. Hodges taught that the antichrists mentioned in 1 John 2:18-19, 22-23 could very well be saved people!

Some of the books by Hodges that present these positions noted above are Hebrews and 1, 2, 3 John in *The Bible Knowledge Commentary, The Hungry Inherit, The Gospel Under Siege, Absolutely Free, Grace in Eclipse,* and *The Epistles of John*.

The polarizing statements from Zane Hodges and Bob Wilkin have essentially negated and removed them and the Grace Evangelical Society from any meaningful contribution to the Lordship debate. Because of the grave concern I have with the teachings of Zane Hodges I decided it would be in the best interest of accomplishing my goals for *In Defense of the Gospel* to make only a brief mention of Hodges, expose his errors, refrain from citing him in response to Lordship Salvation and strongly caution my readers about the reductionist position Hodges articulated on the gospel.

There was at one time a general sense of unity in the Free Grace movement centered on the GES. That unity began to erode beginning with Hodges's and Wilkin's shift on the doctrine of repentance. The disintegration of unity escalated greatly over Hodges's *Crossless* interpretation of the gospel. In my reading of various Lordship related books, websites and blogs I discovered a widespread perception that Zane Hodges, Bob Wilkin and the GES are perceived as the voice of the entire Free Grace movement. This is a serious misnomer! This long running misunderstanding is steadily and successfully being corrected. Today the Free Grace movement is fractured along lines of division over the troubling views of Zane Hodges. Scores of balanced Bible-believing pastors in the Free Grace community, who reject Lordship Salvation, also reject the reductionist teaching of Zane Hodges on the content of saving faith.

The Free Grace Alliance (FGA) is leading the way in the Free Grace community to create distance from and set the GES apart from the rest of the Free Grace movement. In April 2009 the FGA published the following official statement at their website:

> After much discussion and reflection, the FGA Executive Council has concluded that in the light of misunderstandings in our broader Christian community, it is important for us to issue the following statement:
>
> > *The Free Grace Alliance is not associated with the Grace Evangelical Society and does not endorse the GES Gospel (also referred to as "crossless" or "promise only" by some). We invite those who share our heart for the Gospel's clarity and declaration, of both the Person and Work of Christ, to join hands with us.*[7]

The GES is a rapidly shrinking and isolated cell of theological extremists. Because of the egregious errors of Zane Hodges and Bob Wilkin it would be a serious misunderstanding to conclude that either of these men speak for or their reductionist soteriology is representative of the broader Free Grace movement.

For additional articles that detail the troubling teachings of Zane Hodges, Bob Wilkin and the GES please visit my blog *In Defense of the Gospel* at www.indefenseofthegospel.blogspot.com.

ENDNOTES:

1. John MacArthur, *The Gospel According to the Apostles*, p. 14.
2. Ibid, pp. 14-15.
3. Zane C. Hodges, *Harmony With God: A Fresh Look at Repentance*, pp. 53-55.
4. Bob Wilkin, "The Way of the Master," *Grace in Focus* 22 (July/August 2007): 1, 4. See also Zane C. Hodges, "The Sin of Unbelief," *Grace in Focus* 22 (November/December 2007): 4.
5. Grace Evangelical Society, "How Can I Be Saved?" http://www.faithalone.org/gospel.html (accessed January 19, 2010).
6. Bob Wilkin, "The Way of the Master," 4. See also John Niemela, "Objects of Faith in John: A Matter of Person AND Content, Grace Evangelical Society Conference, Dallas, TX, February 28, 2006.
7. Free Grace Alliance, "GES Gospel Statement: The Grace Evangelical Society." http://www.freegracealliance.com/about-fga/ges-gospel-statement (accessed January 19, 2010).

IN DEFENSE OF THE GOSPEL: BIBLICAL ANSWERS TO L*ORDSHIP* S*ALVATION*

INTRODUCTION

---

1 Cor. 15:1-4 Moreover, brethren, I declare unto you the gospel which I preached unto you, which also ye have received, and wherein ye stand; By which also ye are saved, if ye keep in memory what I preached unto you, unless ye have believed in vain. For I delivered unto you first of all that which I also received, how that Christ died for our sins according to the scriptures; And that he was buried, and that he rose again the third day according to the scriptures.

This passage defines the gospel: Jesus, God's Son, died for our sins, was buried, and rose again the third day according to the Scriptures. This is the gospel message, which the Corinthians received from the Apostle Paul.

> Modern Christendom, devoid of the biblical gospel it once preached, leaves men empty and hopeless. Salvation is not to be found in any of the world's so-called 'great religions.' But the glorious good news that 'Christ died for our sins' rings clear across twenty centuries. The death, burial, and resurrection of Christ provides a way by which sinners can be justified with God (Rom. 4:24, 25).[1]

In a heartfelt cry, the Philippian jailer asked, "Sirs, what must I do to be saved?" The answer is the same today as it was centuries ago in that midnight hour when the Apostle Paul replied, "Believe on the Lord Jesus Christ, and thou shalt be saved."

Through the centuries, Satan has tried to confuse, cloud, and complicate the gospel of Jesus Christ. For many the problem begins when one's mind is corrupted from the simplicity that is in Christ.

> 2 Cor. 11:3-4 But I fear, lest by any means, as the serpent beguiled Eve through his subtilty, so your minds should be corrupted from the simplicity that is in Christ. For if he that cometh preacheth another Jesus, whom we have not preached, or if ye receive another spirit, which ye have not received, or another gospel, which ye have not accepted, ye might well bear with him.

There are religious systems that claim to be the way of salvation. Many are foreign to the Bible; others appear to be akin to the biblical plan of salvation. So we are left asking: How can we know what the one true gospel of Jesus Christ is? The acid test is in the simplicity that is found in Jesus Christ. A system that seeks to add a ritual, a sacrament, a commitment to or performance of any good works to the finished work of Jesus Christ can be identified as a false gospel through the addition. The difference boils down to either adding what man must do, or receiving what Christ has done.

Dwight L. Moody (1837-1899) may well have been the most profound evangelist of all time. During his 40-year ministry it is estimated God used him to win a million souls to Christ. He founded the Moody Bible Institute and Moody Church in Chicago, launched a great Christian publishing business, established a world-renowned Christian conference center, and inspired literally thousands of preachers to win souls and conduct revival meetings. It is said that D. L. Moody once rode on a train seated next to a Mormon missionary. They discussed their conflicting views on what they believed to be the gospel. The Mormon explained what his system required man to do to earn the Mormon view of eternal life. D. L. Moody, on the other hand, showed the missionary from the Bible that everything had already been done by Jesus Christ, and all man had to do was believe and receive the free gift of God. After a while Moody said, "Sir, I find our differences can be summed up with just two letters: You are depending on what man must 'do', the Bible says it has been 'done.'" The finished work of Jesus Christ is God's provision for the salvation of mankind.

Is salvation a gift that costs us nothing? Is salvation received by faith alone? Is "unconditional surrender," a "commitment to leave sin" and a "full exchange of self for the Savior" necessary for the reception of eternal life? If we find upfront commitment and surrender are additions to the gospel, then the grace of God is frustrated.

> Galatians 2:21 I do not frustrate the grace of God: for if righteousness come by the law, then Christ is dead in vain.

In the Old Testament as well as in the New Testament, man has always received salvation by faith alone.

> Habakkuk 2:4 Behold, his soul which is lifted up is not upright in him: but the just shall live by his faith.

In Romans 4:3, 9 we read that Abraham was saved by faith:

> For what saith the scripture? Abraham believed God, and it was counted unto him for righteousness... for we say that faith was reckoned to Abraham for righteousness.

Can the Lordship interpretation of the gospel be traced back to New Testament times? Lordship Salvation advocates attempt to trace their theology back to the time of Christ in part by redefining passages such as Luke 9:23; 14:26-7, 33 as though they are evangelistic appeals meant for the unsaved. These passages are in fact meant to give instruction to born again Christians as to how they might live as disciples of Christ. This theme will be fully developed in the following pages.

In 1993 John MacArthur released another apologetic for the Lordship position titled *The Gospel According To The Apostles*. Advocates of Lordship Salvation claim their system is the gospel once preached by the Apostles. Multitudes of evangelicals have rejected Lordship theology as a latecomer and departure from the gospel of grace. Is it possible that these have misunderstood the teaching on Lordship Salvation? A close examination of Lordship theology raises grave concerns over whether this is the gospel of grace as taught in the New Testament, and proclaimed by the Apostles. Is Lordship Salvation the New Testament gospel; or, as many respected pastors and teachers are claiming, is it another deviation from the gospel of Jesus Christ?

The New Testament is very clear: human effort and/or a commitment to the performance expected of a Christian have no role in the definition of the faith that saves or what the lost must do to receive the gift of eternal life. The Bible teaches that a lost man is saved by God's grace when he repents and places his faith in the substitutionary death and bodily resurrection of the Lord Jesus Christ. The Bible says the work of redeeming man from the penalty of sin has been done.

> John 6:28-29 Then said they unto him, What shall we do, that we might work the works of God? Jesus answered and said unto them, This is the work of God, that ye believe on him whom he hath sent.

> To Jewish questioners, obtaining eternal life consisted in finding the right formula for performing works to please God. Jesus directed them to the gift of God that could be obtained by faith in Him. Again there is a similarity to His conversation with the Samaritan woman: "If you knew the gift of God" (John 4:10). Jesus contradicted directly the presuppositions of His interrogators.[2]

Jesus rejected works and taught that one must believe. In verse 29 above, Jesus uses the word *believe*. This is the same Greek word (πιστευω, *pisteuo*) that is found in Romans 10:9. This passage in Romans will be studied later in this book.

> Romans 10:9 That if thou shalt confess with thy mouth the Lord Jesus, and shalt believe in thine heart that God hath raised him from the dead, thou shalt be saved.

The Apostle Paul, under inspiration, taught that our salvation is by faith plus nothing. Paul writes,

> Ephesians 2:8-9 For by grace are ye saved through faith; and that not of yourselves: it is the gift of God: Not of works, lest any man should boast.

The message is the same: salvation is not by works or the resolve to perform works, but by faith. Any message of faith plus works, real or promised, is wrong and condemned by the Lord Jesus Christ, as well as by the Apostle Paul.

ENDNOTES:

1. Fred Moritz, *Preach the Word*, October-December 1999.
2. Merrill C. Tenney, *The Gospel of John*, *The Expositor's Bible Commentary*: Vol. IX, p. 75.

IS UNDERSTANDING THE GOSPEL ESSENTIAL?

Some Lordship Salvation advocates, in my experience, attempt to brush aside legitimate doctrinal queries into what the Lordship gospel really is. They suggest questioning Lordship is a debate over nonessentials. Since a man's eternal destiny hinges on what the biblical plan of salvation is, what could be any more essential than a clear understanding of the gospel?

It is crucial to know what the Bible actually teaches about the gospel. If Lordship Salvation is that gospel, it should be taught at every Bible-believing church, college, and seminary. If, however, Lordship Salvation is a latecomer and a deviation from the biblical plan of salvation, it ought to be rejected and exposed as *another gospel.* In that case, the leadership of Bible-believing churches, colleges, and seminaries would certainly initiate a *ministry of warning* to their congregations and pupils.

> Ecclesiastes 1:3 The thing that hath been, it is that which shall be; and that which is done is that which shall be done: and there is no new thing under the sun.

How is it that John MacArthur, representing the Lordship advocates, has presented, as though it had been lost or neutered, what he contends is the gospel according to Jesus and the apostles, when for many centuries Bible believing pastors and theologians have not arrived at or shared his conclusion? To be sure, the philosophy of Lordship Salvation has roots going back much earlier than 1988 among those who hold to a Calvinistic view of the plan of salvation. This matter is dealt with in a later chapter.

In the foreword from *The Gospel According to Jesus*, Dr. James Montgomery Boice says, speaking of the opponents of Lordship Salvation:

> ...they are mistaken—dreadfully mistaken and they need to be shown their error from Scripture, which is what this book does. They also need to be shown that their view has never been the view of any major Bible teacher or theologian in the church until our own weak times.[1]

Boice is claiming that John MacArthur's interpretation of the gospel is a continuation of the historic, exclusive truth, and all those who disagree with the Lordship position are in doctrinal error.

It is essential to explore the doctrine of Lordship Salvation to determine whether it is truth or error, whether it is the gospel or a perversion of the gospel. Dr. Charles Ryrie wrote:

> The message of faith only and the message of faith plus commitment of life cannot both be the gospel; therefore, one of them is a false gospel and comes under the curse of perverting the gospel or preaching another gospel (Gal. 1:6-9), and this is a very serious matter.[2]

Bible-believing Christians would be wise to thoroughly study this matter. Does the Bible teach that man must add to faith in whom Christ is and what He did to provide salvation a "commitment of life," or a promise of submission to the lordship of Christ in order to be saved? Or does the Bible teach that man's salvation is by grace through faith, apart from any work, promised or performed? Dr. Robert Lightner wrote, "Salvation is either by God's grace or by human effort, commitment, or work. It cannot be by both, anymore than law and grace were both means of salvation in Paul's day."[3]

ENDNOTES:

1. James M. Boice from, *The Gospel According to Jesus*, p. xii.
2. Charles Ryrie, *Balancing the Christian Life*, p. 170.
3. Robert Lightner, *Sin, the Savior, and Salvation*, p. 203.

WHAT IS LORDSHIP SALVATION?

As we begin to look at Lordship Salvation it is imperative that a clear distinction be drawn in regard to where the core area of debate is, and where it is not. The major issue and crux of the doctrinal controversy is over Lordship's definition of how the lost are born again. Concerns in regard to the discipleship of genuine believers are an important discussion, but for me that is not where the main controversy lies. The crux of the Lordship debate is over the **requirements for** salvation, not the **results of** salvation.

One of the central questions that fuels and defines the Lordship debate is: What is required of a sinner that would constitute "saving faith," i.e. the faith that results in his being born again? For a lost man to be born again must his faith in Christ include a "willingness to forsake everything, wholehearted commitment, unconditional surrender and a full exchange of self for the Savior?" Numerous statements to that effect from the advocates of Lordship Salvation are the focal point of the doctrinal controversy. These alleged "overstatements" have never been edited, explained, or eliminated by the men who make them. In fact, over the years, these statements have been reiterated and reinforced.

Most men on both sides of the debate will agree in principle that a new creature in Christ will set out to do the God ordained "good works" (Eph. 2:10) for the believer. Daily submission to the lordship of Christ should follow a genuine conversion to Christ. There is wide spread agreement that born again Christians will grow in the grace and knowledge of their Lord and Savior (2 Peter 3:18). Christians will, however, struggle with the flesh, the warfare between the two natures (Rom. 7:15-25) and the besetting sin (Heb. 12:1). Christians will flop and fail in their walk with God, but growth is typically seen to one degree or another.

As you read on you are going to find, just as I did, that Lordship Salvation touches on numerous Bible doctrines. This makes arriving at a brief definition a difficult, but not impossible undertaking. One editor nearly insisted I provide a single sentence definition within the first two or three pages of the book. Well, I never had it in mind to impress an editor of a publishing firm. My goal has been to demonstrate why Lordship Salvation is wrong and provide the biblical answers to it.

Because Lordship's theology touches on a broad range of Bible doctrines, with practical ramifications, I decided to deal with each doctrine in turn allowing for a complete definition of Lordship Salvation to come forth as the book unfolds. With that said, I also believe it is important to provide a summary definition in the early stages of this book. The following definition is not all encompassing of the Lordship position, but it is a beginning.

Defined briefly: Lordship Salvation is a position on the gospel in which "saving faith" is considered reliance upon the finished work of Jesus Christ. Lordship views "saving faith" as incomplete without an accompanying resolve to "forsake sin" and to "start obeying." Lordship's "*sine qua non*" (indispensable condition) that must be met to fully define "saving faith," for salvation, is a commitment to deny self, take up the cross, and follow Christ in submissive obedience.

John MacArthur released *The Gospel According to Jesus,* in 1988. He has written sequels to this original under the titles *Faith Works: The Gospel According to the Apostles* and

Hard to Believe. The original has been revised and expanded twice. The most recent (2008) is the *20th Anniversary* edition with the subtitle *What is Authentic Faith?* The full title of John MacArthur's original book is *What Does Jesus Mean When He Says, Follow Me? The Gospel According to Jesus.* The title alone should raise concern even before one opens the cover. The point made in the title is that John MacArthur and those who advocate Lordship Salvation believe the Lord's words *Follow Me* are a necessary component of the gospel that first must be committed to for justification and then must be acted upon for "final salvation," i.e., glorification.

> There is no doubt that Jesus saw a measure of real, lived-out obedience to the will of God as necessary for final salvation.... What God will require at the judgment is not our perfection, but sufficient fruit to show that the tree had life-in our case, divine life.[1]

> Endurance in faith is a condition for future salvation. Only those who endure in faith will be saved for eternity.[2]

Lordship Salvation tears at the very heart of the gospel; it corrupts "the simplicity that is in Christ" (2 Cor. 11:3), it is a man-centered message that frustrates grace (Gal. 2:21). Lordship Salvation sets upon the sinner's path to Christ a stumbling block. Lordship Salvation makes rough and uncertain God's simple plan of salvation. We will see that in addition to faith and belief in Christ, Lordship Salvation demands promises of surrender and commitment to fulfill what the Lordship advocates consider genuine saving faith. Surrender and commitment of life in "exchange" for salvation is the doctrine of Lordship Salvation. Those are demands and conditions for salvation placed on the lost that the Bible does not mandate for them.

Why Is It Called "Lordship Salvation?"

The theology known today as "Lordship Salvation" was previously known by other titles such as *Mastery, Commitment,* or *Discipleship Salvation.* It has been my experience to find that some men who hold to the Lordship position on the gospel do not want to be unequivocally, publicly identified with the position by the "Lordship Salvation" label. Once the current title took hold most Lordship advocates did not appreciate its having been attached to their position. For instance, John MacArthur wrote, "Thus there is no salvation except 'lordship salvation.'"[3] In a footnote to that sentence MacArthur continues,

> I don't like the term "lordship salvation." It was coined by those who want to eliminate the idea of submission to Christ from the call of saving faith, and it implies that Jesus' lordship is a false addition to the gospel.[4]

Here MacArthur plainly states that the condition to be met for the faith that saves is "submission to Christ." Later we are going to see that a promise of "submission to Christ" as a definition of saving faith is indeed, "a false addition to the gospel." Marc T. Mueller of Dr. MacArthur's Grace Community Church in Sun Valley, California wrote, "The Saviorhood of Christ is actually contingent on obedience to His Lordship."[5] It is important to note that Mueller identifies obedience to the lordship of Christ as the key element upon which man must act to receive Christ as Savior. This theme is consistent with all pro-lordship advocates.

The position these men espouse places the emphasis on a resolve to surrender and live in obedience to the lordship of Christ. For them the indispensable condition that must be satisfied to be born again is upfront surrender and submission to Christ's lordship. Submission and surrender are given prominence over faith, believing and repentance, although all of these are given consideration in the Lordship interpretation of the gospel.

It becomes clear why many of those who hold to the Lordship position do not like the term, "Lordship Salvation." They are uncomfortable because the term appropriately identifies and labels the position, which they themselves espouse. Upfront "surrender, commitment and obedience to the lordship to Christ" is the heart of their message. It seems only natural then that the term "Lordship Salvation" has come to define their stated position. Opponents of Lordship Salvation, however, feel that the term is in one sense unfortunate because the debate is not over the lordship of Christ, but over the response of a person to the gospel and the conditions that must be met for salvation.

In general, both sides of the debate have come to accept the designation *Lordship Salvation*. On the Grace Community Church web site, (Dr. John MacArthur, Senior Pastor) under *Distinctives*[6] you will find one of the distinctives of the church's teaching is titled, "Lordship Salvation." Here the term *Lordship Salvation* is used without further clarification or apology to define the official theological position of Dr. MacArthur's church in regard to the gospel. So, it does appear the frustration has ceased for most Lordship advocates over the title that defines their position. There are, however, some men who hold to the Lordship philosophy and still bristle when those who oppose this teaching apply the term. The leading Lordship advocate among Baptist missionaries in South Africa detested the term, calling it "unfair and misleading." I have spoken to several Lordship preachers here in the States who dislike the term.

Recently I have spoken with several pastors who, by clear evidence in their own sermons, are men who irrefutably hold to the Lordship position exactly as John MacArthur defines it. In two cases when I asked if they preach Lordship

Salvation, they said, they do not. These men rejected the use of the term "Lordship Salvation" to describe their position on the gospel. When asked, therefore, if they believe Lordship Salvation is their interpretation of the gospel, they believe they are being honest when they say, "no." These men know they hold to the position commonly known as Lordship Salvation, but do not want their position to be identified by that title. Because they do not like the term that has come to identify their position some will steadfastly deny they are advocates of Lordship Salvation.

What is the Motive for Lordship Salvation?

Lordship advocates frequently offer this kind of rationale for their position, "We are trying to answer Easy-Believism." The motive is certainly noble; few preachers care for the "1, 2, 3 pray with me" kind of evangelism. Many share a common frustration over examples we see in our churches today of people who profess Christ as Savior, are genuinely born again, but seem more interested in the world, and live more like the Devil. There are, of course, people in Bible believing churches that profess to know Christ, but have never received Him as Savior.

Answering reductionist interpretations of the gospel and the shallow living of some professing Christians does not justify or excuse taking another extreme position. From his review of *The Gospel According To Jesus*, Dr. Ernest Pickering observed,

> John MacArthur is a sincere servant of the Lord, of that we have no doubt.... We believe in his advocacy of the so-called lordship salvation he is wrong. He desperately desires to see holiness, lasting fruit, and continuing faithfulness in the lives of Christian people. This reviewer and we believe all sincere

church leaders desire the same.... But the remedy for this condition is not found in changing the terms of the gospel.[7]

Dr. Charlie Bing made a similar observation:

> They are motivated by the worthy desire to see those who profess Christ go on to maturity and fruitfulness. Faced with the sad realities of inconsistent behavior, "backsliding," and outright apostasy by some professing Christians, they have proposed a gospel that demands *up front* an exclusive commitment to an obedient lifestyle in hopes of minimizing these problems.[8]

One must always be careful not to bounce off one unbiblical teaching into another. This has sadly been the case of some people who have, with good cause, been frustrated by those who make professions of faith in Christ, but do not live for Christ. We would like to see all new believers begin their walk with God in complete, mature and total submission. The reality, however, is the inner warfare (Rom. 7) and the sin, which doth so easily besets us (Heb. 12:1). This writer shares the distress over those who call themselves Christians, but are weak and seem little interested in the things of the Lord. This frustration, however, does not warrant "changing the terms of the gospel."

What Are Some of the Red Flags?

There are tip-offs to identify a philosophy, doctrine, or cult. For example, Mormons typically use the phrase, "another testament of Jesus Christ." A person who consistently refers to God as Jehovah is probably a Jehovah's Witness. One who says he worships on the Sabbath is most likely a Seventh Day Adventist; one who talks about the "Second Blessing" is a Charismatic.

The following are typical statements made by Lordship Salvation proponents. Such statements should act as signals or alarms that Lordship Salvation is likely being introduced or defended.

1. "You do not make Jesus Lord, He is Lord."
2. In an evangelistic message you might hear appeals such as:
   "You must also submit to the lordship of Christ."
   "Have you taken up a cross to follow after Christ?"
   "It is not enough to believe Jesus died for your sins."
   "Saving faith is acknowledging Christ's right to rule your life."
   "Would you give up your life here to have eternal life?"
   "The gift of eternal life will cost you total commitment of all that you are to the lordship of Christ."
3. Interpreting discipleship passages as strictly evangelistic:

> Luke 9:23-24 And he said to them all, If any man will come after me, let him deny himself, and take up his cross daily, and follow me. For whosoever will save his life shall lose it: but whosoever will lose his life for my sake, the same shall save it.

> Luke 14:26-27, 33 If any man come to me, and hate not his father, and mother, and wife, and children, and brethren, and sisters, yea, and his own life also, he cannot be my disciple. And whosoever doth not bear his cross, and come after me, cannot be my disciple... So likewise, whosoever he be of you that forsaketh not all that he hath, he cannot be my disciple.

Men who hold to Lordship Salvation present these passages from Luke's gospel and similar verses about following Jesus as evangelistic appeals. They are taking verses that teach discipleship and mistakenly apply them to salvation. This issue is dealt with in the chapter, *Salvation and Discipleship: Is There A Biblical Difference?*

How Should You Respond When You Hear the Lordship Gospel?

When you hear someone using terms or expressions indicative of the Lordship view, or clearly presenting the Lordship gospel, you may, depending upon the circumstances, want to query the speaker and request clarification. In any event, you should not automatically assume the worst. It is possible to make a heretical statement without being a heretic. Always begin by giving the benefit of the doubt.

A mature Christian should first be *apt to teach*, not to condemn those who raise a question or make a statement about a doctrinal issue that he/she knows to be heretical. New believers and those with limited exposure to sound and balanced Bible teaching can drift into extremes. A well-meaning believer can and sometimes will adopt a position, which is unbiblical, and not be aware he has done so. There is a great deal of this happening with the explosion of Christian blogs and discussion boards.

It is not uncommon in a Bible college classroom to encounter a young man who is simply unclear on or misinformed about a point of doctrine. In trying to raise a question or in stating his case, he may espouse an unbiblical position and not even realize it. A similar situation may arise in an ordination council. There may be an area of systematic theology, such as eschatology or pneumatology, where the candidate exhibits a deficiency in some of the finer points of these doctrines. Preacher, do you remember the time you were up for ordination? You hoped the men on your ordaining counsel would be gracious to you if you were not exactly on target biblically on a particular point of theology. Is it not right and charitable to extend the same graciousness to your students or to the candidates on whose ordination councils you sit? First seek to clarify rather than condemn, afterward offer instruction and guidance if necessary. Acts 18:24-28 gives us a practical guide on how to handle such cases:

> And a certain Jew named Apollos, born at Alexandria, an eloquent man, and mighty in the scriptures, came to Ephesus. This man was instructed in the way of the Lord; and being fervent in the spirit, he spake and taught diligently the things of the Lord, knowing only the baptism of John. And he began to speak boldly in the synagogue: whom when Aquila and Priscilla had heard, they took him unto them, and expounded unto him the way of God more perfectly. And when he was disposed to pass into Achaia, the brethren wrote, exhorting the disciples to receive him: who, when he was come, helped them much which had believed through grace: For he mightily convinced the Jews, and that publickly, shewing by the scriptures that Jesus was Christ.

From the passage we cannot conclusively determine whether Apollos was preaching false doctrine. The suggestion is that Apollos was on the right track, but not fully *instructed* in the doctrine of Christ. Before he met Aquila and Priscilla, Apollos had been preaching a sincere, but incomplete message. From verse 25, we see that Apollos had been *instructed* κατηξεω (*katecheo*). That means he had received his doctrine by word of mouth. The preaching of

Apollos was limited because his instruction up to that time was limited.

Aquila and Priscilla, therefore, *took him unto them*; they welcomed him in fellowship as a friend and companion. They brought him to a quiet place, likely their home for the Sabbath supper. In that place of privacy and warmth, they simply and tenderly *expounded unto him the way of God more perfectly*. Together they taught Apollos so that his doctrine and message would be exact, complete, and sound. Apollos came away from the instruction of Aquila and Priscilla better prepared to preach the gospel of Jesus Christ. The result was that Apollos *mightily convinced the Jews that Jesus was Christ*.

The example of Aquila and Priscilla ought to be our pattern for today. We ought to befriend, then teach and instruct; instead of assuming the worst and rebuking a sincere, zealous, but not fully instructed believer:

> Priscilla and Aquila heard him interpret the OT scriptures . . . and were greatly impressed by the learning and zeal which he devoted to the defence of the gospel. It was a pity, they thought, that so able a champion of Christianity should not know the fulness of the gospel as they themselves had learned it, and so they invited him to their home in Ephesus and there set forth "the way of God" to him more accurately, making good the gaps which had existed in his understanding of that way hitherto. How much better it is to give such private help to a preacher whose ministry is defective than to correct or denounce him publicly.[9]

When a pastor or any man in leadership presents a strong advocacy of the Lordship gospel, he has likely adopted the Lordship position, and may be attempting to "draw away disciples" (Acts 20:30). Even in this case, you should give benefit of the doubt initially, but you do have genuine cause for concern. At this point, if circumstances warrant, it would be wise to take this man aside and ask him some questions to clarify what you have heard from him. Sample questions can be found in the chapter titled, *Salvation and Discipleship: Is There A Biblical Difference?*

I do believe it would be helpful to forewarn you that it is not uncommon for a Lordship advocate to react angrily if you begin to question him. My approach has been that of one seeking clarification when I have heard a Lordship sermon. I have been careful to be charitable in my approach and not appear as though I am ready to condemn. Even so, I have had encounters with several men who reacted badly, when they realized I knew the issue and desired a clear statement on their position. Two of these men compromised their personal testimony because of the hostility with which they responded to my sincere approach. It is not clear to me why a man will react with anger when he is asked to expand on and clarify his position on a particular doctrine.

Be aware of the red flags that identify Lordship Salvation. When you hear the Lordship gospel, give the benefit of the doubt and be *apt to teach*, but also be determined to seek clarification when clarification is called for.

ENDNOTES:

1. John Piper, *What Jesus Demands From the World*, pp. 160, 221.
2. R. C. Sproul, *Grace Unknown*, p. 198.
3. John MacArthur, *The Gospel According to Jesus* [*Revised & Expanded Edition*], p. 34.
4. Ibid., p. 34.
5. Marc Mueller, *Lordship Salvation Syllabus*, Grace Community Church, 1985.
6. Grace Community Church, http://www.gracechurch.org/distinctives/lordship-salvation, (accessed January 19, 2010)
7. Ernest Pickering, *Lordship Salvation: An Examination of John MacArthur's Book, The Gospel According to Jesus*.
8. Charles Bing, *Lordship Salvation: A Biblical Evaluation and Response*, p. 11.
9. F. F. Bruce, *The New International Commentary on the New Testament: The Book of Acts*, p. 382.

WHAT IS THE CALVINISM CONNECTION?

Lordship Is Rooted In Calvinism

Many evangelicals today might identify Dr. John MacArthur as one of the originators of Lordship Salvation. Dr. MacArthur has written a series of books, which are considered the most comprehensive polemics for Lordship Salvation, but the theology of Lordship Salvation did not originate with him. Before John MacArthur burst on the scene in 1988 with his first edition of *The Gospel According to Jesus* men such as: Martyn Lloyd Jones, J. I. Packer, Walter Chantry and John R. Stott championed the position. We are going to see, however that the origins run much earlier than with modern day theologians. In his doctoral dissertation, Dr. Charlie Bing noted:

> Its history is somewhat difficult to trace since the designation Lordship Salvation is a fairly recent appellation attached to a view that has been implied or demanded by preexisting theological systems.... The clearest expressions of Lordship thought appear in post-reformational theology.[1]

The roots of Lordship Salvation are found in the tenets of Calvinism. Richard P. Belcher explains the connection:

> Lordship Salvation flows from a Calvinistic foundation. God has chosen people and He will save them. He regenerates them and grants them the gifts of repentance and faith. Such a work of salvation transforms them...Through trials, difficulties, and even failures, they are not only eternally secure but will persevere in holiness and faith.²

Kenneth L. Gentry, another Lordship advocate, wrote, "It is largely associated with Reformed or Calvinistic theology, though not exclusively, for Kent, MacArthur, and Thiessen are dispensationalists."³ Lewis Johnson wrote, "The forerunner of the current debate erupted in the late 1950s and early 1960s. Two well-known evangelicals, Everett F. Harrison and John R. W. Stott debated the issue in *Eternity* magazine in September, 1959."⁴ In reference to that debate, in the context of the Reformed origins and current support of Lordship, Dr. Robert Lightner wrote:

> The lordship salvation view did not begin in the 1950s. In reality the view is as old as covenant reformed theology, with which it is very compatible, although not all who embrace a nondispensational theology subscribe to lordship salvation, and some dispensationalists embrace it. Chantry was right when he said lordship salvation "is largely associated with Reformed theology (and rightly so)." Supportive of this is the fact that the most recent full-scale defense of lordship salvation from one who claims to be a dispensationalist cites dozens of Reformed writers such as O. T. Allis, Berkhof, Boice, C. Hodge, J. I. Packer, Pink, and Warfield.⁵

In the latter portion of the quote above Dr. Lightner refers first to Walter J. Chantry who authored *Today's Gospel: Authentic or Synthetic*, a pro-lordship book published in 1970. He then refers to "the most recent full-scale defense of lordship salvation," which is John MacArthur's *The*

Gospel According to Jesus. In regard to the preaching of the gospel, John MacArthur says, "Some will turn away, but it is God who either reveals the truth or keeps it hidden."[6] Later MacArthur writes:

> A second essential element of conversion is revelation. Salvation comes to one who is childlike but only on the basis of revelation from God through Jesus Christ.... The only people who receive it are those who are sovereignly chosen.[7]

Is MacArthur saying that God will allow the gospel truth to be revealed to the elect, but as for those outside the elect, they will be left in spiritual darkness? This would mean the Holy Spirit, promised and sent by Jesus Christ to convince and convict the world of sin, righteous and judgment to come (John 16:7-11), is effectively working only on behalf of those who were unconditionally elected. Does MacArthur mean to suggest God keeps the gospel of Jesus Christ hidden from or blocks its reception from being received by those who are not of the elect? The Scriptures have the answer!

> 2 Corinthians 4:3-6 But if our gospel be hid, it is hid to them that are lost: In whom the god if the world hath blinded the minds of them which believe not, lest the light of the glorious gospel of Christ, who is the image of God, should shine unto them. For we preach not ourselves, but Christ Jesus the Lord; and ourselves your servants for Jesus' sake. For God, who commanded the light to shine out of darkness, hath shined in our hearts, to give the light of the knowledge of the glory of God in the face of Jesus Christ.

The Devil blinds the minds of the entire world's population of unbelievers. But God be thanked for He commands the light of the glorious gospel of Christ to shine upon all men. God does not withhold light or truth from one select group of the world's population. All may receive the gospel, all may choose to believe the gospel, and all may receive Jesus Christ by faith and be born again.

Does Regeneration Precede Faith?

John MacArthur uses the following statement to prepare the way for the *hard demands* of the Lordship gospel: "Thus conversion is not simply a sinner's decision for Christ; it is first the sovereign work of God in transforming the individual."[8] Is MacArthur suggesting that a sinner must first be transformed through regeneration into a child of God before he can believe and respond in faith to the gospel of Jesus Christ?

Regeneration before faith under girds Lordship Salvation. There are a growing number of preachers that believe regeneration occurs prior to and apart from repentance toward God and faith in Jesus Christ. For example Dr. John Piper advocates the position as follows:

> The native hardness of our hearts makes us unwilling and unable to turn from sin and trust the Savior. Therefore conversion involves a miracle of new birth. Thus new birth precedes and enables faith and repentance.... And so when we hear the gospel we will never respond positively unless God performs the miracle of regeneration. Repentance and faith are our work. But we will not repent and believe unless God does his work to overcome our hard and rebellious hearts. This divine work is called *regeneration*.... New birth comes first and enables the repentance and faith of conversion.[9]

On February 28, 2002 at the National Leadership Conference held at Calvary Baptist Seminary in Lansdale, Pennsylvania, Pastor Charles Baker conducted a workshop on Lordship Salvation. In his address he dealt with Calvinistic theology, the regeneration precedes faith issue, and their connection to Lordship Salvation. Pastor Baker said:

> The willingness to let Christ rule over our lives is the result of the working of the Holy Spirit in the life of a regenerated person (Rom. 6:4; 7:4, 6, 18, 22; 2 Cor. 5:17; Eph. 2:10). The Bible makes it clear that the unsaved cannot submit to God's rule (Rom. 8:7). This submission is not a requirement for salvation, but the result of salvation. On this point one can begin to understand why Lordship Salvation is so appealing to those who espouse reformed soteriology.[10]

Regarding the relative order of calling and regeneration Berkhof writes:

> The external call in the preaching of the Word, except in the case of children, precedes or coincides with the operation of the Holy Spirit in the production of the new life. Then by a creative act God generates the new life, changing the inner disposition of the soul. This is regeneration in the restricted sense of the word. In it the spiritual ear is implanted which enables man to hear the call of God to the salvation of his soul. Having received the spiritual ear, the call of God is now brought home effectively to the heart, so that man hears and obeys. This effectual calling, finally, secures the first holy exercises of the new disposition that is born in the soul. The new life begins to manifest itself and issues in the new birth. This is regeneration in the broader sense and marks the point at which regeneration passes into conversion.[11]

Charles Baker writes in response to Berkhof above:

> Thus, in Reformed soteriology, regeneration precedes conversion. It enables the unconverted person to have a new disposition in the soul that willingly submits to the lordship of Christ. The Bible teaches that it is the convicting ministry of the Holy Spirit that brings one to faith in Christ (John 16:8-11). At salvation one becomes a partaker of the divine nature (2 Peter 1:3-4). With God's help the believer can begin to surrender fully to the lordship of Christ in his life.[12]

The Calvinist believes an unsaved man is so "dead" in his sins (Eph. 2:1) that he cannot respond to and cannot believe the gospel. The Calvinist, therefore, comes to the conclusion that God must first regenerate the lost man and then give him the gifts of faith and repentance. This teaching means the lost man must be made spiritually alive, i.e. born again by an act of regeneration prior to believing the gospel and apart from personal faith in the Lord Jesus Christ.

It has been said of Charles Haddon Spurgeon (1834-1892) that he was the greatest preacher since the Apostle Paul. Spurgeon began preaching at the age of 16. At 25 he built London's famous Metropolitan Tabernacle, seating around 5,000. It was never large enough for the crowds he attracted to hear him preach. Wherever he went in the United Kingdom thousands came to hear from him. The London newspapers reprinted his Sunday sermons, which were read by yet thousands more. Spurgeon published thousands of devotionals, commentaries, poems, tracts, sermons and songs. The following quote opens with an excerpt from Charles Spurgeon's sermon, "The Warrant of Faith":

> "In our own day certain preachers assure us that a man must be regenerated before we bid him believe in Jesus Christ; some degree of a work of grace in the heart being, in their judgment,

the only warrant to believe. This also is false. It takes away a gospel for sinners and offers us a gospel for saints...Brethren, the command to believe in Christ must be the sinner's warrant, if you consider the nature of our commission." To deny a universal warrant, and to require subjective experiences before Christ is trusted, is bound to lead to confusion and legality. Such teaching makes men look at themselves instead of the Saviour.[13]

Appendix 'B' is an article by Pastor George Zeller that specifically deals with the *regeneration precedes faith* issue. In that article is the following from Charles Spurgeon, from the same sermon above titled, "The Warrant of Faith." Spurgeon preached this sermon on September 20, 1863 at the Metropolitan Tabernacle.

> If I am to preach the faith in Christ to a man who is regenerated, then the man, being regenerated, is saved already, and it is an unnecessary and ridiculous thing for me to preach Christ to him, and bid him to believe in order to be saved when he is saved already, being regenerate.... So, then, I am only to preach faith to those who have it. Absurd, indeed! Is not this waiting till the man is cured and then bringing him the medicine? This is preaching Christ to the righteous and not to sinners.[14]

It is well worth noting that Spurgeon, who was Calvinistic in his theology, considered the regeneration precedes faith position, held by some Calvinists in his day just as some of them do today as, *absurd* and *false*. Evangelist John VanGelderen wrote:

> Is it "look and live" or "live and look?" Is it "Look unto Me, and be ye saved" (Is. 45:22) or "Be ye saved, and look unto Me?" Is it "He that believeth on Me hath everlasting life" (John 6:47, cf. John 3:15, 16, 36; 5:24) or "He who hath everlasting life believeth on Me?" Did Paul say to the Philippian jailer

"Believe on the Lord Jesus Christ, and thou shalt be saved" (Acts 16:31) or "Thou shalt be saved, and believe on the Lord Jesus Christ?"[15]

Dr. Charlie Bing wrote:

> Is God's invitation to be saved through the gospel is a sincere and legitimate offer only if any and every person can believe it. If God must regenerate people before they can believe the gospel, then the invitation is not really to all people, but only to those already born again. But this is contrary to biblical statements that the gospel is for all (John 3:16; 2 Cor. 5:19-20; 1 Tim. 2:3-6; 1 John 2:2).[16]

Impossible Decision!

> John 16:7-11 Nevertheless I tell you the truth; It is expedient for you that I go away: for if I go not away, the Comforter will not come unto you; but if I depart, I will send him unto you. And when he is come, he will reprove the world of sin, and of righteousness, and of judgment: Of sin, because they believe not on me; Of righteousness, because I go to my Father, and ye see me no more; Of judgment, because the prince of this world is judged.

The Holy Spirit is come to convict the world of "sin" (note singular). What is the "sin" that the Holy Spirit will reprove the world over? That "sin" is explained in verse 10, which is the sin of "unbelief." The lost man needs to be confronted with the Law to bring him/her to know the need for forgiveness through Christ. The book of Galatians is very helpful in this matter. The sin that is damning the lost man to

Hell is "unbelief" and the only act that will result in salvation is "belief" (John 3:16; Acts 16:31).

The Holy Spirit convinces lost men of sin, righteousness and judgment so they might make the decision for, "...repentance toward God, and faith toward our Lord Jesus Christ," (Acts 20:21). There is a fine line of difference, but it is a sharp and clear difference in this matter of submission. Submission is to the conviction of the Holy Spirit, no more, no less. A lost man cannot submit to anything else!

Lordship Salvation's saving faith requires from a lost man an upfront commitment to cross bearing, denying self and following. This requires a decision that is impossible for the lost man to make. Those decisions and commitments are impossible for a lost man because Jesus said, "Apart from me, ye can do nothing," (John 15:5). The Holy Spirit does not indwell this lost man because he is not yet born again. He cannot make decisions of surrender and commitment to the lordship of Christ because he does not yet know the Lord as his Savior.

Because of this dilemma the Lordship advocate must, therefore, come to another view of the order of salvation (*ordo salutis*). Their solution for what is an impossible decision is regeneration, i.e. salvation before faith in Christ. Thus he arrives at a position that insists regeneration, even if only in an instant of time, occurs prior to and apart from believing the gospel and personal faith in Jesus Christ. The Bible has a better answer. After repenting of the sin of "unbelief" the newborn child of God enters into the life of sanctification and begins to repent of his "sins" (1 John 1:8-10).

Which Concept of God Is Greater?

John 16:7-11 and 2 Corinthians 4:3-6 show that the Bible clearly teaches that through the ministry of the Holy Spirit a lost man can come to understand his condition and need of salvation. According to the Bible the light of the glorious gospel of Christ can and does shine without exception on them, which believe not. Some respond in repentance, faith and believing on the Son of God and are miraculously born again.

Isaiah 45:22 Look unto me, and be ye saved, all the ends of the earth: for I am God, and there is none else.

John 6:47 Verily, verily, I say unto you, He that believeth on me hath everlasting life.

John 3:15-16 That whosoever believeth in him should not perish, but have eternal life. For God so loved the world, that he gave his only begotten Son, that whosoever believeth in him should not perish, but have everlasting life.

John 3:36 He that believeth on the Son hath everlasting life: and he that believeth not the Son shall not see life; but the wrath of God abideth on him.

John 5:24 Verily, verily, I say unto you, He that heareth my word, and believeth on him that sent me, hath everlasting life, and shall not come into condemnation; but is passed from death unto life.
John 20:31 . . .that believing ye might have life through his name. —

1 Tim. 1:16 . . . to them which should hereafter believe on him to life everlasting.

> Gal. 3:26 For ye are all the children of God by faith in Christ Jesus.
>
> Rom. 10:9-10, 13 That if thou shalt confess with thy mouth the Lord Jesus, and shalt believe in thine heart that God hath raised him from the dead, thou shalt be saved. For with the heart man believeth unto righteousness; and with the mouth confession is made unto salvation.... For whosoever shall call upon the name of the Lord shall be saved..

The Bible could not be clearer! A lost man, who hears the Word of God, comes under the convicting and convincing work of the Holy Spirit, can respond, if he so chooses, with repentance toward God, faith toward and belief in Jesus Christ (Acts 20:21) and thereby be regenerated, i.e. born again.

Which concept of God is greater: The concept of a God who decrees every detail and decision in all spheres of life and existence because He is sovereign; or the concept of a God who allows his creation the free will and ability to choose, yet He still knows all things, and is sovereign in the whole process? Human freedom is no threat to, does not infringe upon, nor is it a denial of the sovereignty of God. It is a mystery how the divine sovereignty of God and the free will of man can coexist and no damage be done to God's sovereignty. The infinite ways of God will always be a mystery to the finite mind of man (Isaiah 55:8-9).

ENDNOTES:

1. Charles Bing, *Lordship Salvation: A Biblical Evaluation and Response*, pp.6-7.
2. Richard Belcher, *A Layman's Guide to the Lordship Salvation Controversy*.
3. Kenneth Gentry, Jr.: *Lord of the Saved: Getting to the Heart of the Lordship Debate*, p. 8.
4. Lewis Johnson, Jr., "How Faith Works," *Christianity Today*, 11 September 1989, 21.
5. Robert P. Lightner, *Sin, the Savior, and Salvation*, pp. 203-4.
6. John MacArthur, *The Gospel According to Jesus* [Revised & Expanded Edition], p. 115.
7. Ibid., p. 117.
8. Ibid., p. 114.
9. John Piper, *Desiring God: Meditations of a Christian Hedonist*, pp. 65-66.
10. Charles Baker, *Lordship Salvation Issues: Why Is It Still An Issue And How It Is Affecting Us?* p. 4.
11. Louis Berkhof, *Manual of Christian Doctrine*, p. 237.
12. Charles Baker, *Lordship Salvation Issues: Why Is It Still An Issue And How It Is Affecting Us?* p. 5.
13. Iain H. Murray, *Spurgeon vs. Hyper-Calvinism: The Battle for Gospel Preaching*, pp. 76-77, (emphasis mine).
14. Charles Spurgeon, *Metropolitan Tabernacle Pulpit*, volume 9, pp. 531-32, 538, (emphasis mine).
15. John VanGelderen, *Faith Versus Fatalism*, p. 3.
16. Charlie Bing, *"Can an Unregenerate Person Believe the Gospel?"* http://www.gracelife.org/resources/gracenotes.asp?id=46, (accessed January 21, 2010).

SALVATION AND DISCIPLESHIP: IS THERE A BIBLICAL DIFFERENCE?

What is a Disciple?

What is the biblical definition of a disciple? *Disciple* in the Bible is almost always the translation of μαθητης (*mathetes*), which occurs 264 times in the New Testament. This Greek word is always rendered *disciple* in the King James Version of the Bible. While a common word, its usage is restricted to the four Gospels and Acts. The word means *learner* or *pupil* in secular Greek, but has a more specialized usage in the New Testament.

> It is used to indicate total attachment to someone in discipleship. The secular Gk. usage of the word in the sense of apprentice, pupil or student is not found. . . . In many passages it is used in the specifically OT sense of *lamad*, learn the will of God, or learn to direct the whole of one's human existence towards the will of God. . . . It is given a completely new character through its association with Jesus. . . . Following Jesus as a disciple means the unconditional sacrifice of his whole life for the whole of his life.... It is important for understanding discipleship of Jesus to realize that the call to be a disciple always includes the call to service. . . . The disciples would

have been a circle of immediate followers who were commissioned to particular service.... The essence of discipleship lies in the disciple's fulfillment of his duty to be a witness to his Lord in his entire life.[1]

A cost was involved for those early disciples if they would learn of Christ and follow Him in the kind of biblical discipleship as defined above. In Matthew 8:21-22 and John 6:66 discipleship demands *sacrifice* and some were not willing to pay the price. The same is true of believers today. On the other hand, some Christians count the cost and determine to follow Christ no matter what the cost. In a footnote on Matthew 8:21-22, John R. Rice wrote:

> It is no light matter to set out to follow Jesus in a lifetime of service. Jesus wants no half-hearted disciples. Only those who are willing to suffer poverty and to bear the reproach of the Lord Jesus are fit to be His disciples in full-time service. Only those who put Christ before loved ones and family are worthy to follow Him (cf. Luke 14:25-33).[2]

One of the most significant errors with Lordship Salvation is reinterpreting passages meant for the born again disciple of Christ and presenting them as though they are evangelistic appeals directed to the lost. It is from this error where much of the Lordship interpretation of the gospel flows. This error leads to a faulty definition of faith, redefines the role of biblical repentance in salvation, both of which result in a gospel message that frustrates grace.

A Strange Paradox Indeed!

How can the Scriptures teach that salvation is a free gift of God if the human cost to become a disciple, that is, to be born again, is very great as Lordship Salvation advocates insist? Salvation is either the free gift of God, or it is costly to man. The Bible teaches that "the gift of God is eternal life" (Romans 6:23), but discipleship or following Christ is costly (Luke 14:26-27).

> Romans 6:23 For the wages of sin is death; but **the gift of God** is eternal life through Jesus Christ our Lord.
>
> Luke 14:26-27 If any man come to me, and hate not his father, and mother, and wife, and children, and brethren, and sisters, yea, and his own life also, he cannot be my disciple. And whosoever doth not bear his cross, and come after me, cannot be my disciple. For which of you, intending to build a tower, sitteth not down first, and **counteth the cost**, whether he have sufficient to finish it?

Lordship Salvation requires an upfront commitment to discipleship as an indispensable condition for the reception of eternal life. Defining Lordship's discipleship gospel, John MacArthur wrote:

> The gospel Jesus proclaimed was a call to discipleship, a call to follow Him in submissive obedience. . . . Forsaking oneself for Christ's sake is not an optional step of discipleship subsequent to conversion; it is the *sine qua non* of saving faith.[3]
>
> Eternal life is indeed a free gift (Rom. 6:23). Salvation cannot be earned with good deeds or purchased with money. It has already been purchased by Christ, who paid the ransom with his blood. . . . But that does not mean there is no cost in terms of salvation's impact on the sinner's life. Do not throw away

this paradox just because it is difficult. Salvation is both free and costly.[4]

Some paradoxical doctrines in the Bible can be explained, some are difficult to explain, and still others cannot be reconciled. To say that salvation is at the same time both free and costly is not a paradox.

> Under the label of paradox, the Lordship position attempts to maintain theological orthodoxy (justification by faith alone) while demanding a price from the sinner (costly grace). It may cost to be or continue as a Christian, but not to become a Christian. To cite biblical examples where the gospel is presented without cost would be superfluous.[5]

Lordship advocates rationalize the upfront commitment to costly discipleship for salvation by calling it a difficult paradox. These men teach that a commitment to discipleship (cross bearing and following) is as necessary as faith in order to be born again.

> The fact is, Jesus sought more than a superficial following; he sought disciples. In short, the evangelistic call of Jesus was essentially a call to repentance and radical discipleship.[6]

> Jesus never concealed the fact that in His religion there was a demand as well as an offer. Indeed, the demand was as total as the offer was free. If He offered mankind His salvation, He demanded their submission. Jesus gave no encouragement whatever to thoughtless applicants for discipleship.[7]

> The response of faith always embraces the call of discipleship, the call to show forth the reality of a new life and freedom by following in obedience to Christ. The call to faith and to discipleship are the same and cannot be separated.[8]

Who Really Pays?

Lordship advocates have arrived at their costly discipleship gospel as a response to the growing number of people who claim to be Christian, but do not live up to their profession of having placed their faith in Christ. Do advocates of Lordship Salvation believe they can remedy the situation by demanding from the unsaved an up-front commitment to obedient discipleship for salvation? J. I. Packer wrote:

> In our own presentation of Christ's gospel, therefore, we need to lay a similar stress on the cost of following Christ, and make sinners face it soberly before we urge them to respond to the message of free forgiveness. In common honesty, we must not conceal the fact that free forgiveness in one sense will cost everything.⁹

It is true that the redemption of mankind came at a great and infinite price, one paid in full by the infinite Lord Jesus Christ. Creation was simple! Salvation, however, cost God everything—His own dear Son. The Bible speaks of our salvation being purchased with Christ's own blood (Acts 20:28).

> 1 Cor. 6:20 For ye are bought with a price: therefore glorify God in your body, and in your spirit, which are God's.

The finished work of Jesus Christ on the cross and it alone redeems man from sin and death! Salvation is not conditioned on a commitment to or the performance of meritorious works. Salvation is the free gift of God! Only through faith in the Person of Jesus Christ and what He did to provide salvation is man's redemption complete. From that point, through the enabling grace of God, he can begin to live for Jesus as the Lord of his life. A lost man must first come to Christ for salvation; then out of joy and gratitude for the free redemption he has received he follows Christ in discipleship, which is his "reasonable service" (Rom. 12:1-2).

> 1 Corinthians 7:23 Ye are bought with a price; be not ye the servants of men.

W. Harold Mare wrote, "Verse 23 points up the priority of Christ's authority over the Christian. In all earthly service he is to realize that his obedience and service is to Christ, not men. The reason is that God bought us with the price of Christ's blood."[10]

> Romans 10:9 That if thou shalt confess with thy mouth the Lord Jesus, and shalt believe in thine heart that God hath raised Him from the dead, thou shalt be saved.

In commenting on Romans 10:9, John MacArthur says "that it include(s) indisputably the lordship of Christ as part of the gospel to be believed for salvation, and that personal salvation requires a willingness to surrender to [Christ] as Lord."[11] MacArthur is demanding a decision from the lost man that the Bible does not. Lordship Salvation says decisions for full surrender and discipleship are required to be born again. I know of men who will tell sinners they must be willing to give up everything displeasing to God in order to be saved. What is the point of trying to get a lost person to make that kind of promise? He might as well be told to take the Nazarite vow or fulfill the Law of Moses to be saved. At the point of a salvation decision, the sinner does "not know what things those are, nor does the personal worker seeking to point them to Jesus know"[12] Dr. Charles Ryrie wrote:

> The issue is, How can my sins be forgiven? . . . Through faith I receive Him and His forgiveness. Then the sin problem is solved, and I can be fully assured of going to heaven. I do not need to believe in Christ's second coming in order to be saved. . . . But I do need to believe that He died for my sins and rose triumphant over sin and death. I do not need to settle issues that belong to Christian living in order to be saved.[13]

Those who hold to Lordship Salvation blur the biblical distinction between salvation and discipleship by interpreting the following passages as though they are the evangelistic blue print for salvation:

> Luke 9:23-24 If any man will come after me, let him deny himself, and take up his cross daily, and follow me. For whosoever will save his life shall lose it: but whosoever will lose his life for my sake, the same shall save it.
>
> Luke 14:26-27, 33 If any man come to me, and hate not his father, and mother, and wife, and children and brethren, and sisters, yea, and his own life also, he cannot be my disciple. And whosoever doth not bear His cross, and come after me, cannot be my disciple.... So likewise, whosoever he be of you that forsaketh not all that he hath, he cannot be my disciple.
>
> Mark 8:34 And when he had called the people unto him with his disciples also, he said unto them, Whosoever will come after me, let him deny himself, and take up his cross, and follow me.

Dr. Ernest Pickering in his review of the original *The Gospel According to Jesus* stated,

> Salvation is free; discipleship is costly. Salvation comes by receiving the work of the cross; discipleship is evidenced by bearing the cross (daily submission to the will of God). Christ here is not giving instructions about how to go to heaven, but how those who know they are going to heaven should follow Him.[14]

Following is another quotation from the chapter entitled, "The Cost of Discipleship" in MacArthur's *The Gospel According to Jesus:*

> Let me say again unequivocally that Jesus' summons to deny self and follow him was an invitation to salvation, not . . . a second step of faith following salvation. . . . Those who are not willing to lose their lives for Christ are not worthy of Him. . . . He wants disciples willing to forsake *everything*. This calls for full-scale self-denial—even willingness to die for His sake if necessary.[15]

The latter portion of the quotation, "He wants disciples willing to forsake everything," would be fine if John MacArthur stated it in the context of those persons who already believed on the Lord Jesus Christ, were saved by grace through faith, and sought to live as fully surrendered disciples of Christ. MacArthur, however, converts the cost of discipleship into a necessary expense in the form of an upfront commitment to discipleship for the reception of eternal life.

In a 2008 Trinity Broadcasting Network interview, with actor Kirk Cameron, MacArthur was asked to define the gospel. Speaking from Matthew 16 he stated:

> "If anyone wishes to come after Me, let him deny himself." This (the gospel) is not about self-fulfillment, this is about self-denial.... In fact Jesus said this, (paraphrasing) If you come to Me it may cost you your family. But if you're not willing to hate your family you can't My disciple. If you come to Me you might have to give all your possessions away and give them to the poor. If you are not willing to do that you are not worthy to be My disciple.[16]

The initial problem with MacArthur's statement should be immediately evident: The gospel is nowhere to be found in Matthew 16. There is no message of justification by faith in Matthew 16. Yet from this passage MacArthur extracts what he insists is God's redemptive plan for the lost. A lost man does not know what it means to hate his family, to "deny self" and "forsake everything" for Christ. Yet MacArthur insists the willingness to "forsake everything" is required in the "invitation to (*for*) salvation."

A new believer, on the other hand, should but, typically does not immediately forsake all to follow Jesus because he does not know what those things are. Over his lifetime, however, he will learn what those things are as he grows in grace and knowledge (2 Peter 3:18).

The local church I attend has an outreach ministry for people with addictions. Is a man who gets saved through the ministry of that program immediately cured of all his addictions? Will that man immediately forsake every addiction? Of course not, and Lordship advocates understand this. They understand that a new believer will struggle with sin and addictions that will not die easily. Christians who work in a Bible based addictions program know better than to tell the unsaved addict that eternal salvation, as MacArthur defines it, is only for those who are "willing to forsake everything." The personal worker does not tell the newly born again addict, "Only those who endure in faith will be saved for eternity."[17]

The only sense in which salvation is costly is in the fact that Jesus Christ paid the supreme price, his life, for the sinner's redemption. Unfortunately, this is not the focus of Lordship teaching, which finds cost in human conditions for salvation. But to the sinner, salvation is absolutely free. If it were costly to him in any sense, then it could no longer be of grace and Christianity would take its place alongside the rest of the world's religions.[18]

In one of the clearest expressions of portraying discipleship as though it is the key to salvation MacArthur wrote, "Anyone who wants to come after Jesus into the Kingdom of God—anyone who wants to be a Christian—has to face three commands: 1) deny himself, 2) take up his cross daily, and 3) follow him."[19]

That statement opens the door to some valid questions. Does the lost man have to agree to these commands for discipleship to become a Christian? Once I agree to these conditions do I have to remain true to these commands to guarantee my entry into Heaven? These are at the heart of the problem when verses meant for discipleship of the believer are presented as conditions for salvation to the unsaved. One might conclude that MacArthur's costly salvation does not guarantee Heaven for the Christian unless the price is continually paid over time throughout a lifetime. It sounds as though the initial commitment is a down payment on Heaven, and staying committed is the balance due on the agreement.

There is a Cost, But Where is it?

In the original edition of *The Gospel According to Jesus,* John MacArthur titled a section of one chapter, "The Real Cost of Salvation" (p. 139). In the Revised & Expanded and the *20th Anniversary* editions he changed the title to *"The Cost of Following Christ"* (pp. 147, 148). The implications of that section (and the following section titled "Counting the Cost") has not changed. It is simply a new, more palatable banner for the same teaching. In both subsequent editions, just as in the first, John MacArthur has couched his interpretation of the gospel in the biblical terms of discipleship.

It should be remembered that the subtitle of his book, *What Does Jesus Mean When He Says, "Follow Me?" The Gospel According to Jesus* reveals what he believes to be the gospel. When the Lordship advocate speaks of "following Christ," he is speaking of the gospel. When John MacArthur refers to "The Cost of Following Christ," he really means "The Cost to Receive Christ." MacArthur believes there is a "Real Cost of Salvation," or more accurately a "Real Cost *for* Salvation." He believes that the gospel demands a commitment of one's life, and a promise of surrender to the lordship of Christ in an up-front "exchange" for the reception of salvation.

> This is what Jesus meant when He spoke of taking up one's own cross to follow Him. And that is why he demanded that we count the cost carefully. He was calling for an *exchange* of all that we are for all that He is. He was demanding implicit obedience—unconditional surrender to His lordship.[20]

The section titled "The Cost of Following Christ," illustrates the extreme to which the Lordship advocates have taken the matter of a "costly" salvation. Understanding that Lordship advocates equate discipleship with salvation is very important. They require, from a lost person, an upfront promise to perform as a committed disciple of Jesus Christ as a condition for becoming a born again disciple of Jesus Christ.

In the *20th Anniversary* edition of *The Gospel According to Jesus* please note how John MacArthur uses the term "saving faith" in this section (pp. 148-150). He is clearly referring to the salvation experience, i.e., becoming a Christian and what should follow becoming a Christian. The word "exchange" is used twice (pp. 148, 150) in connection with his definition of what constitutes "saving faith."

> That is the kind of response the Lord Jesus called for: wholehearted commitment. A desire for him at any cost. Unconditional surrender. A full *exchange* of self for the Savior. It is the only response that will open the gates of the kingdom. Seen through the eyes of this world, it is as high a price as anyone can pay. But from a kingdom perspective, it is really no sacrifice at all.[21]

"Cost" is the theme of this section. Remember it is not just "the cost of following Christ" in discipleship that John MacArthur refers to as costly, but the reception of salvation (justification) is conditioned by him through wholehearted commitment, desire to and surrender to pay any cost. The Bible, however, teaches that salvation is free; it is the "gift of God."

> Romans 6:23 For the wages of sin is death; but the gift of God is eternal life through Jesus Christ our Lord.
>
> Ephesians 2:8-9 For by grace are ye saved through faith; and that not of yourselves: it is the gift of God: Not of works, lest any man should boast.

Salvation is through personal faith and belief in the Lord Jesus Christ, not a response of "wholehearted commitment...desire...unconditional surrender" coming from the lost man.

> John 20:30-31 And many other signs truly did Jesus in the presence of his disciples, which are not written in this book: But these are written, that ye might believe that Jesus is the Christ, the Son of God; and that believing ye might have life through his name.
>
> John 6:47 Verily, verily, I say unto you, He that believeth on me hath everlasting life.
>
> 1 John 5:5 Who is he that overcometh the world, but he that believeth that Jesus is the Son of God?
>
> 1 John 4:15 Whosoever shall confess that Jesus is the Son of God, God dwelleth in him, and he in God.

The Bible teaches that discipleship, coming after Christ as a believer, is costly. The Luke chapters 9, 14 and Mark chapter 8 define the costly discipleship of the believer. Make no mistake about it: to follow Jesus Christ, to submit your will to His will come with a price. But ask any believer who has submitted his will, to the will of his Savior and you will find he has no regrets. He has found the pathway to blessing and power with God for service.

Some of our most familiar hymns, the hymns we learned as children, speak of this truth. One of my favorites is: *Trust and Obey*, John H. Sammis, 1887. The chorus is:

> *Trust and obey for there's no other way*
> *To be happy in Jesus, but to trust and obey.*

When my children were infants I chose a hymn that I would sing to each of them as a lullaby. For our first child I sang *Great is Thy Faithfulness*. Beginning with the second, through our fifth and last, *Trust and Obey* was their lullaby.

As I look back I have come to believe singing that hymn over and over was more for me than for my children. After all, they were infants and they might have received some comfort from my voice or at least the tones. As for me, however, with each singing I was reminded that as a Christian I would find happiness and direction for living by trusting Him with my life and living in obedience to His commands.

Trust and Obey would have meant nothing to me as an unbeliever. The opening stanza begins, "When we walk with the Lord in the light of His Word." What possible meaning could walking with God have for an unconverted man? I was in sin and rebellion against God. How many of us would have scoffed at that sweet hymn before we knew Christ? Oh, but as a child of God doesn't that tender hymn have great power?

Salvation and discipleship are two separate and distinct issues. Salvation is the gift of God to an undeserving Hell-bound sinner. Discipleship is what ought to flow from the man or woman who through the shed blood of Jesus Christ has been redeemed from sin, death and Hell. Confusing the cost of discipleship for the believer with the gospel of grace through faith is one of the most disconcerting errors of Lordship Salvation.

How are Salvation and Discipleship Distinguished?

The late Dr. J. Vernon McGee had an endearing simplicity in his Bible teaching that has been appreciated by believers for many decades. In the matter of the lordship of Christ, he used to say, "A man ought to make Jesus the Lord of his life, but he had better receive Jesus as his Savior first."

> Luke 14: 26-27, 33 If any man come to me, and hate not his father, and mother, and wife, and children, and brethren, and sisters, yea, and his own life also, he cannot be my disciple. And whosoever doth not bear his cross, and come after me, cannot be my disciple. So likewise, whosoever he be of you that forsaketh not all that he hath, he cannot be my disciple.

In this passage, there are three references to the discipleship of the believer. It is wrong to present these verses as evangelistic appeals to the lost. These things do not save; they are acts of a disciple. The lost must come to Christ for salvation; believers come after Christ in discipleship.

> Salvation is free, discipleship is costly. Salvation comes by simply believing in Christ. By receiving by faith the free gift of salvation through His work on the cross. Discipleship is evidenced by daily submission to the will of God. They are two separate things. The Bible makes a distinction between salvation and discipleship.[22]

Luke 14:26-27, 33 are directed to those who are already saved to instruct them in how to follow Christ as a disciple. In the passage the Lord requires of the disciple that: his love for Jesus ought to make any other kind of love seem like hate; he must bear the cross and come after Christ; and he must forsake all. This passage does not deal with salvation; this is discipleship; and while interrelated there is a distinct biblical difference between them.

> These verses are simply saying that we should put God first. A believer's devotedness to Jesus Christ should be just that, by comparison, it looks as if everything else is hated. . . . A person can be saved by accepting Jesus Christ as Savior, but a person

will never follow and serve Him until he is willing to make a sacrifice.[23]

Luke 9:23-24 And he said unto them all, If any man will come after Me, let him deny himself, and take up his cross daily, and follow Me. For whosoever will save his life shall lose it: but whosoever will lose his life for my sake, the same shall save it.

Dr. J. Vernon McGee wrote, "(Jesus) is not putting down a condition of salvation but stating the position of those who are saved."[24] Lordship advocates, however, consider Luke 9:23-24 an evangelistic passage meant for the unsaved. Lordship advocates believe "take up his cross daily" is a condition that must be committed to for the reception of salvation. If this is a salvation invitation, the sinner is being asked to be willing to die for Jesus in order to be saved.

> If this characterizes saving faith and is made a condition for salvation, as Lordship proponents insist, one must decide to place faith in Jesus as Savior and Lord through surrender everyday without fail. Such an expectation is not found elsewhere in the Bible and makes both salvation and assurance impossible.[25]

Luke 9:24 is a conditional verse. Twice the Lord says, "for whosoever will." Are the demands of Luke 9:24 part of the gospel of Jesus Christ? Are they prerequisites for salvation? Does verse 24 give conditions a man must satisfy to receive God's free gift of salvation? How can the free "gift of God" (Eph. 2:8-9; Rom. 6:23) be conditional on promises of cross bearing, obedience, and submission?

The following is a sermon excerpt from Pastor Doug Van Meter, an American who is senior pastor of the

Brackenhurst Baptist Church in South Africa. He is preaching on Matthew 16:20-21. In the passage Peter rebukes the Lord after He reveals to the disciples His future suffering at the hands of the Jews. The following two excerpts demonstrate just how severely discipleship can be strained to suit the Lordship gospel.

> ...and the Lord did not say, "Oh, Peter let me give you a hug, thank you for loving Me so much." He rebuked him! He said, "Get thee behind Me Satan." He said, "You do not understand the cross; you do not understand the cost of being a Christian." And that is why He said, "If you love your life you are going to lose it, if you hate it you are going to find it." He said, "If you are not willing to take up your cross and follow Me and have some pain, have some cost, you are not worthy of Me." And folks, let me say this, you are not a Christian![26]

Taking Jesus' statement at face value would lead one to question whether Peter was a Christian. Another excerpt from the same sermon also illustrates the severe degree of imbalance in Lordship's teaching on discipleship:

> Years ago when I was in Australia. . . I met a man. . .he gave me two books that really changed my life, they really did. They were written by a fellow named Walter Chantry. [Chantry] talked about believers taking up the cross. I read that book and I discussed it with [the man who had given him Chantry's book] and he showed me from the Scriptures; he said, "Doug, we are messed up when we teach people that you can become a believer and later on a disciple." He said, "If a person does not become a disciple, they are not a Christian." By the way, Christian comes after being a disciple; did you know that? Acts 11:26-the disciples were called Christians first in Antioch. About 20 years after the church started. Christlike and we are teaching people, take Christ as your Savior and later on as your

Lord. If you are doing that you are not getting saved! It is a matter of surrender; there is a cost involved."

I have rarely heard a more definite, categorical, and exegetically unsound sermon as the one above. Another preacher in Australia befriended Pastor Van Meter and gave him the two books by Walter J. Chantry, referred to above. This other man also instructed Pastor Van Meter in the Lordship gospel.

Walter Chantry is a committed Lordship advocate. In Appendix 'F' you will find a review by Dr. Stewart Custer of Walter Chantry's book, *Today's Gospel: Authentic or Synthetic*. A portion of that review states, "It is plain that Mr. Chantry has removed himself from the evangelical tradition. He is not an evangelical; he is a dangerous outsider." Pastor Van Meter said that these books "changed my life." Walter Chantry's books did indeed change him, but it was his soteriology that was radically changed. He was led to believe that passages meant for born again disciples of Christ were instead evangelistic passages directed to the lost. He subsequently abandoned the scriptural position on the gospel for the Lordship position of commitment, submission and surrender in "exchange" for salvation.

Denying one's self, bearing the cross and following Jesus are calls to committed discipleship meant for the believer, not conditions for salvation. Paul expressed what should be the daily attitude of the believer when he wrote, "I protest by your rejoicing which I have in Christ Jesus our Lord, I die daily," (1 Cor. 15:31).

> The term "disciple" is a synonym for "Christian" (Acts 11:26). However, the challenges of this great chapter (Luke 9) cannot be construed as an invitation to salvation. These men were already disciples when Christ called them. By definition they were already believers in Him. . . . That passage (along with its paral-

lels in Matthew 16:24-28 and Mark 8:34-38) follows Peter's great confession of Christ's deity and Christ's first announcement of His coming death. Those words, like the words in Matthew 10:37-39 were spoken to people who were already disciples.... There is no way they can be construed as invitations to salvation. This is not to deny the need for discipleship. Believers should be willing to surrender their wills to Christ and to follow Him wherever He leads them, whatever the cost may be. But that decision cannot be construed as part of the salvation experience. We believe Scripture presents a better answer than demanding lifelong obedience to Christ at the time of salvation.[28]

He . . . made a public declaration about a cross for *every* disciple. . . . Keep in mind that Jesus is talking about *discipleship* and not *sonship*. We are not saved from our sins because we take up a cross and follow Jesus, but because we trust the Saviour who died on the cross for our sins. After we become children of God, then we become disciples.[29]

In John 16:33, the Lord told His disciples, "In the world ye shall have tribulation: but be of good cheer; I have overcome the world." Paul and Barnabas went through Derbe, Lystra, Iconium, and Antioch. Acts 14:22 tells us that they were "Confirming the souls of the disciples, [and] exhorting them to continue in the faith, and that (they) must through much tribulation enter into the kingdom of God." Paul and Barnabas were strengthening the disciples because as believers they would face "tribulation" and affliction, just as Jesus said that His disciples would. Paul and Barnabas, therefore, exhorted them to live in daily submission to Christ, to take up the cross, and follow the Lord in suffering for His sake. These were calls for decisions to be made by believers for total surrender to Christ as true disciples of Christ.

> Romans 12:1 I beseech you therefore, brethren, by the mercies of God, that ye present your bodies a living sacrifice, holy, acceptable unto God, which is your reasonable service.

The Book of Romans is God's blueprint for the gospel. Nowhere in Romans can we find a message of self-denial, forsaking all or cross bearing for salvation, justification. Clearly Romans 12:1 is directed to believers, "brethren," who have already placed their faith in Jesus Christ and are born again. It is a call to sacrifice and commitment for those who are justified. The verse cannot possibly be interpreted as a message for the unsaved. Following Lordship's logic could, however, lead one to conclude that Romans 12:1 is an evangelistic message. Surrender of one's life in "a living sacrifice" to the lordship of Christ should be the response of one who has been saved by personal faith in the Lord Jesus Christ.

> Matthew 7:24-27 Therefore whosoever heareth these sayings of mine, and doeth them, I will liken him unto a wise man, which built his house upon a rock: And the rain descended, and the floods came, and the winds blew, and beat upon that house; and it fell not: for it was founded upon a rock. And every one that heareth these sayings of mine, and doeth them not, shall be likened unto a foolish man, which built his house upon the sand: And the rain descended, and the floods came, and the winds blew, and beat upon that house; and it fell: and great was the fall of it.

The Sermon on the Mount (Matthew 5-7) does not deal with salvation; it talks about discipleship. According to John MacArthur, however, the Sermon on the Mount contains "pure gospel."[30] Jesus Christ is not telling man how to be saved; He is telling the saved man how he ought to live as a disciple of Jesus Christ.

> Matthew 28:19-20 Go ye therefore, and teach all nations, baptizing them in the name of the Father, and of the Son, and of the Holy Ghost: Teaching them to observe all things whatsoever I have commanded you.

Commenting on Matthew 28:19-20, Evangelist John VanGelderen wrote,

> The first "*teach*" means "to make disciples," while the second word "teaching" means to "instruct." Disciples are made by preaching the Gospel and seeing them trust Christ as Savior. The discipleship (learning) process continues by teaching them to observe everything Jesus commanded. Throughout the book of Acts, individual believers and groups of believers are referred to in general as "disciples." These disciples then must be taught to apply the Word of God to their lives.[31]

Dear reader, do not allow the Lordship teacher to rob you of your joy and confidence in the sufficiency of Christ's finished work to save (2 Tim. 1:12). The Christian will not live a perfectly surrendered life. Although he will sin and grieve the Spirit, he should always strive to be holy and blameless. The Apostle Paul struggled in his Christian experience (Romans 7: 14-25), and you will too.

> The ground of assurance of salvation is endangered if surrender to Christ's lordship is a part of that ground. Instead of looking to the sufficiency of Christ and His work of redemption, one is compelled to look within to see if he has yielded himself to the Son of God. If he is conscience of times in his life when

he has denied the lordship of the Master (and who has not?) then he must logically question his standing before God.[32]

Reading the comments of the Lordship Salvation men about their understanding of the requirements for salvation, one seriously has to wonder if they would have us put our ultimate confidence for salvation in our commitment to be crucified with Christ than just solely in Christ's death. Likewise, according to Romans 5:1-10 the term "final salvation" is dependent upon "Christ's life" not mine! Can they not understand what it says, "we shall be saved from wrath through him" and "we shall be saved by his life?" Sadly, these Lordship Salvation men would have us to be consumed with minding our Christian life, our obedience, and our faithfulness in order to have confidence rather than relying on Christ's life. From beginning to end salvation is all of Christ.[33]

When a man tries to carefully introduce verses about discipleship as though they are strictly evangelistic, remember that the Bible teaches that the lost must come to Christ for salvation and then follow after Him in discipleship. Salvation and discipleship are two very different things. We must not use verses intended to teach discipleship to try to lead a man to Christ. To do so creates confusion and frustration. The message becomes a gospel of faith, plus works.

If you are ever in doubt as to what an individual believes and teaches regarding the Lordship gospel, you should seek clarification. Below are questions about a passage in Luke's gospel you can ask to get a clear picture of what the individual's position is.

> Luke 9:23-24 And He said to them all, If any man will come after me, let him deny himself, and take up his cross daily, and follow me. For whosoever will save his life shall lose it: but whosoever will lose his life for my sake, the same shall save it.

1. Does Luke 9:23-24 state conditions I must satisfy to receive God's free gift of salvation?
2. Luke 9:24 is a conditional verse. Twice it says "for whosoever will . . ." Do you view the demands of Luke 9:24 as a part of the gospel of Jesus Christ? Is this a precondition for salvation?
3. Do you believe that becoming a disciple precedes becoming a Christian or is required to become a Christian?
4. As you present the plan of salvation, would you ask the unsaved man, "Are you ready to submit and make a commitment to Jesus as sovereign Lord over your life?"

Salvation has primarily to do with Jesus Christ as Savior; discipleship has primarily to do with Jesus Christ as Lord. Salvation is the new birth, a one-time event in which a man by the washing of regeneration, and renewing of the Holy Ghost (Titus 3:5) is saved from sin, death and Hell. Discipleship is a process, maturing and growing as a believer over a lifetime, "in grace, and [in] the knowledge of our Lord and Savior Jesus Christ" (2 Peter 3:18).

In 1999 I had the privilege of hearing a series of sermons by Rev. Robert Marsh, a South African missionary to the Democratic Republic of Congo. In a sermon taken from Romans 1:16 Robert Marsh spoke on how the believer should not be ashamed of the gospel, for as the passage says, "it is the power of God unto salvation." The missionary illustrated the gospel's power to save men and change their lives from the personal testimony of his own father. The following illustration is only an illustration. I do not elevate the experience of one man to the level of Scriptural authority. Theology based on experience is dangerous, because one can prove anything based on experience. As you read the following account remember: you are reading the application of biblical truth that has been borne out in the preceding pages.

> My father held a good job, but he would come home and he would drink. He never drank on the job, but I always remember him drunk in the evenings. Weekends was the big party, go to his friends...whatever they did they would drink. Christmas was never a happy time in our family. Christmas always we knew would start out very joyous and then everybody would get drunk. I remember days when my father would get so drunk that my mother would take us on a bus to my grandmother's home. I remember days when my father would move his bed into the middle of the garage and slept on his bed because he was a slave to something that controlled his life. Sitting there, sleeping there with his gun under the pillow, but the day came when the power of the gospel changed his life. The day came that my father trusted in Jesus Christ as personal Savior. He went to work, he still had those drinks. He never got drunk like he used to, but the day came when he sat down at the table and he was reading God's Word and the Holy Spirit convicted his life. The power of the gospel said, "you are still in sin, clean up this area, make Christ Lord of your life." That day my father stopped (drinking). He said, "If I am the temple of the Holy Ghost I cannot drink." That day my father surrendered.[34]

That testimony illustrates the biblical order of salvation through faith alone in the Lord Jesus Christ followed by surrender to the Lord in obedience to His Word and the Spirit. That man accepted Christ as his Savior and then, as a born-again man, in gratitude for what Christ had done for him he surrendered a wicked area in his life to the Lord Jesus Christ. The convicting work of the Holy Sprit and the Word of God brought this new Christian to the place of surrender as a disciple of Christ. Rev. Marsh continued the illustration:

> My dad went to work, he worked with people who drank. He said, "I am not going to be ashamed when they ask me why I am not drinking." No it wasn't a hazard, it was because God wanted him to change. My father said, "I make no apologies for being a Christian. Christ has saved me and He has changed my life. He has changed my love from the world to Christ. The gospel has made Christ my Lord and my loyalty is no longer to my flesh and to sin or to this world, but it is to Christ and I must labor for Him."[35]

That dear man was saved by faith in "the simplicity that is in Christ." He surrendered his life to serve his Savior and Lord. Robert Marsh's father came to Christ to be saved exactly as the hymn writer Charlotte Elliott eloquently penned, "Just as I am, without one plea." He then began to follow Christ his Lord as a committed disciple.

> Those who have so trusted Christ can be trained as disciples of the Lord Jesus. They will follow Him in baptism, the first step of obedience to Christ in the Christian life. They will surrender their wills fully to Christ and follow Him. They will be willing to take up a cross, enduring humiliation, suffering, and possible death for the One who literally bore a cross to save them from sin.[36]

One of the most extreme examples of conditioning salvation on a commitment to do the works of a disciple comes from Pastor Steve Lawson.

> If you want to receive this gift it will cost you the total commitment of all that you are to the Lord Jesus Christ. There are many here who think they are saved, but are not; they have never really done business with God.... I want to single you out in the midst of this crowd. Have you taken up a cross in order to follow after Christ? Have you recognized your own sinfulness, acknowledged that God's judgment is true, have you acknowledged Christ's right to rule your life? Have you submitted to the Lordship of Christ? Have you really come to the end of self? Because Jesus does not begin until you end.[37]

Tim Challies confirmed that Lawson's sermon on "true discipleship" from Luke 14:24-33 was an evangelistic appeal meant for the lost. Lawson conditions the reception of "this gift" (the gift of eternal life) on an upfront "total commitment" from a lost man. In the latter portion of the excerpt Lawson is saying that a relation with "Jesus does not begin" until the lost man has come to the end of himself. If in Lawson's message he spoke of following Christ, self denial and cross bearing in the context of a born again believer needing to make those commitments to his Lord and Savior he (Lawson) would be on biblical ground. Lawson, however, took those commands meant for the believer and instead presents them as evangelistic conditions that must be agreed to in exchange for salvation.

> Before you can "come after" Christ in discipleship (Luke 9:23; Matt. 11:29-30), you must "come unto" Christ for salvation (Matthew 11:28). Discipleship is not a requirement for salvation; discipleship is the obligation of every saved person.[38]

By their use of discipleship verses as salvation verses, Lordship teachers have gone beyond the scope of the Bible's simple plan of salvation. It is wrong to apply the verses meant for discipleship to the doctrine of salvation. The word, *disciple* does not appear in the epistles, only in the Gospels and the Book of Acts. In this regard Dr. Ryrie noted:

> This may be because a disciple was expected to physically follow his teacher wherever he went, and this meant leaving his family and occupation so as to be able to be with that teacher all the time. After Christ's resurrection and ascension, this aspect of discipleship was impossible, so the word was used less frequently in the Book of Acts and not at all in the remainder of the New Testament.[39]

Whether or not Ryrie has touched upon a valid reason for the disappearance of the term *disciple*, the concept occurs only occasionally (i.e. *follower*), but when it does it is always in reference to the believer. Since the concept of the disciple is at the heart of Lordship Salvation, the disappearance of the term in the rest of the New Testament should be rather disconcerting to the Lordship advocate.

In August 2007 a friend e-mailed me a statement that was made by a Bible college professor. This professor said, "Luke considered every true believer to be a disciple in some sense of that word. However, he made clear that the demands of discipleship are not conditions to salvation, but are evidences of regeneration and sanctification." This chapter has addressed what I consider one of the most egregious errors of Lordship Salvation. A change of life through submission to the lordship of Christ should come as a result of salvation. It is antithetical to the Scriptures to take what should be the RESULT of salvation and make the resolve to perform those things in discipleship the REQUIREMENT for salvation.

ENDNOTES:

1. "Disciple," *The New International Dictionary of New Testament Theology*, Vol. 1, pp. 486-490.
2. John R. Rice, *Rice Reference Bible*, p. 1,014.
3. John MacArthur, *The Gospel According to Jesus* [Revised & Expanded Edition], pp. 27, 142.
4. Ibid., p. 147.
5. Charles Bing, *Lordship Salvation: A Biblical Evaluation and Response*, p. 160.
6. James G. Merritt, *Evangelism And The Call of Christ in Evangelism In The Twenty-First Century: The Critical Issues*, ed. Thomas S. Rainer, p. 145.
7. John R. Stott, *Basic Christianity*, p. 109.
8. J. Wallis, *Many To Belief, But Few To Obedience*. Sojourners, p. 21.
9. J. I. Packer, *Evangelism And The Sovereignty Of God*, p. 73.
10. W. Harold Mare, "1 Corinthians," *The Expositor's Bible Commentary*, Vol. X, p. 233.
11. John MacArthur, *The Gospel According To Jesus* [Revised & Expanded Edition], p. 203.
12. Ernest Pickering, *Lordship Salvation: An Examination of John MacArthur's Book, The Gospel According to Jesus*.
13. Charles Ryrie, *So Great Salvation*, p. 40.
14. Ernest Pickering, *Lordship Salvation: An Examination of John MacArthur's Book, The Gospel According to Jesus*.
15. John MacArthur, *The Gospel According to Jesus: What is Authentic Faith*, pp. 219, 224.
16. YouTube, "Kirk Cameron Interviews John MacArthur," http://www.youtube.com/watch?v=tNQoOEG8P2I, (accessed January 10, 2010).
17. R. C. Sproul, *Grace Unknown*, p. 198.
18. Charles Bing, *Lordship Salvation: A Biblical Evaluation and Response*, p. 160, (emphasis mine).
19. John MacArthur, *Hard to Believe: The High Cost and Infinite Value of Following Jesus*, p. 6.
20. John MacArthur, *The Gospel According to Jesus:* What is Authentic Faith, p. 149. (Italics added)
21. Ibid., p. 150. (Italics added)
22. Joel Mullenix, *What Is The Gospel?* A sermon recorded at Pensacola Christian College on Nov. 2, 1997.
23. J. Vernon McGee, *Thru The Bible With J. Vernon McGee*, Vol. 4, p. 311.
24. Ibid., p. 287.
25. Charles Bing, *Lordship Salvation: A Biblical Evaluation and Response*, p. 136.

26. Doug Van Meter, *Ear Piercing Time*, a sermon preached at Calvary Baptist Church in Randburg, South Africa on September 25, 1997.
27. Ibid.
28. Fred Moritz, *Preach the Word*, October-December 1999.
29. Warren W. Wiersbe, *The Bible Exposition Commentary*, Vol. 1, p. 207.
30. John MacArthur, *The Gospel According to Jesus: What is Authentic Faith*, p. 202.
31. John VanGelderen, *Preach the Word*, January-March 2000, p. 23.
32. Everett F. Harrison, "Must Christ be Lord to Be Savior—No," *Eternity*, 10 September 1959.
33. Anonymous, "Final Salvation is Dependent on Christ's Life." http://indefenseofthegospel.blogspot.com/2009/11/final-salvation-is-dependent-onchrists.html (accessed Nov. 17, 2009).
34. Robert Marsh, A sermon preached September 19, 1999.
35. Ibid.
36. Fred Moritz, *Preach the Word*, (October-December 1999).
37. Pastor Steve Lawson, *The Cost of Discipleship, It Will Cost You Everything*, Resolved Conference, Feb. 18, 2007. From Challies.com, Resolved Conference VI.
38. George Zeller, *The Relationship Between God's Grace and Lordship Legalism*, http://middletownchurch.org/salvatio/lorsh03.htm (accessed January 10, 2010).
39. Charles Ryrie, *So Great Salvation*, pp. 104-105.

CAN THERE BE A CHRISTIAN WHO IS CARNAL?

1 Corinthians 3:1-4 And I, brethren, could not speak unto you as unto spiritual, but as unto carnal, even as unto babes in Christ. I have fed you with milk, and not with meat: for hitherto ye were not able to bear it, neither yet now are ye able. For ye are yet carnal: for whereas there is among you envying, and strife, and divisions, are ye not carnal, and walk as men? For while one saith, I am of Paul; and another, I am of Apollos; are ye not carnal?

What is the Meaning of the Word "Carnal?"

The word *carnal* (or *carnality*) in the New Testament is the translation of the Greek adjective σαρκικος (*sarkikos*) or one of its two cognates, σαρκινος (*sarkinos*) or σαρχ (*sarx*), which mean *fleshly* and *flesh* respectively. (The only exception to this usage is I Corinthians 3:4, where the word for *man* ανθρωπο is translated *carnal*.) *Sarkikos* has the basic idea of pertaining to flesh.

..."flesh," signifies (a) "having the nature of flesh," i.e. e., sensual, controlled by animal appetites, governed by human nature, instead of by the Spirit of God,... "fleshly;" or as the equivalent of "human," with the added idea of weakness, figuratively of the weapons of spiritual warfare, "of the flesh"... or with the idea of unspirituality, of human wisdom, "fleshly," 2 Cor. 1:12.[1]

The word *carnal* occurs twelve times in the New Testament. Every time it is used as an adjective to describe a person (rather than something impersonal like *mind, things,* or *commandments*), it speaks of a Christian.

Can There Be Both Carnal and Spiritual Christians?

Well-meaning believers will fall into error if they use human logic in their approach to the Bible. Such is the case among Lordship advocates in their interpretation of 1 Corinthians 3:1-4. Although he may express agreement with the passage in a roundabout way by saying, "Christians do behave in carnal ways," he struggles with the biblical truth that there are carnal Christians in the body of Christ. His gospel of total submission for salvation demands total unwavering obedience to the lordship of Christ leaving virtually no room for the possibility of a carnal Christian. Dr. Layton Talbert wrote:

> Some theologians, willing to set aside the stringent logical demands of their theological system, have understood the limitations of logic, the need for balance, and the necessity of sticking with the explicit statements of Scripture. The theological balance is beautiful, allowing every passage to say what it says—no more, no less.[2]

First Corinthians 3:1-4 is clear—there are born again men and women who can and do become carnal Christians and remain carnal for a length of time. How does the Lordship advocate arrive at a position that is contrary to the "explicit statements of Scripture?" The answer may be found in John MacArthur's rejection of the believer having two natures, a new nature and the old nature.

> I believe it is a serious misunderstanding to think of the believer as having both an old and new nature. Believers do not have dual personalities...there is no such thing as an old and new nature in the believer.... Salvation brings about a radical change in the nature of the believer...The old man has ceased to exist.[3]

MacArthur is also on record with what appear to be contradictory statements on the old nature. From the same book as the previous example he wrote:

> A person cannot have two different and opposing natures at the same time.... The passage [Romans 7] is obviously a poignant account of a person's inner conflict with himself, one part of him pulling one direction and another part pulling the opposite. The conflict is real and it is intense.[4]

At the moment of regeneration and conversion the believer receives a new nature. His old nature, however, has not been eradicated or improved. He is going to live out his Christian experience just as Paul did, which was in warfare between the two natures.

> Romans 7:14-25 For we know that the law is spiritual: but I am carnal, sold under sin. For that which I do I allow not: for what I would, that do I not; but what I

hate, that do I. If then I do that which I would not, I consent unto the law that it is good. Now then it is no more I that do it, but sin that dwelleth in me. For I know that in me (that is, in my flesh,) dwelleth no good thing: for to will is present with me; but how to perform that which is good I find not. For the good that I would I do not: but the evil which I would not, that I do. Now if I do that I would not, it is no more I that do it, but sin that dwelleth in me. I find then a law, that, when I would do good, evil is present with me. For I delight in the law of God after the inward man: But I see another law in my members, warring against the law of my mind, and bringing me into captivity to the law of sin which is in my members. O wretched man that I am! who shall deliver me from the body of this death? I thank God through Jesus Christ our Lord. So then with the mind I myself serve the law of God; but with the flesh the law of sin.

In Romans 7:14-25 the Bible makes it very clear that believers will experience struggles between their old sinful flesh and their new spiritual nature. The book to the Romans was written by the Apostle Paul. He was writing about his own struggles with carnality. Paul was a saved man, but he had struggles in his walk with God. Has there ever been a Christian who did not experience both victories over sin and also failures to resist temptation and slip into carnality? There is a very real warfare between the two natures, the flesh and the spirit, in the life of every believer. Sometimes the believer will lose that battle to the old nature, his sinful flesh, and at that moment in his life he is carnal.

> Galatians 5:17 For the flesh lusteth against the Spirit, and the Spirit against the flesh: and these are contrary the one to the other; so that ye cannot do the things that ye would.

Lordship advocates would say, "The distinction commonly made between the carnal Christian and the spiritual Christian is invalid." In addressing this matter, Dr. Ernest Pickering said:

> This is a familiar theme, particularly among Reformed theologians such as Lloyd-Jones. . . . Their impression seems to be that if one admits to the existence of "carnal Christians," one is merely seeking to find a way to excuse the loose living of professing believers. Those who speak of "carnal" Christians are only employing the terminology of Scripture. . . . While brethren may deny the existence of such an individual, we would venture to say that a considerable number of examples could be found in their own churches! One is not going to make "carnal" Christians vanish simply by demanding that saving faith include surrender to the Lordship of Christ. Even if that were done it would not guarantee that the new convert would submit to the Lordship of Christ when confronted with a specific demand. If he did not do so, he would become a "carnal" Christian, walking according to the flesh and not the Spirit.[5]

In the following excerpt Dr. Charlie Bing explains the Lordship position on carnality:

> Many Lordship advocates do not accept the possibility that there can be both carnal and spiritual Christians. While affirming that Christians can fall into sin, and act carnally, one Lordship author proposes that "carnal Christian" is a "contradiction in terms."[6]

Lordship advocate Walter J. Chantry wrote:

> In a panic over this phenomenon [of worldly Christians], the evangelicals have invented the idea of "carnal Christians." These are said to be folks who have taken the gift of eternal life without turning from sin. They have "allowed" Jesus to be their Saviour; but they have not yet yielded their life to the Lord.[7]

In light of 1 Corinthians 3:1-4, it is hard to believe that the "carnal Christian" is an invention of modern-day evangelicals. The Apostle Paul addresses the "brethren" at Corinth. The "brethren" are believers, and Paul calls them "carnal." Not every believer in the church at Corinth was carnal, but certainly there were enough "carnal" Christians to warrant the stern rebukes from the Apostle Paul in his first epistle to them. On the "carnal" Christian John MacArthur says,

> The tragic result is that many people think it is fairly normal for Christians to live like unbelievers. . . . As I noted. . . . contemporary theologians have devised an entire category for this type of person—the "carnal Christian."[8]

While it may be commonplace for "Christians to live like unbelievers," it certainly should not be "normal" for any Christian. The "carnal Christian" is not a category "devised" by "contemporary theologians." It is a category of believers ("brethren") identified in the Word of God, through the inspiration of the Holy Spirit, by the Apostle Paul. Walter Chantry and John MacArthur must ignore the clear teaching of Scripture to arrive at the conclusion that the "carnal" Christian has been "devised," invented or fabricated only in recent times. Dr. Charles Hodge in his commentary on 1 Corinthians makes it clear that there are both carnal and spiritual Christians in the church. He also refers to a third class of Christians who stand out above others in spiritual prominence:

> The apostle tells those whom he admits to be Christians, and whom he calls brethren, that they are not spiritual. He must use the word therefore in a modified sense. This is a very common usage. When we predicate spirituality of a Christian as compared to other Christians, we mean that he is eminently spiritual. But when the distinction is between Christians and the world then every Christian is said to be spiritual. In like manner we speak of some Christians as worldly or carnal, without intending to deny that they are Christians. It is obvious that the apostle uses the terms here in the same manner. He is not speaking of Christians as distinguished from the world, but of one class of Christians as distinguished from another.
>
> Their unfitness to receive any other nourishment than that adapted to children, is proved by their being carnal; and their being carnal is proved by the divisions existing among them. . . . Even Paul said of himself, "I am carnal." This term therefore may be applied even to the most advanced Christians.[9]

From the expanded and updated version of his lengthy article written in 1976, Kenneth L. Gentry writes, "No doubt lordship adherents would regard many 'carnal Christians' to be false converts, who have only an inadequate knowledge of truth at best."[10] Gentry reveals how the Lordship advocate deals with "carnal Christians." According to Lordship advocates, a man who does not live the Christian life in full submission to the Lord Jesus Christ was likely never saved in the first place. The Lordship advocate who sees carnality in the life of a professing believer says, "If he is not living a dedicated Christian life, he may never have been saved." This kind of teaching flows from Calvinism's Perseverance of the Saints. John MacArthur wrote,

I am committed to the biblical truth that salvation is forever. Contemporary Christians have come to refer to this as the doctrine of *eternal security*. Perhaps the Reformer's terminology is more appropriate; they spoke of the perseverance of the saints.[11]

MacArthur continues by quoting A. W. Pink, a Reformed commentator:

[God] does not deal with [believers] as unaccountable automatons, but as moral agents, just as their natural life is maintained through their use of means and by their avoidance of that which is inimical to their well-being, so it is with the maintenance and preservation of their spiritual lives. God preserves His people in this world through their perseverance.[12]

Notice that last sentence: "God preserves His people. . .through their perseverance." Some men might conclude that by Pink's logic a man who cannot save himself in the first place must, after being regenerated, keep himself saved. The Calvinist's idea of genuine salvation, however, does not allow for a non-persevering believer. Does Pink mean that if God's people persevere, God will preserve them and keep them eternally secure? It sounds as if that is his meaning. Pink, on the other hand, might argue that God preserves because the Elect will persevere.

What does the Lord Jesus Christ say? "Verily, verily, I say unto you, He that believeth on me hath everlasting life. . . . And I give unto them eternal life; and they shall never perish, neither shall any [man] pluck them out of my hand," (John 6:47; 10:28). The Bible is clear: man is not saved by promising good works (Eph. 2:8-9), and he is not kept eternally secure by performing good works. Man is saved by God's grace through faith in Christ, and kept secure by the indwelling Holy Spirit (Eph. 1:13).

Ephesians 2:8-9 For by grace are ye saved through faith; and that not of yourselves: it is the gift of God: not of works, lest any man should boast.

Ephesians 1:13 In whom ye also trusted, after that ye heard the word of truth, the gospel of your salvation: in whom also after that ye believed, ye were sealed with that holy Spirit of promise.

Do Carnal Christians Appear in the Bible?

In both testaments of the Bible, we find examples of believers who did not live a life of unwavering submission to the Lord. They were without question righteous, but they did have episodes of carnality during their walk with God. Abraham was certainly a righteous man: "For what saith the scripture? Abraham believed God, and it was counted unto him for righteousness . . . for we say that faith was reckoned to Abraham for righteousness," (Romans 4:3, 9). However, Abraham lied to King Abimelech in regard to his relationship with Sarah (Genesis 20). Abraham said she was his sister because he was worried that the King may kill him to take Sarah for his wife. Furthermore, rather than wait for the promised son (Isaac) that he would have through Sarah in their old age, Abraham, through Sarah's insistence, sought to accomplish God's promise through Hagar.

> Acts 13:22 And when he had removed him, he raised up unto them David to be their king; to whom also he gave their testimony, and said, I have found David the son of Jesse, a man after mine own heart, which shall fulfil all my will.

Children in churches all over the world are taught about the mighty deed of David, when he was just a shepherd boy, that he slew the giant Goliath. David was anointed King of Israel and did many great deeds through the power of God in his life. David also had episodes of carnality in his life. Many know the story of his lust for Bathsheba, his taking her, and arranging the murder of her husband Uriah the Hittite (2 Samuel 11). David tried to cover his sin, but God loved him and sent the prophet Nathan to confront him (2 Samuel 12:1-15). On another occasion David, acting out of pride and against the counsel of his closest advisors ordered the numbering of the people (2 Samuel 24). David is referred to as a man after God's own heart, yet he fell into the kind of sin that one can scarcely imagine a godly man might commit.

> There are in the Bible several clear examples of believers (about whose right relationship to God there can be no question) who were, nevertheless, not completely or continually committed to the Lord. Such examples would seem to settle the issue clearly by indicating that faith alone is the requirement for eternal life. This is not to say that dedication of life is not expected of believers, but it is to say that it is not one of the conditions for salvation.[13]

If a Lordship teacher were to meet the modern-day equivalent of the Apostle Peter, he would possibly conclude that the man had never been saved. The night before the crucifixion, Peter denied his Lord three times. He essentially quit the ministry when he declared, "I go a fishing" (John 21:3). Another time, the Lord appeared to Peter and commanded him, saying, "Rise, Peter; kill, and eat. But Peter said, Not so, Lord" (Acts 10:13-14). There was also Peter's dissimulation at Antioch, when "he withdrew and separated himself, fearing them which were of the circumcision" (Gal. 2:11-ff). Yet in spite of all his shortcomings, Peter was a saved man.

Peter is not the only believer in the New Testament who struggled in his commitment to the Lord Jesus Christ. The Book of Acts tells us about the initial reluctance of the Ephesian believers to abandon their old ways.

> Acts 19:18-19 And many that believed came, and confessed, and shewed their deeds. Many of them also which used curious arts brought their books together, and burned them before all men: and they counted the price of them, and found it fifty thousand pieces of silver.

As Dr. Charles Ryrie writes,

> There were people at Ephesus who became believers in Christ knowing that they should give up their use of magic but who did not give it up, some of them for as long as two years after they had become Christians. Yet their unwillingness to give it up did not prevent their becoming believers. Their salvation did not depend on faith plus willingness to submit to the lordship of Christ in the matter of using magical arts.[14]

Many believers live godly Christian lives; others struggle with the old nature and live carnally. All experience times when they succumb to temptation, fall into sin, and grieve the Holy Spirit. There is daily cleansing available. For the Bible says,

In Defense of the Gospel

> 1 John 1:9 If we confess our sins, he is faithful and just to forgive us our sins, and to cleanse us from all unrighteousness.

Christians can and do struggle in their walk with God to live in submission and obedience to the Lord Jesus Christ. For the children of Israel, crossing the river Jordan was a trek into a land of milk and honey just as God had promised. It was also going to begin as a walk on battleground. The Christian also walks on battleground until he reaches heaven and therefore must "put on the whole armour of God" (Ephesians 6:10-17) to resist and fight successfully in God's power. Charles Spurgeon spoke of the believer's struggle when he realizes that he often lives in less than total obedience to Christ:

> But, saith one, I change so much. I feel sometimes as if I must be a Christian; at other times I feel as if it is out of the question that I could be saved. Yes, and do you not change a great deal as to your bodily life? I do, I know. Why, this heavy, damp, thick atmosphere half poisons me. Lift me up a few thousand feet on a mountain side, with a good stiff breeze blowing, and I feel quite another man. Are these changes reasons for questioning my being alive? Nay, nay. Quite the reverse. The reason why I feel changes is because I am alive, for I reckon that if I were a broomstick or a brick wall the atmosphere would not matter much. If you have no spiritual life you will know few changes, but because you are alive these variations must and will occur.[15]

On November 2, 1997, Dr. Joel Mullenix preached a sermon titled, *"What Is The Gospel?"* This sermon addressed a number of problems with the Lordship gospel. I felt it would be valuable to include the following extended excerpt, which addresses the question, what is a carnal Christian?

> It's interesting as we read through the pages of Scripture that we see many examples of carnal Christians. As we go back to the Old Testament, we meet a man who is very familiar to you. His name is Lot. Lot had a wonderfully privileged life. He grew up in the home of Abraham. As Abraham travelled around the land of promise, which God had called him to, Lot travelled with him. Can you imagine living with Abraham? Lot must have heard Abraham speak of the Lord. He must have heard Abraham speak of the call on his life. Surely Lot heard Abraham's testimony about how God had called him and he had obeyed and had responded. He listened to him speak of the things of God, and Lot placed his own personal trust in God; but Lot became worldly. Lot moved to Sodom as he got his eyes on the things of the world. Lot lived among the Sodomites. Lot was chastened by God! He came to a tragic end. We find him, in the last scene we see of him, in drunken incest with his daughters. As you look at Lot at that point in his life, in fact, as we examine Lot's life in the Old Testament, we would as human beings who cannot see the heart, logically conclude that Lot must not have been a believer; Lot must not have been a saved man. But the Scriptures teach us different. In the New Testament, in II Peter chapter 2 verse 7, the reference is to God's dealing with Sodom; and we read, And [He] delivered just Lot, vexed with the filthy conversation of the wicked: For that righteous man dwelling among them, in seeing and hearing, vexed his righteous soul from day to day with their unlawful deeds. Just Lot, the righteous man, his righteous soul. Looking at Lot's life, you would not have suspected that, but the Scripture makes it absolutely clear; we shall see Lot in heaven some day. Why? Because Lot, at some point in his life, became a carnal Christian.

We meet other characters in the Old Testament. A man who is very familiar to you is the man Samson. Samson grew up in a home with parents who loved the Lord. He heard about the Lord; he knew of God; he called upon God. But Samson was disobedient to his parents. He had a sensual heart. He was blind when it came to the matter of women. And as you study the life of Samson, you see Samson chastened by God, as God always chastens His children when they become disobedient to Him. And so, chastened by God, blinded through the actions of his enemies, Samson dies a tragic death. If you look at Samson's life, you might wonder whether Samson was saved. Samson at times in his life was a carnal Christian. But I'm so glad to remind you that when we come over to Hebrews chapter 11, that great hall of faith of heroes, in verse 32 we have Samson listed as one of those heroes of faith. There is no question that we shall see Samson some day in heaven. Samson was a man who was justified by faith. But Samson in his life became a carnal Christian.

What is a carnal Christian? We meet an interesting case of this in the church at Corinth, a church which was filled with carnal Christians; and in 1 Corinthians chapter 5 verse 5, we meet a Christian man, a believer, a man who had come to know Jesus Christ; and his sins had been forgiven by faith, and faith alone; but now this man is living in sin, and such sin as should not even be named among us—the sin of living in incest. And in 1 Corinthians chapter 5, verse 5, we read these words as Paul gives the instruction to the church at Corinth. He commands them to deliver such a one unto Satan for the destruction of the flesh. That is chastening. Why? That the spirit may be saved in the day of Jesus Christ. Here is a man who has come to God, has been born again, but has wandered off into sin, and is living this terrible life as a carnal Christian.

We meet others in the Bible. David, that great man of God, falls into sin. Who would deny that at that point in his life, David was living the life of a carnal Christian? Peter in the New Testament: Peter, that man who had been in the inner circle, who had been on the Mount of Transfiguration, but as we leaf through the pages of Scripture, we see Peter on the night of the betrayal of the Lord Jesus Christ, denying Him three times, and cursing in his denial. But Peter was a born-again man. Peter was living the life at that time of a carnal Christian.

We even meet people in the Scriptures that we are left with a question in our minds about. King Saul in the Old Testament, a man anointed by God, called by God to be King of Israel, but Saul who gets his eyes on material things, Saul who looks around and becomes caught up in his new calling as king. Saul becomes jealous of David; he becomes disobedient to God in the case of the Amalakites. He seeks information through a medium. One cannot tell from his life whether he is a saved man, and we really don't know for sure to this day because the Bible is silent in his case. He was anointed of God, yet his life did not measure up to that. I would propose to you that perhaps we shall see him in heaven; I don't know for sure. But Saul's life looks like that of a carnal Christian. And how can this be? It can be because it's possible for a Christian to be carnal. The classic passage, which speaks of this in the New Testament, is found in 1 Corinthians chapter 3, and I note especially verses 1 and 3. Paul writes these words to this church which seems to be filled with carnal Christians, and he says in 1 Corinthians chapter 3 verse 1: "And I, brethren, could not speak unto—" Notice that is, "I brethren"; they are saved people he is writing to. "And I brethren could not speak unto you as unto spiritual, but as unto carnal. For ye are yet carnal," he says. "For whereas there is among you envying, [and] strife, and divisions, are ye not carnal, and walk as men?" They all, all the

Christians in that church, started out as all Christians do, as carnal Christians, because that verse references that as babes in Christ, little babies just born again. And they were supposed to grow, and some of them did grow. But some Christians don't grow like they're supposed to, and to look at them in their lives you can't tell from their behavior that they are Christians. And that Corinthian church was full of those carnal Christians, Christians who should have grown but who had never grown in Christ, and their lives look like the world.

That church had such a problem with it that Paul penned these words in 1 Corinthians chapter 11 verses 28 through 32. Paul writes to this church filled with carnal Christians, "But let a man examine himself, and so let him eat of that bread, and drink of that cup. For he that eateth and drinketh unworthily, eateth and drinketh damnation [that's judgment] to himself, not discerning the Lords body. For this cause many are weak and sickly among you, and many sleep." That's the chastening of God in the lives of those carnal Christians. "For if we would judge ourselves, we should not be judged. But when we are judged, we are chastened of the Lord, that we should not be condemned with the world." And in that same letter to Corinth back in chapter 3 verse 15, Paul is discussing the judgment seat of Christ, where we shall all stand one day; and he warns those who are carnal Christians. He says, "If any man's work shall be burned, he shall suffer loss: but he himself shall be saved; yet so as by fire."

So what is the Gospel? The Gospel is that simple message that Jesus the Son of God died for us, and He was buried, and He rose again; and by believing in Him we can be saved. But we have a problem sometimes, because sometimes we as believers, we as Christians, children of God who have been born again by simple faith plus nothing else, sometimes we in our lives live as carnal Christians.[16]

Dr. Ryrie questions the Lordship gospel in light of Bible examples of genuine believers who experience lapses in their obedience to the Lord Jesus Christ:

> Therefore, we ask, how can the lordship of Christ over one's life be a requirement for becoming a child of God? I say again, however, that submission to the lordship of Christ is vital for a developing Christian life; but becoming a child of God and growing up to maturity have different requirements, and lordship over the life is not a requirement for getting into the family of God.[17]

Statements from Notable Commentators

Numerous recognized commentators have acknowledged the reality of carnal Christians based on the teaching of 1 Corinthians 3:1-4. Dr. J. Vernon McGee in his opening remarks on 1 Corinthians 3 wrote:

> As we have seen in chapter 2, Paul has presented two classes of mankind: the natural man and the spiritual man. Now he makes a further division, and it is among believers: carnal Christians and spiritual Christians. Their status as carnal or as spiritual will manifest itself in their lives and in their Christian service.[18]

Dr. McGee continues as he comments on verse 1:

> The carnal Christian is the one who hasn't grown up spiritually, and it is evident that he lacks spiritual discernment—not because he doesn't have the Holy Spirit dwelling within him, but because he is not growing in grace and in the knowledge of Christ. This unnatural man, this carnal Christian, (sic) is a babe in Christ.[19]

Dr. Charles Ryrie wrote:

> ... we know experientially and from Scripture that flesh and Spirit battle in the believer, which seems to indicate that there are areas of both carnality and spirituality in the person at the same time (Galatians 5:17). Rather than thinking of varying degrees of carnality and spirituality, perhaps we should think of areas of carnality *and spirituality* as the experience of a growing believer.[20]

Dr. H. A. Ironside said of 1 Corinthians 2:14-3:8:

> In this passage we have three men brought before us: the natural, the carnal, and the spiritual. What are we to understand by these expressions? We often say that there are only two classes of people in the world, those who are saved and those who are lost; and of course that distinction stands. But here the apostle divides mankind into three classes: the natural, the carnal, and the spiritual. . . . Now a carnal man, strange as it may seem, is a fleshly believer. There are many such persons. The carnal man has been regenerated, he has received a new nature, his spirit has been quickened into newness of life, and that spirit that fell into the basement is being elevated into its proper place by divine power, but the man finds he is still under the power of that old carnal fleshy nature in a large measure.[21]

Dr. Warren Wiersbe wrote on 1 Corinthians 3:1-4:

> Paul already explained that there are two kinds of people in the world-natural (unsaved) and spiritual (saved). But now he explains that there are two kinds of saved people: mature and immature (carnal). A Christian matures by allowing the Spirit to teach him and direct him by feeding on the Word. The immature Christian lives for the things of the flesh (*carnal* means flesh) and has little interest in the things of the Spirit.

Of course, some believers are immature because they have been saved only a short time, but that is not what Paul is discussing here.[22]

Dr. G. Campbell Morgan wrote:

First, he addresses them as brethren . . . he is writing to them as brethren, those who are his fellow believers, who are babes. That shows the presence of life. He is not writing to those dead. . . . He is not writing to men of the world, outside the Christian fact. He is writing to those within the Christian fact, to those born again, who have life. Yes, he says, they are babes, but they are brethren. The trouble with them is that they are not spiritual, but are carnal. . . . Writing to these Corinthians, Paul says, I will tell you what is the matter with you Corinthian people. I cannot write unto you as unto spiritual—you are not living in that realm—but as to carnal. You are living under the mastery of the flesh. Oh, you are children, you are babes. You are born again. You have life, but you are yielding yourself to the carnal side of your nature, instead of the spiritual.[23]

Lordship advocates who struggle with the reality of carnal Christians in the church would do well to read again First Corinthians 3:1-4. They would do well to let the Bible say what it says, without the trappings of logic and rationalizations to make it fit their system. They would do well to refrain from trying to force the Scriptures into conformity with the presuppositions of Lordship Salvation. The Bible is clear; a man can be genuinely born again, indwelled with the Spirit of God, and live as a carnal Christian at the same time.

> Galatians 5:17: For the flesh lusteth against the Spirit, and the Spirit against the flesh: and these are contrary the one to the other: so that ye cannot do the things that ye would.
>
> Romans 7:14, 18, 21: For we know that the law is spiritual: but I am carnal, sold under sin. For I know that in me (that is, in my flesh,) dwelleth no good thing: for to will is present with me; but how to perform that which is good I find not. I find then a law, that, when I would do good, evil is present with me.

Christians will experience episodes of carnality in their lives. As we saw earlier in this chapter David, the man after God's own heart, did not always live a godly life. Neither will you or I live apart from episodes of carnal, sinful behavior or thoughts. Christians, because of the old sin nature, are capable of committing sin and suffering dire consequences just as David did. Although David became carnal, the Bible tells us that he also sought God's forgiveness:

> Psalm 51:1, 10, 12: To the chief Musician, A Psalm of David, when Nathan the prophet came unto him, after he had gone in to Bathsheba. Have mercy upon me, O God, according to thy lovingkindness: according unto the multitude of thy tender mercies blot out my transgressions. Create in me a clean heart, O God; and renew a right spirit within me. Restore unto me the joy of thy salvation; and uphold me with thy free spirit.

A believer will sometimes be carnal, but if his heart is tender toward God, he will be convinced of his sin and rebellion against the Lord, confess his sin, and be restored to a sweet fellowship with God. That a person sometimes struggles in his walk with God and may experience doubts about his salvation is usually a good indication that the individual is saved. One can hardly imagine an unsaved person expressing concern over the assurance of his salvation.

Evidence of a changed life ought to be seen, to some degree, in the life of any genuinely born again man. There should be genuine evidence of regeneration and a new life born of the Spirit of God. I do not make room for and I do not stand for the loose living of professing believers. The sad, reality, however, is that we will always have carnal Christians in our churches. These need to be counseled, prayed for and guided to live a life that is a shining testimony of the grace of God in their lives. The Christian will struggle with sin as he learns to "lay aside every weight, and the sin which doth so easily beset us" (Hebrews 12:1).

> We may take comfort about our souls if we know anything of an inward fight and conflict. It is the invariable companion of genuine Christian holiness. . . . Do we find in our heart of hearts a spiritual struggle? Do we feel anything of the flesh lusting against the Spirit and the Spirit against the flesh, so that we cannot do the things that we would? Are we conscious of two principles within us, contending for the mastery? Do we feel anything of war in our inward man? Well, let us thank God for it! It is a good sign. It is strongly probable evidence of the great work of sanctification. . . . Anything is better than apathy, stagnation, deadness and indifference.[24]

ENDNOTES:

1. W. E. Vine, *Vine's Expository Dictionary of Biblical Words*, p. 169.
2. Layton Talbert, "*Salvation: Divine Determination or Human Responsibility?*" Preach the Word (April-June 1998), pp. 24-25.
3. John MacArthur, *Freedom from Sin*, pp. 31-33.
4. John MacArthur, *Romans 1-8*, 344, 378.
5. Ernest Pickering, *Lordship Salvation: An Examination of John MacArthur's Book, The Gospel According to Jesus.*
6. Charles Bing, *Lordship Salvation: A Biblical Evaluation and Response*, p. 177.
7. Walter Chantry, *Today's Gospel: Authentic or Synthetic*, p. 54.
8. John MacArthur, *The Gospel According to Jesus: What is Authentic Faith?*, p. 138.
9. Charles Hodge, *A Commentary On 1 & 2 Corinthians*, p. 48, 50.
10. Kenneth Gentry, Jr. *Lord of the Saved*, p. 7.
11. John MacArthur, *The Gospel According to Jesus* [Revised & Expanded Edition], p. 105.
12. A. W. Pink, *Eternal Security*, p. 15, in *The Gospel According to Jesus* [Revised & Expanded Edition], p. 105.
13. Charles Ryrie, *Balancing the Christian Life*, p. 170.
14. Ibid., p. 172.
15. Charles Spurgeon, *The Treasury of the New Testament*. Vol. II, p. 701.
16. Joel Mullenix, *What Is The Gospel?* A sermon recorded Nov. 2, 1997. Sermon printed by permission.
17. Charles Ryrie, *Balancing the Christian Life*, p. 173.
18. J. Vernon McGee, *Thru The Bible With J. Vernon McGee*, Vol. 4, p. 16.
19. Ibid., p. 16.
20. Charles Ryrie, *So Great Salvation*, p. 64, (italics his).
21. H. A. Ironside, *1 Corinthians*, pp. 106-107, 112-113.
22. Warren Wiersbe, *Be Wise*, pp. 43-44.
23. G. Campbell Morgan, *The Corinthian Letters of Paul*, pp. 53-55.
24. J. C. Ryle, *Holiness*, p. 82.

WHAT IS BIBLICAL REPENTANCE?

Preface

The doctrine of repentance is a subject to which entire books have been dedicated. This single chapter is not meant to fully develop all that defines this vital doctrine. My primary goal is to succinctly define and illustrate what biblical repentance is and is not as it pertains to the Lordship Salvation debate. This chapter is the most heavily revised of any from the original edition of this book. Interaction with the advocates of Lordship Salvation showed me areas in which the original chapter needed tightening through revision, elimination and addition. I understand there will be some from both sides, and others somewhere in the middle of the Lordship Salvation discussion that will disagree with some elements of this important chapter. This is, however, presently my best effort to briefly define biblical repentance as I understand it.

In the Lordship Salvation controversy the doctrine of repentance probably draws more attention, scrutiny and debate than any other doctrine in the debate. Men on both sides of the Lordship debate agree that repentance has a role in salvation. They disagree sharply on the exact role and definition of repentance, but agree that repentance is involved in the salvation experience. Zane Hodges and Bob

Wilkin are notable exceptions to this general consensus on repentance. The teaching of these men entirely eliminates repentance toward God as a condition of salvation. Furthermore, Hodges and Wilkin reject the almost universally held "change of mind" definition of repentance. Elements of this teaching can be found in Zane Hodges's book *Absolutely Free*, but it is primarily articulated in his later work *Harmony With God*.

Ironically, Wilkin's 1985 doctrinal dissertation is titled *Repentance as a Condition for Salvation in the New Testament*. At that time Wilkin held the "change of mind" view and believed repentance was a condition for salvation. The influence of Hodges eventually led Wilkin to abandon the position he defended in his dissertation. At the 1998 Grace Evangelical Society's National Conference Bob Wilkin revealed he had a "change of mind" about repentance. Hodges and Wilkin defined repentance as "turning from sin" and also announced their view that repentance (by any definition) is not a condition for salvation.

What Biblical Repentance Is Not...

We live in a day in which scandals among politicians and professional athletes are rampant. Hardly a month goes by when gambling, drugs, drunk driving, immoral behavior or arrests and convictions are not reported. The misdeeds and abuse of power among political figures is legendary. In the opinion of many the use of steroids and human growth hormones raises the most controversy and ire among professional athletes, owners, coaches, fans, and sportswriters.

An athlete who has been accused of (and especially if they have been subsequently found to have been) using performance-enhancing drugs will often face a hostile press, an investigative panel or the judiciary. Some of these athletes respond defiantly, although some do express remorse and regret for their past actions. The question, however, is whether or not the latter are truly repentant.

Repentance is not simply knowing you are a sinner. It is not confessing and feeling sorrow about some sin. Confession and remorse may indicate only that one is sorry that his sin was discovered and will do it again the next time he gets a chance. Repentance is not making a resolution and turning over a new leaf with the intent to do better with one's life. True biblical repentance is not making a decision to stop committing sin or a specific list of sins. That is reforming the life. Reformation or the commitment to reform toward better performance in life does not save. A commitment to reform as a requirement for salvation frustrates the grace of God.

> Galatians 2:21 I do not frustrate the grace of God: for if righteousness come by the law, then Christ is dead in vain.

How Does the Lordship Advocate Define Repentance?

Dr. John MacArthur, Lordship's most prolific apologist, defines repentance as turning from one's sins. You find this teaching on pages 177-180 in the *20th Anniversary* edition of *The Gospel According to Jesus*. MacArthur's view of repentance implies that the lost man must come to Christ for salvation with the intention of turning from sin and continuing to strive against sin throughout his lifetime.

In a Trinity Broadcasting Network interview John MacArthur was asked what must take place before a lost man can become a Christian after he understands his sin, guilt before God and need to be forgiven. He replied:

...add to that the fact that I (the lost man) am so crushed... disturbed...broken...battered. I'm so humiliated by that condition; I am so helpless to change it myself that all I can do is cry out to God. And in that cry I am not only saying that I want to be delivered from the person that I am, kill me, but I want to TURN TO RIGHTEOUSNESS.... This is about **turning from sin** to Christ and then of course believing the facts of the gospel is the way all of that actually becomes a divine miracle and transaction.[1]

Rev. Nathan Busenitz is the personal assistant to Dr. John MacArthur. In 2006 Nathan invited me to enter a series of what grew into protracted discussions at the Shepherd's Fellowship blog *Pulpit Magazine* over the Lordship Salvation interpretation of the gospel. The repentance question became a very important and revealing discussion because it is with repentance that the Lordship advocate takes some of his most serious doctrinal missteps. Through my interaction with Nathan we get a clearer picture of the Lordship advocate's view of repentance. During our public discussions for example Nathan wrote:

> Lordship sees repentance as more than just a change in *dependence*. It is also **a change of allegiance**. It includes a **willingness to submit** to the authority of Jesus Christ.... Lordship Salvation defines sin as rebellion or 'lawlessness' (which is how 1 John 3:4 defines it). To turn from (or forsake) one's rebellion is (by definition) to begin submitting.
>
> If I truly **hate my sinfulness**, and am broken over it, I will be simultaneously inclined to **stop doing it**. And as I earlier pointed out, the inclination (or desire or willingness) to stop sinning is the inclination **to start obeying**. And an inclination to start obeying is a change of allegiance (from self to God).[2]

Nathan's definition of repentance requires a lost man to be "inclined" (i.e. make a decision) to "stop doing it" (sinning) and "start obeying" to receive the gift of eternal life. This is to tell a lost man that to be born again he must be willing to turn over a new leaf. Nathan's repentance is telling a lost man that he must make a commitment to change his behavior, which is telling him that he must repent toward the *performance* of good works. Lordship's repentance, as MacArthur and Busenitz define it, demands a commitment for reformation of life to receive the gift of eternal life.

Lordship Salvation's repentance confuses sanctification (growth of a believer) with justification (God declaring/making a sinner righteous). For Lordship advocates anything short of a "complete turnaround" in behavior following a resolve to stop sinning and "start obeying" is not repentance and would leave the lost man dead in his sins, no matter what he believed about his guilt before God or the death, burial, and resurrection of Jesus Christ. Upfront and lifelong commitment to the kind of behavior expected of a spiritually mature Christian is the Lordship advocates practical definition of repentance to salvation.

In Nathan's comment above he wrote, "Lordship sees repentance as more than just a change in *dependence*. It is also a change of allegiance." As soon as I saw Nathan's use of "allegiance" in his definition of repentance I had an immediate concern. I followed up with two questions for Nathan based from a passage of Scripture.

> John 12:42-43 Nevertheless among the chief rulers also many believed on him; but because of the Pharisees they did not confess him, lest they should be put out of the synagogue: For they loved the praise of men more than the praise of God.

The Bible says they were not open about, and would not confess a "change of allegiance." Did they biblically repent; were they believers?

I posted the above twice to Nathan's attention at *Pulpit Magazine*, but he never replied to it. It is a question Lordship advocates cannot answer. Lordship's repentance, which calls for commitment, submission, and allegiance infringes on the finished work of Christ. A commitment to "start obeying" is misplaced dependence. That is depending on behavior for salvation. That is works dependence!

Nathan also wrote, "Lordship teaches that repentance includes a turning from lawlessness and rebellion, which necessarily means a willingness to surrender, and a turning to God." Nathan's order is wrong! Lost man cannot turn from sin, but he can turn to God to deliver him from the penalty and power of sin (Romans 6).

Classic Lordship Salvation contends that repentance is turning from sin(s) or the resolve to turn from sins. Repentance is viewed as a commitment to discipleship and fruit bearing. Scripture has a better answer. The Bible teaches that the Savior saves "the ungodly" (Rom. 5:6) in their sin, and believers from the power of sin (Rom. 6:1-ff; Gal. 5:16). Jurist theologian Ron Shea (Th.M., J.D.) explains that Lordship's front-loading of the gospel is fundamentally a *bilateral contract at law*.

> In this view, eternal salvation is not dependent on the performance of a work, but only the promise of future works. In the minds of those determined to adhere to salvation by works, this distinction supposedly allows the works of the law to be somehow added to the equation of salvation without annulling the doctrine of grace. Paul's Epistle to the Romans would disagree. "For if they which are of the law be heirs, faith is made void, and the promise is of none effect." The...expres-

sion of "saving repentance" is nothing more than a specific form or expression of Bilateral Contract Salvation . . . "*a promise for a promise.*" The lost sinner "*promises*" future obedience in exchange for God's "*promise*" of eternal life. This errant understanding of the term "*repentance*" is the most common and pervasive form of "Lordship Salvation" taught within Christendom throughout the world.[3]

Lordship advocates I interact with do not teach a form of repentance that overtly conditions salvation on the performance of "good works" (Eph. 2:10). They do, however, view repentance as a commitment to "stop sinning, start obeying," as a promise for the performance of "good works." Whether one is required to actually *perform* good works, or required to promise the *performance* of works to be born again, the conclusion is the same, grace is frustrated (Gal. 2:21).

Is repentance a condition for receiving eternal life? Yes, if it is repentance or changing one's mind about Jesus Christ. No, if it means to be sorry for sin or even to resolve to turn from sin, for these things *will not save*.[4]

Repentance for salvation, as Lordship advocates view it, is defined as the sinner's willingness to stop sinning in thought and deed, and to start obeying. The problem with this view is the emphasis is wrongly put on a change in personal behavior, not a change of mind toward God where the emphasis should be.

What is the Meaning of the Word "Repentance?"

Thus far we have examined what repentance is not and the Lordship Salvationist's error on repentance. Now let's begin to biblically define this important doctrine.

The Hebrew word translated "repent" in the Old Testament is *nacham*, which means "*to draw a deep breath*," an expression of deep feeling of either relief or sorrow (Girdlestone, *Synonyms of the Old Testament*, p. 87). The meaning "*to repent*" or "*to regret*" in the Old Testament is nearly always used of God rather than man, but not exclusively (Job 42:6; Jeremiah 8:6; 31:19).

> Job 42:6 Wherefore I abhor myself, and repent in dust and ashes.
>
> Jeremiah 8:6 I hearkened and heard, but they spake not aright: no man repented him of his wickedness, saying, What have I done? every one turned to his course, as the horse rusheth into the battle.
>
> Jeremiah 31:19 Surely after that I was turned, I repented; and after that I was instructed, I smote upon my thigh: I was ashamed, yea, even confounded, because I did bear the reproach of my youth.

G. Michael Cocoris identifies a key factor in the Old Testament usages:

> The conclusive evidence that repentance does not mean to be sorry for sin or to turn from sin is this: in the Old Testament, *God* repents! To illustrate: in the King James Version of the Old Testament, the word *repent* occurs forty-six times. Thirty-seven of these times, God is the one repenting (or not repenting). If repentance means sorrow for sin or turning from sin, God is a sinner.[5]

The noun μετανοια (*metanoia, repentance*) and its verb form μετανοεω (*metanoeo, to repent*) are the New Testament counterparts to the Old Testament *nacham*. It would be incorrect, however, to view the two words as identical in meaning. That the use of μετανοεω (*metanoeo*) in the LXX differs from its use in the New Testament demonstrates the development of a precise theological meaning for μετανοια (*metanoia, repentance*) in the New Testament. For an explanation of this development, see "Conversion" in *The New International Dictionary of New Testament Theology*.

In the New Testament μετανοια (*metanoia, repentance*) expresses the root meaning of the word "repentance," which is a change of mind. The etymology of the word also brings out this idea. Regarding the prefix μετα (*meta*), which is generally translated *after*, Thayer states,

> ... a preposition ... and hence prop. *in the midst of, amid*, denoting association, union, accompaniment. ... In composition, [when prefixed to another word as with *metanoia*] *meta* denotes 1. Association, fellowship, participating, with ... 2. Exchange, transfer, transmutation.[6]

The root *noia* comes from the word νους (*nous*), which means *mind*. The connection between *meta* and *nous* leads us to define "repentance" as "afterthought, change of mind." Thayer defines *metanoia* thus:

> *a change of mind*: as it appears in one who repents of a purpose he has formed or of something he has done, ... esp. the change of mind of those who have begun to abhor their errors and misdeeds, and have entered upon a better course of life, so that it embraces both a recognition of sin and sorrow for it and hearty amendment, the tokens and effects of which are good deeds.[7]

It is important to note the distinction that Thayer makes between true repentance, a change of mind with consequent results, and the "tokens" or fruit of true repentance, amended deeds. The deeds are the evidence, not the substance of repentance. Repentance is an attitude that should result in action. I once heard a preacher express the sentiment this way, "the fruit of repentance must follow the root."

> It is agreed that true repentance *should* and *probably will* result in a visible change of conduct because it is the new inner disposition of a person and indicates a new desire and bearing. However, to make outward transformation essential to the meaning of repentance itself is to confuse the two beyond biblical validity.[8]

By using terms such as "better course of life" and "amendment" in the latter part of his definition, Thayer seems to suggest the opposite—that repentance is an action. The cloudiness of Thayer's definition makes it possible for the latter portion to be misused.

John MacArthur cites the same passage from Thayer to bolster his Lordship gospel emphasis on behavior rather than believing. He focuses on a change of life and behavior. I do not believe Thayer would agree with MacArthur's interpretation of his meaning. Genuine biblical repentance should produce a change of life evidenced by a new behavior as one yields to the working of God's Spirit. Without a preceding changing of the mind, however, there will be no genuine change of life.

To be born again, a man must transfer his dependence from the works of the law (Galatians 2:16) to the finished work of Christ (Romans 10:4).

> Galatians 2:16 Knowing that a man is not justified by the works of the law, but by the faith of Jesus Christ, even we have believed in Jesus Christ, that we might be justified

by the faith of Christ, and not by the works of the law: for by the works of the law shall no flesh be justified.

Romans 10:4 For Christ is the end of the law for righteousness to every one that believeth.

1 Thessalonians 1:9-10

> For they themselves show of us what manner of entering in we had unto you, and how ye turned to God from idols to serve the living and true God; And to wait for His Son from heaven, whom he raised from the dead, even Jesus, which delivered us from the wrath to come.

This is one passage of Scripture that virtually always comes up in the discussion of repentance with Lordship advocates and needs to be carefully explained at this point. How does John MacArthur, for the Lordship view of repentance, interpret the first verse of this passage?

> As *metanoia* is used in the New Testament, it *always* speaks of a change of purpose, and specifically a turning from sin. In the sense Jesus used it, repentance calls for a repudiation of the old life and a turning to God for salvation. Such a change of purpose is what Paul had in mind when he described the repentance of the Thessalonians: "You turned to God from idols to serve a living and true God" (1 Thessalonians 1:9). Note the three elements of repentance: turning to God, a turning from evil, and the intent to serve God. No change of mind can be called true repentance if it does not include all three elements. The simple but all too often overlooked fact is that a true change of mind will necessarily result in a change of behavior.

> Repentance is not merely shame or sorry over sin, although genuine repentance always involves an element of remorse. It is a redirection of the human will, a purposeful decision to forsake all unrighteousness and pursue righteousness instead.⁹
>
> What is the gospel, after all, but a call to repentance (Acts 2:38; 3:19; 17:30)? In other words, it demands that sinners make a change—stop going one way and turn around to go the other (1 Thess. 1:9).¹⁰

Those quotes represent Lordship's classic misuse of 1 Thess. 1:9. MacArthur starts by addressing the Greek word *metanoia* as it is used in the New Testament, and then quotes a verse that does not even contain the word *metanoia*. The Greek word for "to turn" is completely different; it is επιστρεπηο (*epistrephō*) and means simply "to turn, turn to or toward." *Epistrephō* does not mean "to repent."

Through the balance of this section I am going to draw from the *Inspired Commentary*, the Word of God, to bring out the meaning and context of 1 Thess. 1:9. Before we can draw a conclusion on 1 Thess. 1:9 we need to begin by reviewing Paul's initial evangelistic ministry to the Thessalonians. In Acts 17:1-4 we find Paul arriving at Thessalonica and, "as his manner was," preaching the gospel. He was preaching Jesus who suffered and rose again. He said, "...Jesus, whom I preach unto you, is Christ." He is exhorting the Thessalonians, in their unsaved condition, to change their mind about Jesus. In verse four we see that some were persuaded, "some of them believed," but some "believed not." What was it in Paul's preaching that some were persuaded of and believed? That Jesus, who suffered, died and rose again, was the Christ. In Paul's evangelistic appeal to the Thessalonians is there any call or exhortation for "turning from evil" or the "intent to serve" for salvation? No, there is not! MacArthur is forcing "turning from evil (sin) and the intent to serve God...to forsake all unrighteousness" into the narrative of Paul's sermon.

Those who "believed not" set in motion a wave of persecution against the new believers (Acts 17:5-9). The events at Thessalonica set a pattern for what we find in Paul's two epistles to the Thessalonian believers.

In 1 Thessalonians 1 Paul acknowledges and praises them for their "work of faith" and "labor of love." They set an example for others of what Bible Christianity should look like. Their fine example was being set with "patience" (v. 3) in the face of "much affliction" (v. 6; Acts 17:5-9). They were setting the right example for fellow believers (Macedonia and Achaia, vv. 7-8) to emulate how to go through persecution. The reputation of the Thessalonian church preceded Paul in his missionary travels; therefore he did not need to speak of it (v.8). Their testimony of faith and patience in the face of persecution was a living example and a sermon without words. With respect to Lordship Salvation, this raises a serious problem. If the example of the Thessalonians in their willingness to change their behavior after they believed is considered the necessary condition of true saving faith, then in what way were the Thessalonians "examples to all that believe in Macedonia and Achaia" (v. 7)? How could they be the example to all other believers when all believers in Christ will necessarily live and behave just like the Thessalonians as Lordship advocates insist?

1 Thess. 1:9 opens with, "For they... ." The "they" is their "faith to God-ward," which became known abroad. The Thessalonians "turned to God," which put them in a position for the capacity to serve God. The example they became to other believers was the result of their believing the message Paul preached unto them—the One who suffered and rose again is the Christ. The "patience of hope" (v. 3) is defined in verse 10, "And to wait for his Son from heaven." While they expected and patiently

waited for Him to come they kept working out their faith and labored in love. Today when so many are occupied with His coming, we would do well to learn from the Thessalonians that we should keep occupied (doing something for Him) until He comes.

Lordship advocates who use this passage as an illustration of repentance only quote verse 9, "and how ye turned (*epistrepho*) to God from idols to serve the living and true God." Grammatically, however, there are two parallel infinitives of purpose, which are found in verses 9 and 10. The sentence structure, therefore, if breaking it down into main points and sub points, could be visualized this way:

v9, For
    they themselves shew of us
        - what manner of entering in we had unto you
        and
        - how ye turned to God from idols
            - **to serve** (*douleuein*) the living and true God

v10,   **and**
        - **to wait** (*anamenein*) for His Son
    from heaven,
        -whom He raised from the dead, even Jesus,
        - which delivered us from the wrath to come.

There is a major problem for the Lordship position in claiming that 1 Thess. 1:9 is making the intent "to serve" a necessary description (thus condition) of genuine repentance/faith. If "to serve" is a condition/necessary description, then syntactically so must the phrase "to wait" be as well. Wait for what? "His Son from heaven," i.e. the Second Coming of Christ. There is no other passage in Scripture that conditions the reception of eternal life on believing in Christ's Second Coming or waiting for it!

There is simply no way the two infinitive clauses can be separated. They are both present tense, active voice, infinitives, and they are both subordinate, dependent clauses that are parallel to one another and dependent upon the main, independent clause of 1:9, "how ye turned to God from idols."

To be born again do the lost need to believe in the Second Coming of Christ? If we accept MacArthur's view that the Thessalonians were saved by "turning from evil and the intent to serve," then the Scriptures also demand waiting for the second coming of Christ as a third condition for conversion.

There is, however, an even larger point with 1 Thess. 1:9-10. This passage is not even describing their initial, saving faith. The emphasis of the passage is clearly upon describing their faithful example in following the Lord subsequent to their initial, saving faith. In 1 Thess. 1:9 Paul is not speaking of how to become a believer; he wrote to them about their growth and testimony as believers.

This interpretation fits perfectly with Paul's introductory description of these Thessalonians in 2 Thess. 1:3-4. Notice there too they are described not as to their initial, saving faith, as if Paul is saying to them there, "Your conversion was genuine." No, he is pleased with the fact that their "faith groweth exceedingly" (1:3) and that they were exercising "patience and faith" amidst the trials they were enduring (1:4).

This interpretation, furthermore, fits perfectly with the *Inspired Commentary* on the Thessalonian Epistles that we have in Acts 17, where the Thessalonians' initial, saving faith is described in 17:1-4, esp. v. 4 "persuaded" (*peitho*) or "believed" (KJV) and v. 5 "were not persuaded" (*apeitho*) or "believed not" (KJV). The content of their faith is described in v. 3, that is, they believed in Christ's substitutionary death and bodily resurrection, which were according to the

Scriptures (1 Thess. 4:14; 1 Cor. 15:3-4). There is no mention of turning from idols, serving the living God, waiting for the Second Coming, etc. Instead, what we see is that immediately upon believing, these baby Christians in Thessalonica were persecuted for their faith (Acts 17:5-9), particularly by Jewish unbelievers (1 Thess. 2:14-16).

From the Scriptures we can firmly conclude that 1 Thess. 1:9-10 is a post conversion passage. Paul is addressing the things that followed their conversion. He was teaching them post conversion truth. In verse ten he concerns himself with their growth in light of the Lord's imminent return. At the time of their persecution Paul and Silas were ministering to them as new believers (1 Thess. 2:8). In both epistles to the Thessalonians Paul is ministering to them as new believers. Every chapter in 1 Thessalonians ends with Paul referencing the Second Coming of Christ, which is a vital truth for believers. In 2 Thessalonians 1 we find Paul speaking of their growing faith, charity toward one another and patience in persecution. Paul is commending them for their faith that grew out of their believing the gospel.

Lordship's repentance, as MacArthur defines it, is to "stop going one way," i.e. stop sinning and replace sinning with the "intent to serve," i.e. do the "good works" (Eph. 2:10) expected of a born again believer. MacArthur changes the gospel from repentance toward God and faith in the Lord Jesus Christ to a man-centered message that conditions the reception of eternal life on the lost man's, "purposeful decision to forsake all unrighteousness," which is an upfront commitment to certain expected levels of behavior. Believing the gospel should result in some form of a change in behavior as one grows in grace. However, nowhere in Scripture is the gospel for the reception of eternal life defined by a sinner's intention, commitment or resolve to change his behavior.

Discussing Three Aspects of Repentance

There are three aspects involved in most discussions of biblical repentance. They are intellect, emotion and volition, but do these aspects define biblical repentance unto eternal life?

- Intellectually, repentance may involve a change of view toward one's past action. I can remember episodes from my early years, prior to the time I received Christ as my Savior. There were times when I behaved in an ungodly way, but at the time I had no sense of guilt, shame or remorse. At the time of my conversion I looked back, and saw my sin as God saw my sin. The realization of my guilt and shame before God became very real. It was, however, more than a realization; it was an acknowledgment and agreement with God about my sinfulness. One might say, "My mind is made up, I am a sinner!" My sins are forgiven, I am a child of God and on my way to Heaven, but I can remember that afternoon coming to grips with my sin, my guilt before God and that I was headed for Hell.

While we were living in South Africa, my wife home schooled our children. My wife taught Bible as part of the daily lesson plan and on this occasion she was teaching Peter, who was a first grader at the time, about sin. After a careful explanation of sin and God's view of sin, she asked Pete if he understood the lesson. Pete said that he did. Liz was encouraged to think that Pete was beginning to grasp the sinfulness of man. So, Liz then asked, "Now Pete, are you a sinner?" Pete replied, "Nope, I'm an American!" We still laugh at that and will always remember it. That story does illustrate that Pete had not come to the point of understanding his sin condition and his need of the Savior. In his mind there was nothing over which he needed to "change the (his) mind."

Often I have spoken to Christians who sometimes wonder how people can behave badly and think nothing of it. My typical reply is the unsaved person is only doing what comes naturally to him. The bad behavior is only the symptom of the real problem, which is their sin nature. They have not been pricked in their heart. The reality of guilt before a holy and just God has not dawned on them. On the day of Pentecost God used His Word through Peter's preaching to bring many of the listeners to the realization of their guilt before Him.

> Acts 2:37-38 Now when they heard this, they were pricked in their heart, and said unto Peter and to the rest of the apostles, Men and brethren, what shall we do? Then Peter said unto them, Repent, and be baptized every one of you in the name of Jesus Christ for the remission of sins, and ye shall receive the gift of the Holy Ghost.

- Emotionally, repentance may produce a display of sorrow for sin and a desire for pardon. Thinking back again to the day that I received Christ and was born again I vividly recall my heart gripped with sorrow for my sin. The pastor showed me from the Bible that I was a sinner. God was using His Word to bring me to a sense of shame for what I had been and done. I was not able to speak much at all as the pastor explained God's judgment for sin and His pardon offered to me. My guilt and shame was very real as I came to know I was a Hell-bound sinner, and deserved Hell.

Sorrow may produce repentance, but repentance is not sorrow for sin. Esau (Hebrews 12:16-17) wept over what he had lost, but "found no place of repentance." The Roman Catholic can feel or express sorrow for sin, do penance for sin, but that is not repentance to salvation. Man may sorrow and not repent. Sorrow may, however, lead to repentance as with the Corinthians.

> 2 Corinthians 7:9-10 Now I rejoice, not that ye were made sorry, but that ye sorrowed to repentance: for ye were made sorry after a godly manner, that ye might receive damage by us in nothing. For godly sorrow worketh repentance to salvation not to be repented of: but the sorrow of the world worketh death.

In my experience there was genuine emotion and sorrow, but sorrow is not always evident and it is not essential for salvation. Dr. H. A. Ironside noted,

> When some change their minds, there may be emotions—and there may not be. When people change their mind, a change of action is expected, but both of these things are *results* of repentance, and not the nature of repentance. Nowhere is man exhorted to feel a certain amount of sorrow for his sins in order to come to Christ.[11]

- Volitionally, repentance is a change of will and disposition.

> Luke 15:21 And the son said unto him, Father, I have sinned against heaven, and in thy sight, and am no more worthy to be called thy son.

What is apparent in the passage above is a conscious choice or decision was made. In Luke 15 the prodigal son had come to see what he had become through rebellion against his father and God. When he came to his senses (*intellect*) his thoughts (*emotions*) turned toward his father, then he arose (*volition*) and went back to his father.

Concerning man's choice or volition, we know from Scripture that repentance, just like saving faith, is not automatic as a result of being one of God's elect. Though God does speak of granting "repentance to Israel" (Acts 5:31) and "to the Gentiles" (Acts 11:18), this simply means that God grants them the *opportunity* to repent, which in His justice He doesn't even have to do. Since we are all under sin, He would have the right to justly condemn us all (Rom. 3:9-20). Instead He gives us the opportunity to repent out of His inherent goodness and grace (Rom. 2:4-5). But if repentance was God's gift given only to the elect, then why didn't everyone in Israel repent about Christ in the Book of Acts if God gave "repentance to Israel" as a gift? The human will or volition is involved in repentance just as it is in saving faith. That is why in Scripture repentance is a command from God that all must heed (Acts 17:30). That is also why *metanoeo* is used in the imperative mood when addressing unregenerate audiences (Acts 2:38; 3:19). Though God does convict the lost of their sin (John 16:8-9), the sinner must concede to this truth from God via his own volition rather than willfully resist His convicting work (Acts 7:51-54). In this sense, biblical repentance involves our individual will or volition.

Can Repentance and Faith Be Separated?

Repentance and Faith are two-sides of the same theological coin. The Apostle Paul clearly states that repentance and faith are his theology of conversion.

> Acts 20:21 Testifying both to the Jews, and also to the Greeks, repentance toward God, and faith toward our Lord Jesus Christ.

Repentance and faith should not be viewed chronologically. Thiessen wrote, "There is, of course, no chronological sequence; conversion, justification, regeneration, union with Christ, adoption, all take place at the same instant."[12]

Repentance and Faith should not be separated. True repentance never exists apart from faith. As a person turns to God, he turns from his sin of unbelief and dependence on works.

There must be a balance in our theology when we come to repentance and faith. The sinner who turns in repentance toward God and faith in Jesus Christ (Acts 20:21) is born again. Faith without a corresponding understanding or emphasis on repentance can lead to Zane Hodges's reductionist *Crossless* interpretation of the gospel. Repentance without a corresponding understanding of the true nature of faith can lead to John MacArthur's *Lordship Salvation*. Tendencies to emphasize one side of the repentance/faith theological coin more than the other will lead to an out of balance view of the gospel and consequently to the corresponding extremes.

Further Explanation of Repentance

The New International Dictionary of New Testament Theology sees a distinction in meaning between *metamelomai* and *metanoeo*.

> The example of Judas makes it clear that *metamelomai* and *metanoeo* do not have identical meanings in the NT. Judas recognized that Jesus had been wrongly condemned. He regretted his betrayal (Matt. 27:3), but he did not find the way to genuine repentance. We find the same differentiation in 2 Cor. 7:8-10. Paul did not regret that he had written a sharp letter to the Corinthians, for the sorrow caused to its recipients had led them to true repentance (metanoia), to an inner turning to God.[13]

Please note that Judas repented about his sin of betraying Jesus, but he never biblically repented unto salvation. Why? Though he was sorry for his sin and even admitted it was wrong, he never changed his mind about Jesus being the Christ, his Savior!

> Matthew 27:3-4 The Judas, which had betrayed him, when he saw that he was condemned, repented (*metamelomai*) himself, and brought again the thirty pieces of silver to the chief priests and elders, Saying, I have sinned in that I have betrayed the innocent blood.... .

Though Judas acknowledged his sin and that Jesus was "innocent," this is far from having a change of mind to "believe Jesus is the Christ, the Son of God" (John 20:31). This is really brought out in Acts 2:36-38 where repent (*metanoeo*) is used in v. 38. The whole point of the passage is to show Israel that the One whom they crucified was actually the Messiah. God wanted them to "know assuredly" something (2:36), specifically that "God hath made this same Jesus, whom ye have crucified, both Lord and Christ." This clearly indicates a change of mind specifically about Jesus Christ. Though Lordship advocates may be able to reason that this still involved recognition of their sin in crucifying their Messiah ("whom ye have crucified"), conspicuously absent, however, is any call of Peter to turn from their sins. Rather, in this passage Peter focuses on only the one sin of rejecting Jesus as their Messiah, the true Christ. At no point through 2:22-38 does Peter mention their sins (plural). Instead he focuses them on the true identity of the Christ, the One whom they had crucified.

Dr. H. C. Thiessen adds this note on *metanoia*,

> Repentance must not be presented as a "work" to perform. This is the teaching of the Roman Catholic Church . . . but it is unscriptural. Confession of sin, and reparation for wrongs done to men are fruits of repentance; but they do not constitute repentance.[14]

Conditioning salvation upon man's "unconditional surrender," his commitment to or promise of obedience is not the gospel. This is the point upon which some who reject Lordship Salvation consider it the first cousin of Roman Catholicism's sacramental works salvation.

When repentance is defined as "turning from sin" its basic nature is changed from what occurs in the heart and mind to an action. A commitment to certain behavior expected of a Christian turns the gospel of grace on its head. Salvation then is no longer "the gift of God," but instead a works based message that frustrates grace (Eph. 2:8-9; Gal. 2:21). Sin is the problem for every lost man, and Hell is the inevitable consequence. Lordship's "turning from evil," the "desire to stop sinning" or the "intent to serve" is not the solution; Christ is the answer!

Repentance is a change of mind where one recognizes he is a hopeless, Hell-bound sinner before a just and holy God. When he agrees with the convincing and convicting work of the Holy Spirit that he is a sinner (John 16:7-9) and transfers his dependence to the Lord Jesus Christ for his salvation—he has biblically repented. Biblical repentance is a change of mind that should produce the fruit of a change in direction from self and sin toward God. The fruit that should follow is distinct from repentance itself. In Acts 26:20, Paul summarizes his ministry to King Agrippa by indicating he calls people to a change of mind where they turn to God, and once they've turned to God, been saved, they should do the "good works" (Eph. 2:10) that are fitting of that change of mind and dependence on the Lord. This is distinct from Judaism which was teaching people should do works to get saved, but Paul also emphasized people should "have...fruit unto holiness" (Rom. 6:22) once they have been saved. Dr. Fred Moritz wrote:

> Repentance is a change of mind. That is a momentous change! The lost person changes his mind about his sin, his rebellion against God, and his relationship to God. Paul taught the elders at the church of Ephesus that repentance is directed toward God. He says that his message in Ephesus was, "Testifying both to the Jews and also to the Greeks, repentance toward God, and faith toward our Lord Jesus Christ" (Acts 20:21). Repentance is the change of mind that produces faith in Christ. It is as if the lost person says, "God is right, I am wrong." The other side of the coin is that when the lost person recognizes his own sinfulness, he is ready to trust Christ as the only Savior.[15]

A truly repentant man no longer trusts in anything other than the finished work of Christ for his salvation. Once he has repented and placed his faith in Christ, he is born again. The result of repentance, genuine salvation and the new life in Christ should be the evidence of a changed life. His behavior should change because he has a new desire in him to grow in Christ. Following a genuine conversion some sin typically drops off immediately. Unsaved adults who look down the path of sin they have trod, see Jesus, and turn to Him finding forgiveness for and freedom from sin in Him. If they stop looking to Jesus they could and probably will go right back into trouble—not positionally, but practically.

Through the Word of God and prayer, the Holy Spirit will show him areas where he needs to take steps of faith and growth. As he responds to the Spirit, he continues to grow by God's grace and will show new evidences of a changed life. But this is not automatic or the necessary result of a person having initially repented about Jesus Christ at the time of new birth. It requires the on-going exercise of our volition in a willingness to "change our mind" about areas of our lives that are sinful and in conflict with the will of God as it is revealed to us through His Word and wooing of the Holy Spirit. In this sense, there is a need for daily repentance specifically "from sin" after a person is born again in order for practical sanctification and spiritual growth to occur (2 Cor. 12:21). But this is distinct from the repentance required by God in saving faith, which is the focus of this chapter.

> Ephesians 2:8-10 For by grace are ye saved through faith; and that not of yourselves: it is the gift of God: Not of works, lest any man should boast. For we are his workmanship, created in Christ Jesus unto good works, which God hath before ordained that we should walk in them.

In Ephesians 2:8-10 the Word of God sets out the order of things. Verses 8-9 teach that a man is saved by God's grace through personal faith. Verse 10 teaches that since he has been born again by the power of God, he will now be in a position to do good works ordained by God for him and these will be pleasing to God.

> Philippians. 2:12-13 Wherefore, my beloved, as ye have always obeyed, not as in my presence only, but now much more in my absence, work out your own salvation with fear and trembling. For it is God which worketh in you both to will and to do of his good pleasure.

The working out of one's salvation is a demonstration to others that a person has already received salvation and is progressing in sanctification. This occurs as the believer routinely repents through a renewing of the mind (Rom. 12:1), coupled with gratitude for God's mercy and a new desire "both to will and to do of His good pleasure." A proper understanding of repentance can only be drawn out of a study of its precise theological usage in the New Testament, and must be based upon its primary meaning, a "change of mind."

ENDNOTES:

1. YouTube, "Kirk Cameron Interviews John MacArthur," http://www.youtube.com/watch?v=M_YYNuMN5II&NR=1, (accessed January 10, 2010).
2. Nathan Busenitz, Pulpit Magazine, http://www.sfpulpit.com/category/lordship, (accessed January 11, 2010).
3. Ron Shea, *Repentance and Salvation in Scripture: Confusion Over Repentance*, p. 3. (emphasis his).
4. Charles Ryrie, *So Great Salvation*, p. 99.
5. G. Michael Cocoris, *Repentance: The Most Misunderstood Word in the Bible*, p. 12, (emphasis his).
6. Joseph Thayer, *A Greek-English Lexicon of the New Testament*, pp. 402, 404.
7. Ibid., pp. 405-406.
8. Charlie Bing, *Lordship Salvation: A Biblical Evaluation & Response*, p. 86.
9. John MacArthur, *The Gospel According to Jesus: What is Authentic Faith*, p. 178.
10. John MacArthur, *Faith Works: The Gospel According to the Apostles*, p. 33.
11. H. A. Ironside, *Except Ye Repent*, p. 12.
12. Henry Thiessen, *Lectures in Systematic Theology*, p. 352.
13. *The New International Dictionary of New Testament Theology*: Vol. 1, p. 356.
14. Henry Thiessen, *Lectures in Systematic Theology*, p. 354.
15. Fred Moritz, *Preach the Word*, (October-December 1999).

WHAT IS BIBLICAL SAVING FAITH?

What is the Meaning of the Word "Faith?"

*F*aith (*belief*) is a very common word in the New Testament. It is the translation of the Greek πιςτις (*pistis*), and occurs 245 times, and is almost always translated *faith*, but is occasionally rendered *believe*, *belief*, *assurance*, or *fidelity* in the King James Version of the Bible.

The meaning of the Greek word is very similar to its English counterpart. Faith is basically a trust or confidence in someone or something. Dr. Zodhiates' definition is: "Being persuaded, faith, belief. In general it implies such a knowledge of, assent to, and confidence in certain divine truths, especially those of the gospel."[1] Faith is a child-like trust in God, which accepts the record He has given of His Son.

> 1 John 5:10-11 He that believeth on the Son of God hath the witness in himself: he that believeth not God hath made him a liar; because he believeth not the record that God gave of his Son. And this is the record, that God hath given to us eternal life, and this life is in his Son.
>
> Hebrews 11:1 Now faith is the substance of things hoped for, the evidence of things not seen.

The faith that saves man from the penalty of his sin cannot include any kind of meritorious works. The Bible is very clear on this point.

> Ephesians 2:8-9 For by grace are ye saved through faith: and that not of yourselves: it is the gift of God: Not of works lest any man should boast.
>
> Titus 3:5 Not by works of righteousness which we have done, but according to His mercy He saved us, by the washing of regeneration, and renewing of the Holy Ghost.

Salvation is obtained through faith in the finished work of Jesus Christ. Man is saved by faith, plus nothing! The faith that saves, however, is more than simple acknowledgment.

> Saving faith goes beyond understanding one's sinfulness, his deserved judgment in hell, and his only hope being in Christ. It goes beyond agreement with all this. . . . Understanding and agreement would simply be acknowledgment. However, saving faith goes beyond acknowledgment to dependence on Christ for salvation from sin and hell. . . . When one chooses to cast his dependence on Christ for salvation from sin and hell, he goes beyond acknowledgment to an act of the will. Acknowledging Christ is not salvation; depending on Christ is.[2]

Why Does Lordship Focus on the "Kind" of Faith?

As we begin look at "saving faith" in light of Lordship Salvation we must remember when the Lordship advocate speaks of "saving faith" you must determine if he is speaking in terms of what he believes is **required for** salvation or what should be the **result of** salvation. Lordship Salvation blurs those lines of distinction just as, we have seen earlier, it blurs the lines of distinction between salvation and discipleship. Lordship advocates confuse sanctification with the event of justification, which is why they define "saving faith" in terms of commitment and surrender. There is little disagreement that true faith in Christ for salvation should result in a genuine desire to live for Christ. James 2:14-26 is very clear; a genuine conversion should evidence itself in genuine results.

Lordship advocates correctly state that Jesus Christ must be the *object* of saving faith. Although one quickly learns that the key issue is not the *object* of faith, but rather the *kind* of faith. To them the *kind* of faith that "does not save" is any faith that does not meet their Lordship definition of saving faith. Most Lordship advocates leave no room for the possibility of a balanced position on the gospel. They consistently use terms such as "Easy-Believism" or "cheap grace" as a blanket label for any gospel presentation that falls short of the Lordship requirements for saving faith. They cannot acknowledge that many, who reject Lordship Salvation, preach a gospel message that balances faith and repentance. Dr. Fred Moritz explains the shortcomings of the Lordship advocate's lack of balance in definitions:

> The student of logic will spend some time studying fallacies. One of the logical fallacies people use in an attempt to prove their point is sometimes called the "false dilemma." This fallacy occurs "when the two alternatives are presented, not all the possibilities have been explored." This fallacy presents itself in the current debate. Those who advocate the lordship salvation position see only the mental assent or "easy believism" position as an alternative. Likewise those who hold to Hodges's mental assent position decry all others as advocates of lordship

salvation... There is a balanced, biblical position on the issue of salvation.³

In his review of *The Gospel According to Jesus,* Dr. Ernest Pickering writes about saving faith:

> A number of times, in various ways, this emphasis is given. Saving faith is "more than just understanding the facts and mentally acquiescing," (*The Gospel According to Jesus*, p. 31). We do not know any fundamental preachers of the gospel who would disagree with that statement. We have never heard any reputable gospel preacher ever teach otherwise. The old Scofield Bible declared that "faith is personal trust, apart from meritorious works, in the Lord Jesus Christ" (p. 1,302 Scofield Bible). *The Ryrie Study Bible* declares, "Both Paul and James define faith as a living, productive trust in Christ" (note on James 2:14).⁴

Following is John MacArthur's definition of saving faith from the original edition of *The Gospel According to Jesus*: "Saving faith is a commitment to leave sin and follow Jesus at all costs. Jesus takes no one unwilling to come on those terms."⁵ In his *Revised & Expanded Edition,* John MacArthur reworked the above statement as follows, "Saving faith does not recoil from the demand to forsake sin and follow Jesus Christ at all costs. Those who find his terms unacceptable cannot come at all."⁶ In the *20ᵗʰ Anniversary* edition of *The Gospel According to Jesus* the same section appears this way, "Saving faith does not recoil from the demand to forsake sin and self and follow Christ at all costs. Those who find His terms unacceptable cannot come at all. He will not barter away His right to be Lord."⁷

The message MacArthur conveys is consistent in all three editions of *The Gospel According to Jesus.* Only in the third edition, however, does the final sentence appear as shown above. The Lord most certainly will not barter away His lordship or sovereignty. Neither is eternal salvation something that can be gained through barter, but is Lordship Salvation's interpretation of how a lost man is born again a barter system?

Is Lordship's "Saving Faith" a Barter System?

In each of the quotes above notice Dr. MacArthur is speaking in terms of coming to Christ. The obvious implication is of a lost man coming to Christ for salvation. You can read those quotes, apply them to a personal evangelism setting, and you have a lost man being told that he must come to Christ with a promise to "leave/forsake (stop committing) sin," and follow Jesus at any cost to receive the gift of eternal life. These quotes, which run like a thread through all three editions of *The Gospel According to Jesus*, remove any doubt that MacArthur conditions the reception of eternal life on a definition of "saving faith" that includes an upfront commitment to performance. Again from his original edition MacArthur wrote,

> Thus in a sense we pay the ultimate price for salvation when our sinful self is nailed to a cross. . . . It is an exchange of all that we are for all that Christ is. And it denotes implicit obedience, full surrender to the lordship of Christ. Nothing less can qualify as saving faith.[8]

Faith and believe appear many times in Scripture as the condition for salvation. MacArthur's first error, therefore, is his import of the term "surrender" as a necessary co-condition with faith to be born again. Second, please note carefully that MacArthur speaks of paying "the ultimate price for salvation," i.e. paying the price to become a Christian.

Does the Bible call on the lost to, "pay the ultimate price for salvation?" Is receiving the gift of eternal life conditioned on an "exchange" of "obedience" and "full surrender?" Dr. MacArthur's saving faith not only implies, it demands the "exchange" of a commitment to life long obedience and submission to the Lord to receive His free gift of salvation. At salvation there only has to be surrender to what the Holy Spirit is convincing and convicting of at the moment. Future issues of discipleship may not even be on one's mind.

Lordship Salvation, according to John MacArthur's definition of saving faith, is a barter system. From my on line debates with the advocates of Lordship Salvation and from Dr. MacArthur's own books I have documented that his interpretation of the gospel does indeed demand an "exchange" of "obedience" and "full surrender" for the reception of eternal life. Lordship advocates are, however, quick to cry, "straw man." The straw man argument is a logical fallacy based on misrepresentation of an opponent's position. To set up a straw man or set up a straw-man argument is to create a position that is easy to refute, and then attribute that position to the opponent. The call for upfront promises to stop sinning, for "obedience" and "full surrender" in "exchange" for salvation is found in Dr. MacArthur's Lordship books and on line sources. Lordship's exchange/barter system does not need to be artificially attributed to Dr. MacArthur because it is his position. There is, therefore, no straw man! Claiming "straw man" does nothing to negate the clear, incontrovertible evidence of Lordship Salvation's barter system.

Did the Apostles Preach Lordship's "Saving Faith?"

Charles H. Spurgeon wrote as follows about the "saving faith" of the Apostles' preaching:

> Certain persons have been obliged to admit that the apostles commanded, and exhorted, and besought men to believe, but they tell us that the kind of believing that the apostles bade men exercise was not a saving faith. Now, God forbid we should ever in our zeal to defend a favorite position, be driven to an assertion so monstrous. Can we imagine for a moment apostles. . . going about the world exhorting men to exercise a faith which after all would not save them? When our Lord bade His disciples go into all the world and preach the gospel to every creature, and added, "he that believeth and is baptized shall be saved," the faith which was to be preached was evidently none other than a saving faith, and it is frivolous to say otherwise.[9]

Lordship teachers do not claim that the Apostles preached a faith that does not save. Instead, they assert that their Lordship gospel is the historic gospel of the Apostles. In 1993 John MacArthur released a sequel to *The Gospel According To Jesus* **titled** *Faith Works: The Gospel According To The Apostles***. In this book he claims that the present day Lordship interpretation of the gospel is the very gospel message preached by the Apostles of Jesus Christ. Does the New Testament bear this out?**

I have done a simple key word search of the New Testament (KJV) beginning with the Book of Acts through Revelation. The words I searched for are: "commit," "surrender" and "follow." These words appear, 54, zero and 45 times respectively. At no point in the New Testament, from the Book of Acts through Revelation, do any of these terms commonly used to define the Lordship gospel, by its present day advocates, appear in an evangelistic context. We do find the words "faith" and "repent" frequently, but never in conjunction with or in the context of commitment, surrender and following.

The Lordship gospel of commitment and surrender is not found in the preaching of the Apostles. That is because when

Jesus preached commitment, surrender and following He was preaching discipleship, not salvation! The Bible simply does not support the contention that the Apostles taught or preached an evangelistic message like that of modern day Lordship Salvationists. The Lordship interpretation of the gospel certainly is not the gospel of the Apostles, nor the gospel according to Jesus.

All of the world's religions and false cults claim that men must contribute something of their own to receive or hold on to eternal life. The churches of Galatia to which the Apostle Paul wrote also fell prey to the same error

> Galatians 1:6 I marvel that ye are so soon removed from him that called you into the grace of Christ unto another gospel.
>
> Galatians 2:21 I do not frustrate the grace of God: for if righteousness come by the law, then Christ is dead in vain.
>
> Galatians 3:1-3 O foolish Galatians,. Received ye the Spirit by the works of the law, or by the hearing of faith? Are ye so foolish? having begun in the Spirit, are ye now made perfect by the flesh?

In his commentary on the Epistle to the Romans, Dr. H. A. Ironside writes,

> The Apostle is not trying to draw a fine distinction, as some preachers do, between believing with the head and believing with the heart. He does not occupy us with the *nature* of belief; he *does* occupy us with the *object* of faith. . . . To *call* upon the name of the Lord is, of course, to invoke His name in faith. His name speaks what He is. He who calls upon the name of the

> Lord puts his trust in Him, as it is written, "The name of the Lord is a strong tower, and the righteous runneth into it and is safe."[10]

One comes to the Lord Jesus Christ by faith to be saved from his sin. As a Christian, he then lives for Christ as his personal Savior and Lord.

> Romans 10:17 So then faith cometh by hearing, and hearing by the word of God.
>
> Hebrews 11:1 Now faith is the substance of things hoped for, the evidence of things not seen.

Dr. Michael Bere wrote, "Faith is not so foolish nor a blind faith. Our faith is based on substance, on the evidence, on the eternal Word of God. The Christian trusts in the One he has never seen. That is faith!"[11]

Why is the "Object" of Our Faith Essential?

> John 20:28-29 And Thomas answered and said unto him, My Lord and my God. Jesus saith unto him, Thomas, because thou hast seen me, thou hast believed: blessed are they that have not seen, and yet have believed.

After the crucifixion of Jesus the disciples hid themselves behind locked doors. They feared the Jews and what might become of them. Jesus appeared to his disciples in that room, but Thomas was absent. When Thomas returned the others told him of the Lord's appearing to them, but he would not believe. Thomas said, "Except I shall see in his hands the print of the nails, and put my finger into the print of the nails, and thrust my hand into his side, I will not believe," (John 20:25b). A short time later the Lord appeared again and removed any doubt Thomas had. Dear reader, every generation yet to come was on the Lord's mind when He spoke to Thomas.

> John 20:27-29 Reach hither thy finger, and behold my hands; and reach hither thy hand, and thrust it into my side: and be not faithless, but believing. And Thomas answered and said unto Him, My Lord and my God. Jesus saith unto him, Thomas, because thou hast seen Me, thou hast believed: blessed are they that have not seen, and yet have believed.

You are "blessed" if you have believed on Him without having seen Him. Have you believed? Have you placed your faith, your trust, your hope, and your confidence in the Lord Jesus Christ to save you? Your faith, your belief in Him, your dependence on who Jesus Christ is and what He has done for you has saved you.

Jesus Christ must be the object of man's faith. This makes all the difference. If Jesus is not the object of faith then there has been no saving faith. Faith in churches, sacraments, righteous living, men, angels, or miracles is not saving faith. A personal commitment of "full surrender" to the lordship of Christ is not saving faith. All of these are false additions to dependence on Christ alone! The Bible is very clear; there is no other way and no other name by which man can be saved.

> John 14:6 I am the way, the truth, and the life: no man cometh unto the Father, but by Me.

Acts 4:12 Neither is there salvation in any other: for there is none other name under heaven given among men, whereby we must be saved.

The Bible says faith as tiny as a mustard seed can move mountains. God is far more interested in seeing men saved from their sins than He is in moving mountains into the sea. If mustard-seed faith can move a mountain, surely it is sufficient for a man to be saved if the Son of God, the Lord Jesus Christ, is the object of his faith.

> If thy faith be fixed on Christ, though it seems to be in itself a line no thicker than a spider's cobweb, it will hold thy soul throughout time and eternity. For remember, it is not the thickness of this cable of faith, it is the strength of the anchor which imparts strength to the cable.[12]

Examples of Saving Faith

Luke 7:36-50
"Seest thou this woman?"

Luke 7:36-50 And one of the Pharisees desired him that he would eat with him. And he went into the Pharisee's house, and sat down to meat. And, behold, a woman in the city, which was a sinner, when she knew that Jesus sat at meat in the Pharisee's house, brought an alabaster box of ointment, And stood at his feet behind him weeping, and began to wash his feet with tears, and did wipe them with the hairs of her head, and kissed his feet, and anointed them with the ointment. Now when the Pharisee which had bidden him saw it, he spake within himself, saying, This man, if he were a prophet, would

> have known who and what manner of woman this is that toucheth him: for she is a sinner. And Jesus answering said unto him, Simon, I have somewhat to say unto thee. And he saith, Master, say on. There was a certain creditor which had two debtors: the one owed five hundred pence, and the other fifty. And when they had nothing to pay, he frankly forgave them both. Tell me therefore, which of them will love him most? Simon answered and said, I suppose that he, to whom he forgave most. And he said unto him, Thou hast rightly judged. And he turned to the woman, and said unto Simon, Seest thou this woman? I entered into thine house, thou gavest me no water for my feet: but she hath washed my feet with tears, and wiped them with the hairs of her head. Thou gavest me no kiss: but this woman since the time I came in hath not ceased to kiss my feet. My head with oil thou didst not anoint: but this woman hath anointed my feet with ointment. Wherefore I say unto thee, Her sins, which are many, are forgiven; for she loved much: but to whom little is forgiven, the same loveth little. And he said unto her, Thy sins are forgiven. And they that sat at meat with him began to say within themselves, Who is this that forgiveth sins also? And he said to the woman, Thy faith hath saved thee; go in peace.

The woman had just washed His feet with her tears, and "did wipe them with the hairs of her head, and kissed His feet, and anointed them with the ointment." Jesus acknowledges to the Pharisees what the woman had just done unto Him. Then Jesus said, "Wherefore I say unto thee, her sins, which are many, are forgiven; for she loved much: but to whom little is forgiven, the same loveth little" (Luke 7:47). Jesus says that it was her "faith," not a submissive action or attitude that saved her. There is no upfront commitment to discipleship, no surrender of every area of life, no promise of future obedience; she is saved by faith alone!

Luke 18:35-43
The Healing of Bartimeus

> And it came to pass, that as he was come nigh unto Jericho, a certain blind man sat by the way side begging: And hearing the multitude pass by, he asked what it meant. And they told him, that Jesus of Nazareth passeth by. And he cried, saying, Jesus, thou Son of David, have mercy on me. And they which went before rebuked him, that he should hold his peace: but he cried so much the more, Thou Son of David, have mercy on me. And Jesus stood, and commanded him to be brought unto him: and when he was come near, he asked him, Saying, What wilt thou that I shall do unto thee? And he said, Lord, that I may receive my sight. And Jesus said unto Him, Receive thy sight: thy faith hath saved thee. And immediately he received his sight, and followed him, glorifying God: and all the people, when they saw it, gave praise unto God.

The corresponding passages are found in Matthew 20 and Mark 10. From those passages we learn more details of this incident that Luke relates in his gospel. In Mark's gospel we learn that the man's name is Bartimeus, meaning "son of Timeus." In Matthew, we learn that there were two blind men.

Although there are some minor differences in the synoptic gospels' description of this event, the expression "Son of David" appears in each of the three gospels. All three gospel accounts show that the blind man acknowledged

Jesus as his Messiah: "Thou Son of David, have mercy on me." The blind man calls upon Jesus by His Messianic title, "Son of David." The blind man may not have been fully aware of the significance of the title he was using. He does, however, appear to be expressing worship when he calls on Jesus as "Son of David." Jesus, the Messiah, is the object of the man's faith.

In Luke's account we read,

> Luke 18:40-42 And Jesus stood, and commanded him to be brought unto him: and when he was come near, he asked him, Saying, What wilt thou that I shall do unto thee? And he said, Lord, that I may receive my sight. And Jesus said unto him, Receive thy sight: thy faith hath saved thee.

The One whom this man had heard, who heals the sick of every malady and makes the blind to see was within shouting distance. He cries out trying to be heard above the din that surely was present almost everywhere Jesus went. Hearing the man's pitiful cry Jesus stops and has him brought near. Jesus asks, "What wilt thou that I shall do unto thee?" The blind man asked for and received his sight. From that moment he followed Christ. Imagine the unceasing gratitude of this once blind, now seeing man. Jesus Christ did for him what no one else could have done.

Notice the chronological sequence: the blind man calls on his Messiah, and then he is brought near. Then the Lord says, "Receive thy sight: thy faith hath saved thee." It was his faith in Jesus Christ that saved him. He was "saved" spiritually because of his belief that Jesus was the promised Messiah. He had placed his faith in Christ and expressed it in his heartfelt cry for mercy from the Lord. That was saving faith! His faith was rewarded, and from that point he followed Christ as a seeing man, giving God glory for the miracle. Like blind Bartimeus, any one who, conscious of his own helpless condition, believes in who Jesus is, what He did to provide salvation and cries out to Him in faith for mercy, will just as assuredly be received of Him and healed of spiritual blindness.

The order of events in the conversion of Bartimeus upsets the Lordship gospel of commitment, surrender, and promised obedience for salvation. Luke 18:38-39 says,

> And he cried, saying, Jesus, thou Son of David, have mercy on me. And they which went before rebuked him, that he should hold his peace: but he cried so much the more, Thou Son of David, have mercy on me.

This blind man acknowledged Christ as Messiah and his faith, according to Jesus, saved him. Only after he was saved by faith alone in his Messiah did he follow Christ as a committed disciple.

> Luke 18:43 And immediately he received his sight, and followed him, glorifying God: and all the people, when they saw it, gave praise unto God.

The Lord did not precondition the gift of salvation by making demands of this man before granting him the gift. His sight is restored because of his faith, not in "exchange" for personal promises of obedience and submission. **He is following because he has been saved; he is not following to become saved!** His faith in the Savior resulted in his becoming a follower, a disciple.

The Apostle Paul, under inspiration, taught that our salvation is by faith plus nothing. Paul repeatedly emphasized this doctrine through his Epistles:

> Romans 3:28 Therefore we conclude that a man is justified by faith without the deeds of the law.
>
> Romans 4:2-3 For if Abraham were justified by works, he hath [whereof] to glory; but not before God. For what saith the scripture? Abraham believed God, and it was counted unto him for righteousness.
>
> Ephesians 2:8-9 For by grace are ye saved through faith; and that not of yourselves: it is the gift of God: Not of works, lest any man should boast.
>
> 1 Cor. 15:14, 17 And if Christ be not risen, then is our preaching vain, and your faith is also vain. And if Christ be not raised, your faith is vain; ye are yet in your sins.
>
> Galatians 2:16 Knowing that a man is not justified by the works of the law, but by the faith of Jesus Christ, even we have believed in Jesus Christ, that we might be justified by the faith of Christ, and not by the works of the law: for by the works of the law shall no flesh be justified.
>
> Galatians 3:2 This only would I learn of you, Received ye the Spirit by the works of the law, or by the hearing of faith?
>
> Galatians 3:11 But that no man is justified by the law in the sight of God, it is evident: for, The just shall live by faith.

Galatians 3:24 Wherefore the law was our schoolmaster to bring us unto Christ, that we might be justified by faith.

Philippians 3:9 And be found in him, not having mine own righteousness, which is of the law, but that which is through the faith of Christ, the righteousness which is of God by faith.

Colossians 2:7 Rooted and built up in him, and stablished in the faith, as ye have been taught, abounding therein with thanksgiving.

2 Timothy 3:15 And that from a child thou hast known the holy scriptures, which are able to make thee wise unto salvation through faith which is in Christ Jesus.

Hebrews 11:13 These all died in faith, not having received the promises, but having seen them afar off, and were persuaded of them, and embraced them, and confessed that they were strangers and pilgrims on the earth.

Paul speaks of a saving faith in Christ without mentioning commitment, surrender, or works. The Apostle Peter continues,

1 Peter 1:5, 9 Who are kept by the power of God through faith unto salvation ready to be revealed in the last time. Receiving the end of your faith, even the salvation of your souls.

The appropriation of Jesus Christ as Savior is taught in John 1:12, "But as many as received him, to them gave he power to become the sons of God, even to them that believe on his name." By faith a man receives the Lord Jesus and is thereby saved and born into the family of God. J. Gresham Machen notes:

> When a man...accepts Christ, not in general but specifically, as he is offered to us in the gospel, such acceptance of Christ is saving faith.... The true reason why faith is given such an exclusive place by the New Testament, so far as the attainment of salvation is concerned, over against love and over against everything else in man . . . is that faith means receiving something, not doing something or even being something. To say, therefore, that our faith saves us means that we do not save ourselves even in the slightest measure, but that God saves us.[13]

The message is the same: salvation is not by the performance of works or the promise of future works, but by faith in the Lord Jesus Christ. Those who teach Lordship Salvation frontload faith with commitments to do the "good works" (Eph. 2:10) expected of a mature Christian to become a Christian. This is an addition of what man must do to the finished work of Christ on the cross, which He has done once for all (Heb. 10:10). This is a message that frustrates grace (Gal. 2:21) and corrupts the simplicity that is in Christ.

---

2 Corinthians 11:3 But I fear, lest by any means, as the serpent beguiled Eve through his subtilty, so your minds should be corrupted from the simplicity that is in Christ.

ENDNOTES:

1. Spiros Zodhiates, *The Hebrew Greek Study Bible*, p. 1,749.
2. John VanGelderen, *Engine Truths*, p. 10.
3. Fred Moritz, *Preach the Word*, Oct. – Nov. 1999, p. 10.
4. Ernest Pickering, *Lordship Salvation: An Examination of John MacArthur's Book, The Gospel According to Jesus*.
5. John MacArthur, *The Gospel According to Jesus*, p. 87.
6. John MacArthur, *The Gospel According to Jesus [Revised & Expanded Edition]*, p. 95.
7. John MacArthur, *The Gospel According to Jesus, What is Authentic Faith*? p. 99.
8. John MacArthur, *The Gospel According to Jesus*, p. 140.
9. Charles Spurgeon, *The Treasury Of The New Testament*, Vol. IV, pp. 576-577.
10. H. A. Ironside, *Lectures on Romans*, p. 130-131, (emphasis his).
11. Michael Bere, *Bible Doctrines For Today*. Book 2, p. 35.
12. Charles Spurgeon, *The Treasury of the New Testament*, Vol. II, p. 836.
13. J. Gresham Machen, *What Is Faith*: pp. 161, 173.

THE RICH YOUNG RULER

Matthew 19:16-22 And, behold, one came and said unto him, Good Master, what good thing shall I do, that I may have eternal life? And he said unto him, Why callest thou me good? there is none good but one, that is, God: but if thou wilt enter into life, keep the commandments. He saith unto him, Which? Jesus said, Thou shalt do no murder, Thou shalt not commit adultery, Thou shalt not steal, Thou shalt not bear false witness, Honour thy father and thy mother: and, Thou shalt love thy neighbour as thyself. The young man saith unto him, All these things have I kept from my youth up: what lack I yet? Jesus said unto him, If thou wilt be perfect, go and sell that thou hast, and give to the poor, and thou shalt have treasure in heaven: and come and follow me. But when the young man heard that saying, he went away sorrowful: for he had great possessions.

The account of Christ's encounter with the rich young ruler (Matthew 19:16-22; Mark 10:17-22; Luke 18:18-23) is a passage often used by the Lordship advocates to support their view of the gospel. This passage is a mainstay of John MacArthur's *The Gospel Accord to Jesus* and Walter Chantry's *Today's Gospel: Authentic or Synthetic*.

Eternal Life and Salvation

This passage is without a doubt an episode of direct evangelism. The focus of the young man's question is achieving salvation and eternal life. I do not challenge the Lordship advocate when he interprets this passage as having to do with salvation; on that point we agree. It has been my experience, however, that Lordship advocates, to bolster the Lordship gospel of submission and commitment, misinterpret the meaning of this passage. Properly understood, the Lord intended to bring this rich young man to the point of realizing that his own sinful nature was keeping him from receiving eternal life.

The Young Man's Approach

The manner in which the young man approached Christ is noteworthy. In Mark's gospel we read, "There came one running, and kneeled to him." He did not stride up to Christ like a self-righteous man full of himself and his riches. At least it does not at first appear to be his problem. He ran to the feet of Jesus and knelt before Him. The way in which this young man approached Christ looks sincere enough. He appears to be in urgent need and kneeling as though he is worshiping Christ. In the previous chapter we saw blind Bartimeus calling out to Jesus using one of His Messianic titles, "Thou Son of David, have mercy on me," (Luke 18:39). Others had come before Christ in similar humility and appearing to worship Him (Mark 1:40; John 9:38).

Without a doubt this young man wanted to know that he was right in the sight of God and on his way to Heaven. Even though he probably had all that the world could provide, he knew that he lacked the most important thing: the hope and expectation of eternal life. But he approached Jesus on the basis of his own good works. He assumed he could do enough good things to deserve eternal life. He had to learn that his good works were not going to be good enough, and Jesus was about to teach him this lesson.

He saluted Jesus this way: "Good Master, what good thing shall I do, that I may have eternal life?" Certainly he was honoring Jesus, but what was his motive in calling Jesus, "Good Master?" Was he trying to address Jesus as a respected rabbi and teacher? Regardless of the motive, Jesus used that salutation to get this young man thinking in the right direction.

The Lord's initial response was, "Why callest thou me good? there is none good but one, that is, God." Jesus answered him with a question of His own to help the young man comprehend His divine nature. He did not recognize that Jesus is the Christ, the Son of God. Jesus then directed the man to the Law of Moses. Commenting on this transition, Dr. Warren Wiersbe wrote:

> He wanted him to see himself as a sinner bowed before the holy God. We cannot be saved from sin by keeping the Law (Gal. 2:16-21; Eph. 2:8-10). The Law is a mirror that shows us how dirty we are, but the mirror cannot wash us. One purpose of the Law is to bring the sinner to Christ (Gal. 3:24), which is what it did in this man's case.[1]

If this young man had recognized Jesus as God, he would have realized that he could not meet God's standard of perfection. Jesus, the God-man, is that perfection, and all men fall short of it.

> Romans 3:23 For all have sinned, and come short of the glory of God.

All men must come to Christ as helpless, undeserving, Hell-bound sinners if they are going to receive forgiveness and eternal life.

A Sincere Question: Or Is It?

> "Good Master, what good thing shall I do, that I may have eternal life?"

When the young man said, "good thing," what he really meant was "good work." There is little doubt that the young man's question shows that he believed he could in some way earn or merit eternal life. This man sincerely desired eternal life, but he was focused on works not faith. He had to learn that he could not receive eternal life by any "good thing" or work he had ever done or would do.

The First Set of Commands and the Man's Response

When this young man came to Christ seeking to justify himself, he was immediately confronted with the demands of perfect righteousness from the Law of Moses. At first, Jesus simply told this young man, "...if thou wilt enter into life, keep the commandments." The young man replied, "Which?" Now, this young man certainly was not ignorant of the Law of God. Could it be that the Lord's instruction, "keep the commandments," had a chilling impact on him? He certainly knew that he had not kept all the Law of Moses perfectly. It appears that he was trying to escape the broad sweeping force of the Lord's words.

Jesus then cited the latter section of the Ten Commandments, the five commands that deal with man's relations to other men. The Lord was using the Law to help this young man see that he was a sinner and without hope before a holy God. Jesus, however, did not name the tenth commandment yet. Instead, the Lord cited Leviticus 19:18: "Thou shalt not avenge, nor bear any grudge against the children of thy people, but thou shalt love thy neighbour as thyself: I am the LORD."

> Jesus did not give him the last of those six commandments dealing with man's relationship to man in the list of the Ten Commandments . . . Jesus did not give him the commandment that said, "thou shalt not covet," because that is where the young man's problem was.[2]

The young man in response said, "All these things have I kept from my youth up." As far as this young man was concerned, he had met the standard. It is not very likely that he was telling the Lord an outright lie. What is more likely is that he did not fully understand God's perfect standard and his failure to meet it. Jesus did not challenge his claim. The young man was about to find out, however, that he was far from blameless in his relationship to a holy God. In his commentary on Matthew 19:16-26, H. A. Ironside observes:

> If men would seek eternal life by doing good, the law challenges them to perfect obedience. Because all have sinned, it is not possible for anyone to be justified by the deeds of the law. The law speaks with awful force to an awakened conscience, giving one to realize the hopelessness of ever obtaining eternal life by human merit.[3]

Dr. Ironside then goes right to the heart of the problem with the rich young man's assertion:

> No doubt these words came from a sincere heart, but they give evidence of lack of real exercise of conscience. Who, knowing himself, could so speak? Outwardly, the life may have been blameless, but if conscience had been active there would have been confession of sin. It was the smug self-righteousness of one who prided himself on his own morality and did not realize the corruption of his heart. The question, "What lack I yet?" in itself indicates how complacent he was—how self-satisfied.[4]

No one has ever kept the Law from his youth. This young man had not perfectly obeyed and honored his parents throughout his lifetime. For a moment, let us assume that he had kept all the commands that the Lord had just cited to him. Even so, there were many others he had not kept:

> Obviously, he had broken the very first commandment of the Decalogue. He worshipped the god of money as well as the God of Israel (Exodus 20:3). He certainly did not love the Lord with all his heart, soul, and might (Deuteronomy 6:5). His love of possessions kept him from that kind of total love for the Lord. Because he apparently did not share his wealth, he also violated the command to love his neighbor as he loved himself (Leviticus 19:18).[5]

> The young ruler did not see himself as a condemned sinner before the holy God. He had a superficial view of the Law of God, for he measured obedience only by external actions and not by inward attitudes. As far as his actions were concerned, he was blameless (see Phil. 3:6); but his inward attitudes were not blameless, because he was covetous. He may have kept some of the commandments, but the last commandment caught him: "Thou shalt not covet!"[6]

Now we are learning that this young man was very confident in himself and his righteousness. He thought he could do something more than he had done already that would ultimately earn for him eternal life. Such was the mindset of the Jews in that day. In the gospel of John, the Jews asked Jesus, "What shall we do, that we might work the works of God" (John 6:28)? To which Jesus replied, "This is the work of God, that ye believe on him whom he hath sent" (John 6:29).

> Recognizing in Jesus a supreme goodness he did not possess, this rich young man asked the Lord what he had to do to gain eternal life. The question reflected the Jewish perspective of the time. One had to do something great in order to merit eternal life.[7]

There is no good thing that man can do to earn or deserve eternal life. In our day, many believe they can do some good deed to merit favor with God and ensure eternal life. Still others believe that if they have done nothing bad enough to deserve God's wrath and judgment they will receive eternal life. The hope of many is that when life is over, the good they have done will outweigh the bad, and they will make it to Heaven. According to God's Word, at life's end a man's work will not add up to eternal life.

> Isaiah 64:6 But we are all as an unclean thing, and all our righteousnesses are as filthy rags.

Jesus showed this rich young man that he could not earn Heaven through any good work. The Lord was going to show him that he was a sinner and condemned already (John 3:18).

The Lord's Convicting Words

> Matthew 16:21 Jesus said unto him, If thou wilt be perfect, go and sell that thou hast, and give to the poor, and thou shalt have treasure in heaven: and come and follow me.

Jesus had previously omitted the commands that relate to God. He had also omitted the tenth commandment. It was the tenth commandment that would convict the rich young man of his sin. The Lord was now using that commandment to bring this young man face to face with his sin: "Thou shalt not covet" (Exodus 20:17).

> Now Jesus . . . puts His finger on the very spot in this young man's life where the Law would condemn him. So, now the young man senses his condemnation by the Law. Now he's been brought to the place to face the fact that he is a sinner, and he needs a sacrifice; the sacrifice of the "Good Master" who perfectly kept all the Law and then shed His blood as the Lamb of God . . . to pay the penalty of this young man's sin and our sin. Now this young man can no longer depend on his works. Salvation is a free gift! He realized his condemnation under the Law, under living a life of works.[8]

To "covet" means to desire, take pleasure in, or to delight in. The young man coveted his wealth more than he coveted the things of God. We know this because he walked away from God, in the person of Jesus Christ who stood before him, rather than be willing to sell his possessions. In this he was also guilty of violating the first of the Ten Commandments, Exodus 20:3: "Thou shalt have no other gods before me."

We know from the Scriptures that the Law can't save. Jesus was bringing this young man to the Law so that the Law would serve its function as the schoolmaster, and show this young man that he was condemned by the very thing he was trusting.[9]

Keeping the Law of God does not save anybody. No man or woman from Adam and Eve until our time ever has kept or ever will keep the Law perfectly. The Law is our schoolmaster; it shows us that we are sinners in the sight of God. The keeping of the Law does not lead to regeneration or salvation. The Law condemns and shows us that if we are going to be saved we need help from Almighty God through the person of Jesus Christ.

> ...the sinner *cannot* (a) by a single volition bring his character and life into complete conformity to God's law; (b) change his fundamental preference for self and sin to supreme love for God; nor (c) do any act, however insignificant, which shall meet with God's approval or answer fully to the demands of law.[10]

Salvation is not by the works of the Law; it comes by faith. No man can perfectly keep the Law!

> Job 9:20 If I justify myself, mine own mouth shall condemn me: if I say, I am perfect, it shall also prove me perverse.

> Romans 3:20-28 Therefore by the deeds of the law there shall no flesh be justified in his sight: for by the law is the knowledge of sin. . .Therefore we conclude that a man is justified by faith without the deeds of the law.

> Galatians 2:16 Knowing that a man is not justified by the works of the law, but by the faith of Jesus Christ, even we have believed in Jesus Christ, that we might be justified by the faith of Christ, and not by the works of the law: for by the works of the law shall no flesh be justified.

Not of Works!

When the rich young ruler approached Christ, he asked, "Good Master, what good thing shall I do, that I may have eternal life?" That "good thing" is works. In commenting on this passage John MacArthur writes,

> Our Lord gave this young man a test. He had to choose between his possessions and Jesus Christ. He failed the test. No matter what points of doctrine he affirmed, because he was unwilling to turn from what else he loved most, he could not be a disciple of Christ. Salvation is only for those who are willing to give Christ first place in their lives.[11]

That citation from the revised and expanded edition of *The Gospel According to Jesus* is a sanitized revision of the original in which MacArthur stated:

> Our Lord gave this young man a test. He had to choose between his possessions and Jesus Christ. He failed the test. No matter what he believed, since he was unwilling to forsake all, he could not be a disciple of Christ. Salvation is for those who are willing to forsake everything.[12]

From *Hard to Believe* MacArthur wrote:

> And he needed to be willing to submit to the Lord Jesus, even if it meant he had to give up all his earthly possessions. He might not ask, but the requirement for eternal life is the willingness to give it all up if he does.[13]

During a Trinity Broadcasting Network interview MacArthur stated:

> In fact Jesus said this, "If you come to Me it may cost you your family. But if you're not willing to hate your family you can't be My disciple. If you come to Me you might have to give all your possessions away and give them to the poor. If you are not willing to do that you are not worthy to be My disciple."[14]

For a moment let's say the man confessed his sin of covetousness, asked Jesus to forgive him. He also expressed a willingness to give away all that he had, but Jesus did not ask him to do so at that moment. Is he a saved man? Did he meet Lordship's "requirement for eternal life" as MacArthur defines it? Assuming he becomes saved the man begins to follow Jesus and some time later Jesus turns to him and says, "Today, I want you to give all that you have to the poor." If that man hesitates to obey this command, what does it mean? Is he is in danger of losing his salvation? Was he never saved in the first place? If one concludes he was never saved in the first place then any act of disobedience, in the life of a professing believer, must raise the same question.

When I lived in Florida there was a period of time when I was witnessing to a young man who worked at a fast food restaurant. His name was Tom and he was interested in spiritual things. My wife remembers how I would visit Tom late at night, actually in the hours just after midnight, at his restaurant and we would pour over the Bible. I was very clear about his sin, God's wrath and his need to born again through faith in Jesus Christ as his only hope for salvation. After a number of weeks Tom believed the gospel and received Jesus Christ as his personal Savior.

He began to take steps of growth that one might expect of a new believer. One day, right out of the blue, he asked me what I thought about his hair. Now Tom had long flowing hair. His hair was not dirty or sloppy, just long and not what you would call the best testimony for Christ. His hair was not an issue as a lost man, his sin and guilt before God was. A few weeks after receiving Christ, during his personal reading of the Bible, he came across this passage.

> 1 Corinthians 11:14 Doth not even nature itself teach you, that, if a man have long hair, it is a shame unto him?

So, for Tom his hair had become an issue. The Lord had pricked Tom's heart about his hair. Tom felt as though the verse meant for him that he should get a haircut. I told him that if he felt God wanted that for him then he should obey. Tom said he would get his hair cut that week. Tom knew he should get his hair cut, he wanted to get his hair cut, but just could not bring himself to do it. Tom became unwilling to get his haircut: Does this mean he was never saved in the first place, or has he fallen into carnality?

A short time later Tom moved to one of the western states. I knew from the first time I met him he would be moving soon, which is why I was urgent about seeing him as often as possible to present the gospel. In my heart I think Tom probably got that hair cut some where along the way. Tom's hair was not the issue for receiving or keeping eternal life no more than the giving away possessions was for the rich young ruler.

Giving up earthly possessions or even the willingness to do so does not bring anyone closer to eternal life. Salvation is a free gift! The gift of God is not conditional on haircuts, forsaking possessions, station in life or performing personal acts of charity. The Scriptures are very clear: Man cannot be saved by any personal work of righteousness (Titus 3:5). Attaching the performance of and/or promise to perform the works of discipleship to faith in Christ corrupts "the simplicity that is in Christ" (2 Cor. 11:3) and will "frustrate the grace of God" (Gal. 2:21). Man is saved through personal faith in Jesus Christ alone!

In his quote above John MacArthur says, "no matter what he believed." Taking that at face value leads one to the conclusion that John MacArthur is suggesting that believing on the Lord Jesus Christ (Acts 16:31) is insufficient for salvation. For the Lordship advocate, even if the young man believed that Jesus was the Messiah, believed that Jesus was the Savior, and expressed dependent faith in Christ, that would be insufficient to save him. It is clear that John MacArthur, representing the Lordship position, conditions the lost man's reception of eternal salvation not on simple belief alone, but also on an upfront promise to "forsake everything." In the case of this rich young ruler, the Lordship advocate would state that his salvation depended on the willingness to surrender his riches. Dr. Charles Ryrie wrote:

> Is eternal life gained by keeping the commandments, even by keeping them perfectly, if anyone could do that? Paul answered that very question at the conclusion of his synagogue message in Antioch in Pisidia. He said that only through Jesus is everyone who believes justified and that no one could be justified by the Law of Moses (Acts 13:39). . . . So even if the rich young man's claim were true that he had kept the

commandments the Lord mentioned, he still could not have gained eternal life, even if he had kept them perfectly.[15]

Does Charitable Giving Lead to Salvation?

Are we to assume that if the rich young ruler had obeyed the command to, "sell that thou hast, and give to the poor," he would have earned salvation? Representing the Lordship position, John MacArthur answers the question this way:

> Do we literally have to give away everything we own to become Christians? No, but we do have to give Christ first place (cf. Col. 3:18) [sic]. That means we must be willing to forsake all for him (Luke 14:33)—that is, we cling to nothing that takes precedence over Christ. . . . Jesus' request of this man was simply to establish whether he was willing to submit to the sovereignty of Jesus over his life.[16]

In the chapter *Salvation and Discipleship: Is There A Biblical Difference* we have dealt with the Lordship error of interpreting discipleship passages as evangelistic appeals. In the above quote from MacArthur, one can see that the Lordship advocates arrive at their costly salvation because they confuse discipleship with salvation. John MacArthur cites Luke 14:33 as a cross-reference. Jesus says, "So likewise, whosoever he be of you that forsaketh not all that he hath, he cannot be my disciple." John MacArthur says of Christ's encounter with the rich young ruler,

> At first sight, we might wonder what kind of message Jesus was trying to give this young man. A closer look reveals clearly what it was. If we could condense the truth of this entire passage into a single statement, it would be Luke 14:33: "So

therefore, no one of you can be My disciple who does not give up all his own possessions."¹⁷

John MacArthur has misinterpreted the message that Jesus gave the rich young ruler. The Luke 14 passage is not dealing with salvation, but instead the good works one might expect of the believer. "Giving up all his own possessions" or even the willingness to do so would not have brought the rich young man any nearer to eternal life than keeping the Law, getting baptized, or joining and financially supporting a local church. If the lost man is told that he must resolve to do anything toward his salvation: forsaking all or surrendering "all his own possessions," the message becomes works based and thereby non-saving. Salvation is either through what Christ has DONE or Lordship's insistence on what man must be inclined toward or resolved to DO.

Matthew 19:23-24 Then said Jesus unto his disciples, Verily I say unto you, That a rich man shall hardly enter into the kingdom of heaven. And again I say unto you, It is easier for a camel to go through the eye of a needle, than for a rich man to enter into the kingdom of God.

The young man had just departed in sorrow. Now the Lord was commenting on and instructing his disciples on the importance of what had just taken place. The disciples were at first perplexed at the Lord's words. Most commentators agree that the "eye of a needle" was in reference to a small door found in the larger gates to a city. The door was only large enough for a human to pass through. The door would have been too small for a camel. Dr. Charles Ryrie explains:

No way could a camel with or without its humps squeeze through the eye of a needle. The disciples understood that the Lord was saying that it is impossible for anyone who trusts in riches to enter the kingdom—unless God intervenes and offers a way of salvation that is unrelated to human resources and abilities. But the young man did not stay around long enough to hear that message. He would not acknowledge his need of outside help, so he did not receive it. But he could have, for the Lord said that with God all things are possible—even the salvation of this rich man. But not on the basis of giving away his wealth.[18]

Salvation has never been dependent upon what man does with his riches. Jesus never conditioned the gift of eternal life on this man's willingness or promise to give away his riches. As noted above, the Lord used the young man's riches to show him that he was covetous and worshipped his money above God. If that young man had given all his wealth to the poor, that act would not have bought him eternal life. The Lord brought him to realize that he was a sinner who needed a sacrifice that not even all of his riches and good works could buy. Dr. J. Vernon McGee wrote:

> Money will buy anything except the most valuable thing—eternal life. This discourse reveals the impossibility of a rich man entering into heaven by his riches. It is impossible for any man to enter heaven by his own means.[19]

Dr. McGee makes another interesting observation regarding the Lord's instruction to the young man:

> Jesus asked him to separate himself from his riches and follow him. Where would this lead him? Well, at this time the Lord Jesus is on the way to die for the sins of this man. Had he followed Jesus, he would have come to the cross for redemption.[20]

What does the Bible say about trusting the works of man for salvation?

> Isaiah 64:6 But we are all as an unclean thing, and all our righteousnesses are as filthy rags.
>
> Romans 3:10, 23 As it is written, There is none righteous, no, not one . . . For all have sinned, and come short of the glory of God.
>
> Titus 3:5 Not by works of righteousness which we have done, but according to his mercy he saved us, by the washing of regeneration, and renewing of the Holy Ghost
>
> James 2:10 For whosoever shall keep the whole law, and yet offend in one point, he is guilty of all.

In light of these passages one must conclude from Jesus' encounter with the rich young ruler, that the Lord was not requiring that he perform, or promise to perform, a work of charity on behalf of the poor to receive eternal life.

Conclusion

This rich young ruler had erred in three vital areas.

- First, he failed to recognize Jesus as the Messiah, the Son of God. He had an incomplete knowledge of who Jesus was. His understanding, like many others in that day, was limited to Christ being no more than a great and respected teacher.

- Second, he believed that he could by "good things" (works) earn for himself eternal life. He learned that he had not kept the Law perfectly and was, therefore, condemned by the Law.

- Third, he did not remain with Christ and by faith accept Him as Savior, the only hope for eternal life. The Bible says, "he went away sorrowful." He not only left a disheartened man, he left an unsaved man. He remained unsaved because he trusted in his own righteousness. He was shown his sin of coveting and refused to acknowledge or repent of it.

The error in the Lordship proponents' interpretation of the passage is this: they come to the passage requiring a costly salvation because they confuse the cost of discipleship with the free gift of salvation through the finished work of Christ on the cross. They say, on the one hand, salvation is by faith alone; and then, on the other hand, they require the hard demands of submission, commitment and surrender in "exchange" for God's saving grace. The Lordship advocate claims to preach a gospel of salvation by grace through faith plus nothing. How their interpretation of the encounter between Jesus and the rich young ruler is not a faith plus works message is difficult to grasp.

> Thus, the account of the rich young ruler does not teach that to be saved the ruler must meet the demands of discipleship, surrender to Christ's lordship in the area of covetousness and love for others, or repent of particular sins. The issue of riches was raised to show that the ruler had not fulfilled the righteous requirements of the law and that he was really trusting in the merit of his wealth and position. . . . The forsaking of one's possessions, or the willingness to do so is never made a condi-

tion of salvation in other evangelistic encounters in the New Testament.[21]

ENDNOTES:

1. Warren Wiersbe, *The Bible Exposition Commentary*, Vol. I, p. 146.
2. Joel Mullenix, *What Is The Gospel?* A sermon recorded at Pensacola Christian College on November 2, 1997.
3. H. A. Ironside, *Notes on Matthew*, pp. 245-246.
4. Ibid., p. 246.
5. Charles Ryrie, *So Great Salvation*, p. 83.
6. Warren Wiersbe, *The Bible Exposition Commentary*, Vol. I, p. 146.
7. Charles Ryrie, *So Great Salvation*, p. 81.
8. Joel Mullenix, *What Is The Gospel?* A sermon recorded Nov. 2, 1997.
9. Ibid.
10. A. H. Strong, *Systematic Theology*, p. 640.
11. John MacArthur, *The Gospel According To Jesus [Revised & Expanded Edition]*, p. 85.
12. John MacArthur, *The Gospel According To Jesus*, p. 78.
13. John MacArthur, *Hard To Believe: The High Cost and Infinite value of Following Jesus*, p. 9.
14 YouTube, "Kirk Cameron Interviews John MacArthur," http://www.youtube.com/watch?v=tNQoOEG8P2I, (accessed January 10, 2010).
15. Charles Ryrie, *So Great Salvation*, p. 82.
16. John MacArthur, *The Gospel According To Jesus [Revised & Expanded Edition]*, p. 94.
17. Ibid., p. 85.
18. Charles Ryrie, *So Great Salvation*, p. 86.
19. J. Vernon McGee, *Thru the Bible with J. Vernon McGee*, Vol. IV, p. 205.
20. Ibid., p. 205.
21. Charles Bing, *Lordship Salvation: A Biblical Evaluation and Response*, pp. 149-150.

ROMANS CHAPTER TEN

Romans 10:9 That if thou shalt confess with thy mouth the Lord Jesus, and believe in thine heart that God hath raised Him from the dead, thou shalt be saved.

Romans 10:9 is a favorite of the Lordship advocates in support of their evangelistic message of commitment and surrender in exchange for salvation. This chapter is dedicated to a careful examination of and commentary on this important verse. Key words from the verse will be studied and compared. The purpose of this chapter is to demonstrate that Romans 10:9 does not support the Lordship Salvation interpretation of the gospel.

What is Confession and What Are We to Confess?

Confess is the translation of ομολογεω (*homologeo*). In this usage of this word, the meaning is clearly understood by examining the etymology, which is composed of two parts. The prefix ομο (*homo*) is the adjective ομος (*homos*), meaning "same," as illustrated by certain English words such as *homogenous*. The stem of the word *confess* is the verb λεγω (*lego*), which means "to say" or "to speak." Many who have never studied Greek will nonetheless recognize the noun form of this verb, λογος (*logos*), meaning "word," a name or title of Christ used by the Apostle John in the first verse of his gospel. By adding the prefix "same" to the root "speak," the etymological meaning emerges "to say the same thing."

Thayer defines "confess" as follows: "to say the same thing as another, i.e. *to agree with, assent.*"[1] Vine defines it similarly: "to speak the same thing, to assent, accord, agree with . . . (c) to declare openly by way of speaking out freely, such confession being the effect of deep conviction of facts."[2]

When the word *confess* is used of sin, it means to say the same thing God says about our sin. Biblically defined sin literally means a missing of the mark. All mankind falls short of sinless perfection and therefore all mankind is guilty of sin before a holy God. Genuine biblical confession occurs when we recognize and acknowledge in genuine agreement with what God says about our sin.

Romans 3:10, 23 As it is written, There is none righteous, no, not one. For all have sinned, and come short of the glory of God

---

If a man is going to receive mercy and forgiveness from God he had better start by acknowledging and confessing he is guilty of sin. If he does not come to the place of acknowledging his sinful condition, he will not recognize his need of a Savior. Romans 10:9 speaks of "confessing" Christ. Biblical confession involves an agreement regarding the object of the confession with the one to whom the confession is being directed. To confess the Lord Jesus means to agree with God about the Person and works of the Lord Jesus Christ. It does not, however, involve an upfront commitment of life or act of personal surrender to be born again.

How Does the Bible Define "Believe?"

> John 3:36 He that believeth on the Son hath everlasting life: and he that believeth not the Son shall not see life; but the wrath of God abideth on him.

To better understand how the word "believe" from Romans 10:9 cannot support the Lordship interpretation of the gospel, an initial look at John 3:36 is necessary.

The active word in this verse is *believe*. If a man will believe on the Son (of God), he will have eternal life. John MacArthur cites this verse in a footnote on p. 33 of *The Gospel According to Jesus*. The meaning of the verse, however, is distorted to favor the Lordship Salvation view. He cites the verse as follows: "He who does not obey the Son shall not see life. . . ."[3]

John MacArthur chooses John 3:36 to support the Lordship gospel by citing the second usage of the word "believeth" (from the KJV) as "obey," but he does not cite the first half of John 3:36, which is the key to the context. The first usage of the word "believeth" in John 3:36 is identical to the word "believe" in the Romans 10:9 passage. While the word "believeth not" απειθων, (*apeithon*) is a different word than the first usage of the word "believeth," and can mean "obey" in some cases, the context of John 3:36(a) demands unbelief, not disobedience. The correct meaning of "believeth not" (απειθων) is to refuse or withhold belief. Or, we could say that disobedience in itself is unbelief. Taking the whole context into consideration, the second part of the verse cannot be referring to a person's actions, but rather to his unbelief.

In reference to John 3:36, Spiros T. Zodhiates defines *Apeitheia* thus: "from the negative *a* (1), without, and *peitho*

(3982), to persuade. Not to believe, to disbelieve implying disobedience; also to disobey as through unbelief."[4]

Obey is a legitimate translation of *believe*, but to render it thus in this verse does not clearly convey what sort of obedience is required. Refusing to believe in Christ is, in essence, disobedience.

Lordship teachers say that Romans 10:9 explicitly demands personal submission from a lost man; a belief in and acceptance of the lordship of Christ as Ruler of his own life in order to be saved. For example, Stott writes:

> We may believe in the deity and the salvation of Christ, and acknowledge ourselves to be sinners in need of his salvation; but this does not make us Christians. We have to make a personal response to Jesus Christ, committing ourselves unreservedly to him as our Savior and Lord.[5]

Referring to Acts 2:21, 2:36, 16:31; and Romans 10:9-10, John MacArthur said:

> All of these passages include indisputably the lordship of Christ as part of the gospel to be believed for salvation.... it is clear that people who come to Christ for salvation must do so in obedience to Him, that is, with a willingness to surrender to Him as Lord.[6]

Kenneth L. Gentry wrote:

> To "believe on the Lord Jesus Christ" involves more than knowledge, assent and trust (reliance). True, one must know about God's provision, he must assent to the truth of the gospel and he must rely on Christ to save him. But to believe on the Lord Jesus Christ means more than to believe that he is Lord and more than to rely on Him to give eternal life. It also means to receive Christ as one's own Lord, the ruler of one's own life.[7]

Gentry's definition of *believe* goes beyond the scope of Acts 16:31, "believe on the Lord Jesus Christ, and thou shalt be saved" and Romans 10:9-10. From the definitions above one concludes that the unbeliever must make an up-front commitment of personal surrender and submission to Christ in every area of life to be born again.

In Acts 8:35-38, the Ethiopian Eunuch desired baptism. This Eunuch, a man of importance, was on his way home from Jerusalem. He was in his chariot reading a scroll of the prophet Isaiah, which he evidently purchased in Jerusalem. The Eunuch did not understand what he was reading. God called Philip the Evangelist away from a great work in Samaria and directed him to a wilderness road where Philip then saw this Eunuch. The Spirit of God told Philip to draw near the chariot. Once near Philip could hear the Eunuch reading Isaiah's prophecy. (It was a common practice in that day to read out loud.) Philip asked the Eunuch if he understood what he was reading, and the Eunuch said he did not. So, Philip joined the Eunuch and began to explain the portion of Isaiah he was reading. The Acts passage says:

> Then Philip opened his mouth, and began at the same scripture, and preached unto him Jesus. And as they went on their way, they came unto a certain water: and the eunuch said, See, here is water; what doth hinder me to be baptized? And Philip said, If thou believest with all thine heart, thou mayest. And he answered and said, I believe that Jesus Christ is the Son of God. And he commanded the chariot to stand still: and they went down both into the water, both Philip and the eunuch; and he baptized him.

The Eunuch's confession was enough, and Philip baptized him. There was no mention of a "wholehearted commitment" to discipleship, no promise of submission, only that he believes. Believe what? "Jesus Christ is the Son of God." The Eunuch humbled himself and accepted the deity of the Lord Jesus Christ.

It is also interesting to note that the word *believeth* in Philip's question and *believe* in the confession by the Eunuch are identical words. They are also the same as the word *believe* in Romans 10:9. *Pisteuo* means "to believe, to be mentally persuaded, knowledge of and confidence in." Vine writes on *believe* as used in Romans 10:9, "to believe, also to be persuaded of, and hence to place confidence in . . . reliance upon and not mere credence."[8] Dr. Spiros T. Zodhiates defines *believe* as, "to believe, to have mental persuasion . . . to believe in or on Christ, implying knowledge or assent to and confidence in Him."[9]

The Eunuch was saved and baptized because of his confession (*to agree, admit, assent with Philip*) that Jesus is the Son of God. Philip did not seek a commitment or promise from the Eunuch that he would live in obedience to the lordship of Christ in Ethiopia before administering believer's baptism. The Eunuch was born again upon his confession of and belief in the deity of the Lord Jesus Christ. The truth the Eunuch confessed about Christ, that He is the Son of God, was why the Jews sought to have Christ crucified.

John 19:7 The Jews answered him, We have a law, and by our law he ought to die, because he made himself the Son of God

---

Note Vine's statement on the position of Christ within the Triune God:

> The Son of God, in His eternal relationship with the Father, is not so entitled because He at any time began to derive His being from the Father...but because He is and ever has been the expression of what the Father is.... Thus absolute Godhead, not Godhead in a secondary or derived sense, is intended in the title.[10]

Adding to the gospel so much as a commitment to do the "good works" (Eph. 2:10) expected of a Christian, no matter how noble the motivation may be, distorts the good news of salvation by grace through faith. The Bible is abundantly clear that a man is saved from his sin and on his way to Heaven solely by believing in, and faith depending on the finished work of Christ.

> Act 16:31 And they said, Believe on the Lord Jesus Christ, and thou shalt be saved, and thy house.
>
> Romans 4:4-5 Now to him that worketh is the reward not reckoned of grace, but of debt. But to him that worketh not, but believeth on him that justifieth the ungodly, his faith is counted for righteousness.
>
> Romans 10:3-4 For they being ignorant of God's righteousness, and going about to establish their own righteousness, have not submitted themselves unto the righteousness of God. For Christ is the end of the law for righteousness to every one that believeth.

> Ephesians 2:8-9 For by grace are ye saved through faith; and that not of yourselves: it is the gift of God: Not of works, lest any man should boast.
> 1 John 5:1 Whosoever believeth that Jesus is the Christ is born of God.
>
> John 9:35-38 Jesus heard that they had cast him out; and when he had found him, he said unto him, Dost thou believe on the Son of God? He answered and said, Who is he, Lord, that I might believe on him? And Jesus said unto him, Thou hast both seen him, and it is he that talketh with thee. And he said, Lord, I believe. And he worshipped him.

From the ninth chapter of John's gospel we read that the man born blind received physical sight by a miracle of Jesus; but spiritual sight came when Jesus asked, "Dost thou believe on the Son of God?" He answered, "Lord, I believe." Jesus made belief the condition, and the man met that condition by believing. Here we do not see Christ demanding from the blind man a commitment to follow Him in order to be saved. The man believed, he worshipped the Lord, and Christ accepted the worship of this man who had believed on Him.

In The Context Of Romans 10:9- What is the Meaning of the Word, "LORD?"

> Romans 10:9 That if thou shalt confess with thy mouth the Lord Jesus, and shalt believe in thine heart that God hath raised him from the dead, thou shalt be saved.

From the verse *Lord* is the rendering of the Greek κυριος (*kurios*), which is one of the most common words in the New Testament. This usage of *Lord* occurs hundreds of times and in every New Testament book with the exception of the first and third epistles of John. Dr. H. C. Thiessen defines it this way:

> The term is used in four different senses. It is used of God the Father; as a title of courtesy; as a name for a master; and as a title of address to, or as a name for, Christ (Matt. 7:22; 8:2; 14:28; etc).. . . . It is clear, then, that already in the New Testament times the name "Lord" came to be applied to Christ in the sense of deity.[11]

For those who hold to Lordship theology, confession of and belief in Christ's deity does not completely define the gospel invitation of Romans 10:9. Is that a fair representation of the Lordship position? Note the following statement from Dr. Marc T. Mueller, a professor from John MacArthur's Master's Seminary. He has written, "The saviour hood of Christ is actually contingent on obedience to His lordship."[12]

The obvious and disturbing implication of this teaching is two fold. First, the lost must make a commitment of obedience to the lordship of Christ to be born again. Second, he then must live up to his commitment of obedience to Christ's lordship or he will not ultimately realize Christ as Savior, i.e., he will not reach Heaven. Proponents of the Lordship view hold that the title *Lord* when applied to Jesus necessitates the lost man's submission to the rule and reign of Christ over his life, in sanctification, for both *initial* salvation (justification) and *final* salvation (glorification). John MacArthur says that Romans 10:9 explicitly demands submission to Christ's sovereign authority.

> It is important to keep in mind that MacArthur sees much more than deity and sovereignty in the term "Lord" as applied to Christ for salvation. He insists it means the sinner must promise

to serve Christ and allow Him to be Master over every area of his life, all his life.[13]

The designation *Lord* in Romans 10:9 teaches that the acceptance of Christ's deity is necessary for salvation. There are many cultic religions that would have you believe Jesus was a good man, a great teacher and a worker of miracles. However, they will not recognize Jesus as God, the Creator, equal with the Father. Occasionally I have representatives of these cult religions at my door seeking a dialogue with me. The only dialogue they receive from me is this, "Jesus is equal with God the Father and as long as you regard Jesus as less than God, I can tell you from the authority of the Bible, you are dead in your sins and on your way to eternal damnation in Hell!" Jesus is nothing to us if He is not God of very God. In Colossians 2:9 the Bible says, "For in Him dwelleth all the fullness of the Godhead bodily." If He is not God, He is not the Savior. John 8:24 says, "I said therefore unto you, that ye shall die in your sins: for if ye believe not that I am He, ye shall die in your sins." By Christ's saying, "I am," He was clearly indicating His deity. The same truth is presented in John 8:58 where Jesus said, "Verily, verily, I say unto you, Before Abraham was, I am." Dr. Charlie Bing comments on Romans 10:9 in the context of verses 9-13:

> It should be noted that though Rom. 10:9-13 has universal application ("whosoever," v. 11, 13; "Jew and Greek," "all," v 12), confession of the deity of Christ had special significance to the Jews, who were the primary subjects in view. Jesus' deity was particularly offensive to them, not His mastery (John 5:18; 10:33). To admit His deity was to acknowledge His identity as Messiah, Savior, and King of the Jews.[14]

Dr. Charles C. Ryrie asks:

> Do these verses [Romans 10:9-10] mean that one must confess Jesus as Master of his life in order to be saved... is Paul saying in this passage that in order to be saved a person must receive Christ as the Sovereign of the years of his life on earth?[15]

No! Romans 10:9-10 does not demand a personal upfront commitment to Jesus as Master of life for salvation! This passage does not require "unconditional surrender" to the lordship of Christ in order to be saved. Romans 10:9 requires a confession—literally "to speak the same thing"—that Jesus Christ is Lord, that Jesus is deity. In *The Expositor's Bible Commentary*, Everett Harrison writes:

> Paul's statement in vv. 9-10 is misunderstood when it is made to support the claim that one cannot be saved unless he makes Jesus the Lord of his life by a personal commitment. Such a commitment is most important; however, in this passage, Paul is speaking of the *objective lordship* of Christ (His deity), which is the very cornerstone for faith, something without which no one could be saved.[16]

In salvation, a man calls upon the name of the Lord to do for him what he cannot do for himself. It is not by works of righteousness that a man is born again; nor is it by the promise of future righteous works that a man is saved. God has judged our righteous works in the Bible.

> Isaiah 64:6 But we are all as an unclean thing, and all our righteousnesses are as filthy rags.

Harrison continues on the deity of the Lord Jesus:

> Intimately connected as it was with the resurrection, which in turn validated the saving death, it proclaimed something that was true no matter whether or not a single soul believed it and built his life on it.[17]

Christ's title *Lord* clearly denotes His rulership, His mastery and His sovereignty. His rulership, however, is denoted only because *Lord* first and foremost denotes Christ's deity. Dr. Charlie Bing wrote:

> As deity, Kurios also denotes many other functions of Christ. The Lordship argument that insists on rulership as a condition of salvation to the exclusion of the other functions of Christ as God is inconsistent with the biblical data that also call Him Judge, Son of Man, Creator, Savior, Christ, etc.
>
> But the main flaw of the Lordship argument is its insistence that the use of the title "Lord" in salvation passages demands the unbeliever's personal submission of every area of life. The leap from the objective to the subjective is insupportable . . . the passages that speak of Jesus as both Lord and Savior do not justify the subjective demand of a personal submission to Christ's lordship.
>
> When a sinner trusts in Jesus as Savior, it can be affirmed that he implicitly submits to the authority of Jesus Christ to forgive sin. Thus it is not denied that the logical and biblical implications of trusting in the divine Savior for salvation should lead one also to submit to Him as divine Master. However, the issue in salvation is salvation, not mastery.[18]

H. C. G. Moule writes concerning the result, the evidence of having received Christ, "But then this empty hand, holding Him, receives life and power from Him. His Rescuer vivifies the man. He is rescued that he may live, and that he may serve as living."[19] Moule is correct in his teaching that service for the Lord who saved him ought to follow a man's salvation experience. Paul in Ephesians 2:10 says, "For we are his workmanship, created in Christ Jesus unto good works, which God hath before ordained that we should walk in them." That is, Christ accomplished our salvation; as His workmanship, we can then set about to do "good works" for Christ that would be expected from a committed disciple.

What Do Notable Men Say About Romans 10:9?

A number of widely respected expositors have made definitive statements on Romans 10:9. In his *Expository Dictionary,* Vine says,

> KURIOS . . . signifying having power. . . . Christ Himself assumed the title, Matt. 7:21-22; 9:38; 22:41-45; Luke 19:31; John 13:13, apparently intending it in the higher senses of its current use, and at the same time suggesting its O. T. associations. . . . Thomas, when he realized the significance of the presence of a mortal wound in the body of a living man, immediately joined with it the absolute title of Deity saying, "My Lord and my God," John 20:28.[20]

Dr. A. T. Robertson translates Romans 10:9, "Confess Jesus as Lord." He continues,

> The idea is the same, the confession of Jesus as Lord as in I Corinthians 12:3; Philippians 2:11. No Jew would do this who had not really trusted Christ, for *Kurios* in the LXX is

used of God. No Gentile would do it who had not ceased worshipping the Emperor as *Kurios*. The word *Kurios* is the touchstone of faith.[21]

H. A. Ironside wrote,

The gospel has been proclaimed; they have heard it; they are familiar with its terms. The question is: do they believe and confess the Christ it proclaims as their Lord? For in verses 9 and 10 he epitomizes the whole matter in words that have been used of God through the centuries to bring assurance to thousands of precious souls. . . . To *call* upon the name of the Lord is, of course, to invoke His name in faith. His name speaks of what He is. He who calls upon the name of the Lord puts his trust in Him, as it is written, "The name of the Lord is a strong tower, and the righteous runneth into it and is safe."[22]

F. F. Bruce declared,

When Paul gives Christ the title "Lord," he does so because God the Father Himself has given Him that title as the name above every name (Phil. ii. 9) . . . the confession "Jesus Christ is Lord" means "Jesus Christ is Jehovah" . . . the confession "Jesus Christ is Lord" is man's acknowledgment of the supreme honor to which God has exalted Him.[23]

H. C. G. Moule wrote,

Let us mark and cherish its insistence upon "*confession*," "*confession with the mouth that Jesus is Lord*." This he specifically connects with "*salvation*," with the believer's preservation to eternal glory. . . . Is faith after all not enough for our union with the Lord, and for our safety in Him? Must we bring in something else, to be a more or less meritorious makeweight in the scale? If this is what he (Paul) means, he is gainsaying the whole argument of the Epistle on its main theme.

No; it is eternally true that we are justified, that we are accepted, that we are incorporated, that we are kept, through faith only; that is, that Christ is all for all things in our salvation, and our part and work in the matter is to receive and hold Him in an empty hand.[24]

Everett F. Harrison said,

The creedal statement before us pertains to the person of Christ rather than his redeeming work. "Jesus is Lord" was the earliest declaration of faith fashioned by the church (Acts 2:36; 1 Cor. 12:3). This great truth was recognized first by God in raising his Son from the dead—an act then acknowledged by the church and one day to be acknowledged by all (Phil. 2:11).[25]

J. Gresham Machen demonstrates a significant fact,

The ancient Greeks used their word for "lord" (kurios) to describe a master who rules over slaves. But the early Church, the apostles, and the New Testament used "kurios" to refer to absolute deity, or as a synonym for "God." Thus, when the early Church, apostles, or New Testament declared Jesus is Lord, they meant He is God.[26]

Warren W. Wiersbe wrote,

Paul gave us the spiritual understanding of this admonition. . . . He told us that God's way of salvation was not difficult and complicated. . . . The sinner need not perform difficult works in order to be saved. All he has to do is trust in Christ. He made it clear in Romans 10:9-10 that salvation is by faith—we believe in the heart, receive God's righteousness, and then confess Christ openly and without shame.[27]

From the above quotations and the biblical evidence the consensus is confession with the mouth of Christ's position as Lord is required for salvation, not a promise of future obedience to Him as Lord.

Evangelicals on both sides of the lordship issue agree—no one can have Christ as a substitute for sin and become a child of God who does not acknowledge Him as such. Lordship salvation people go a step further and say the sinner must turn his entire future life over to Jesus as Lord before he can receive forgiveness of sin. **Nowhere in Scripture is making Jesus lord of one's life a requirement to receive salvation from the Savior.**[28]

ENDNOTES:

1. Joseph Thayer, *Greek-English Lexicon of the New Testament*, p. 446, (emphasis his).
2. W. E. Vine, *Vine's Expository Dictionary of Biblical Words*, p. 224.
3. John MacArthur, *The Gospel According to Jesus*, p. 33.
4. Spiros Zodhiates, *The Hebrew Greek Key Study Bible*, p. 1,691.
5. John Stott, *Basic Christianity*, 2d ed,. p. 107. Also see p. 121.
6. John MacArthur, *The Gospel According to Jesus*, p. 207.
7. Kenneth L. Gentry, Jr., "The Great Option: A Study of the Lordship Controversy." *Baptist Reformation Review* 5, Spring 1976: 49-79.
8. W. E. Vine, *Vine's Expository Dictionary of Old and New Testament Words*, p. 116.
9. Spiros Zodhiates, *The Hebrew Greek Key Study Bible*, p. 1,749.
10. W. E. Vine, *Vine's Expository Dictionary of Old and New Testament Words*, pp. 16-17.
11. Henry Thiessen, *Lectures in Systematic Theology*, pp. 141-142.

12. Marc Mueller, *Lordship/Salvation Syllabus*, Grace Community Church, 1985, p. 20, (emphasis his).
13. Robert Lightner, *Sin, the Savior, and Salvation*, p. 205.
14. Charles Bing, *Lordship Salvation: A Biblical Evaluation and Response*, p. 111.
15. Charles Ryrie, *So Great Salvation*, pp. 70-71.
16. Everett F. Harrison, "Romans," *The Expositor's Bible Commentary*, Vol. X, p. 112.
17. Ibid., p. 112.
18. Charles Bing, *Lordship Salvation: A Biblical Evaluation and Response*, pp. 6-7, (emphasis mine).
19. H. C. G. Moule, *Romans*, p. 272.
20. W. E. Vine, *Vine's Expository Dictionary of Old and New Testament Words*, pp. 16-17.
21. A. T. Robertson, *Word Pictures in the New Testament*, Vol. IV, p. 389.
22. H. A. Ironside, *Lectures on Romans*, pp. 130-131.
23. F. F. Bruce, *Tyndale New Testament Commentaries, Romans*, pp. 187, 205.
24. H. C. G. Moule, *Romans*, p. 272, (emphasis his).
25. Everett Harrison, *Romans, Expositor's Bible Commentary*, Vol. X, p. 112.
26. J. Gresham Machen, *The Origin of Paul's Religion*, pp. 306, 309.
27. Warren Wiersbe, *The Bible Exposition Commentary*, Vol. I, p. 547.
28. Robert Lightner, *Sin, the Savior, and Salvation*, p. 209, (emphasis mine).

ACTS 16:30-31

And brought them out, and said, Sirs, what must I do to be saved? And they said, Believe on the Lord Jesus Christ, and thou shalt be saved, and thy house.

The Philippian magistrates had beaten Paul and Silas because of the complaints of an angry mob. The jailer was charged with keeping Paul and Silas locked up through the night. At midnight, while Paul and Silas were praying and sang praises to God, an earthquake struck. The bonds fell from all the prisoners and the jail doors flung open. The jailer rushed in to find all the cell doors wide open and supposed all the prisoners had escaped. Based on Roman law the jailer knew his life was forfeit. He drew his sword and was about to take his own life, but Paul cried out, "Do thyself no harm: for we are all here," (Acts 16:28). The jailer rushed in, he was trembling, fell to his knees and asked Paul and Silas, "Sirs, what must I do to be saved?" The response was quick and positive: "Believe on the Lord Jesus Christ, and thou shalt be saved, and thy house."

Does *believe* mean one must surrender every area of his life to the lordship of Christ to be born again? Does

Paul mean the jailer must commit himself to a life of godly behavior to be saved? Or does Paul mean for the jailer to rest in and depend on the finished work of the Lord Jesus Christ? The latter is the gospel; the former are works.

Paul and Silas preached the gospel to the jailer and those in his house; they believed and were saved. What is the gospel that saves when believed? It is, first of all, "that Christ died for our sins;" second, "that He was buried;" and third, "that He rose again the third day" (1 Cor. 15:3-4).

How Does Lordship Confuse "Believe" With Submission?

Lordship teachers insist this condition, *believe*, demands more than faith in Christ as Savior; that it also demands submission to Him as Ruler and Master of one's life in order to be saved. For example, Kenneth Gentry wrote:

> The lordship view expressly states the need to acknowledge Christ as Lord and Master of one's life in the act of truly receiving Him as Savior. These are not two different, sequential acts (or successive steps), but rather one act of pure, trusting faith.[1]

Dr. Bing notes, "The major flaw of the Lordship Salvation argument about Christ's Lordship, however, is its confusion of the objective position of Jesus Christ as Lord with the subjective response of the individual."[2]

Lordship advocates argue that submission is inherent to the concept of *believe*, a conclusion that can be drawn by implication only. We must be careful to avoid drawing doctrinal conclusions through what may be implied. For example, infant baptism is taught and practiced because some believe that it is implied in Acts 16:14-15.

> And a certain woman named Lydia, a seller of purple, of the city of Thyatira, which worshipped God, heard us: whose heart the Lord opened, that she attended unto the things which were spoken of Paul. And when she was baptized, and her household, she besought us, saying, If ye have judged me to be faithful to the Lord, come into my house, and abide there. And she constrained us.

The Roman Catholic Church built an entire dogma on infant baptism because they found the concept inherent in verse 15. Their reasoning is that Lydia must have had infants or little children in her household. Therefore, they say, these young ones must have been baptized with her. Other religions base infant baptism on this passage,

> Matthew 19:14 But Jesus said, Suffer little children, and forbid them not, to come unto me: for of such is the kingdom of heaven.

Baptism is not even implied in the verse, but some conclude it is and therefore create an entire doctrine and practice. Similarly, demands for surrender in exchange for salvation are based on implication, nothing more.

> In Lordship reasoning, the jailer would have to comprehend and concede to the implication of not only Jesus' lordship, but the humanity of Jesus as well as Jewish messianic theology in order to be saved.[3]

The latter part of the preceding quotation raises an issue that Dr. Charles Ryrie explains more fully:

> Incidentally, why is it that those who teach that you cannot receive Jesus without receiving His personal mastery over the years of one's life do not also insist that we must receive Him as Messiah (the meaning of Christ) with all that the concept of Messiah entails? That would mean, for starters, that in order to be saved one must believe that Jesus is Israel's promised deliverer, the One who fulfills many Old Testament prophecies, and the One who is the coming King over the earth. Is the acknowledgment of all that Messiah means part of the necessary content of faith for a genuine salvation experience?[4]

To be genuinely saved, a man would have to acknowledge that Jesus is the Creator, that the creation is held together by Him (John 1:3; Col. 1:16-17), and that it is Jesus who will sit in judgment of the believers (Rom. 14:10; 2 Corinthians 5:10). What Lordship Salvation, through implication and inference, demands does not encompass all that Christ's title "the Lord Jesus Christ" denotes.

> It should also be apparent that to ask a pagan Gentile soldier to comprehend, much less submit to, the implications of Jesus Christ's Lordship could be considered unreasonable and theologically flawed. Submission of one's life is expected of believers on the basis of an understanding of God's grace (Rom. 12:1; Titus 2:11-12). The jailer, as any unbeliever dead in sin, was incapable of making such a mature decision.[5]

Regarding the Philippian jailer, Acts 16:34 states, "And when he had brought them into his house, he set meat before them, and rejoiced, believing in God with all his house." The man had believed and was now rejoicing in his salvation. Everett F. Harrison made a penetrating observation when he wrote, "A faithful reading of the entire book of Acts fails to reveal a single passage where people are pressed to acknowledge Jesus Christ as their personal Lord in order to be saved."[6] Commenting on Acts 16:30-31, Warren Wiersbe writes,

> "What must I do to be saved?" is the cry of lost people worldwide, and we had better be able to give them the right answer. The legalists in the church would have replied, "Unless you are circumcised according to the custom of Moses, you cannot be saved"(Acts 15:1, NKJV). But Paul knew the right answer—faith in Jesus Christ. In the Book of Acts, the emphasis is on faith in Jesus Christ alone (Acts 2:38-39; 4:12; 8:12, 37; 10:10-43; 13:38-39).[7]

According to Dr. Robert Lightner,

> The term Lord in Acts 16:31—or anywhere else it is used of Christ—does not mean Master over one's life. Rather it is a descriptive title of who He is—the sovereign God. It is one of many character-revealing names ascribed to Him, not a condition for salvation. The saving the jailer asked about was conditioned upon his believing (the verb). He had to believe Jesus was who He claimed to be—the sovereign Son of God who died as his substitute.[8]

What is the Biblical Order?

Man comes to Christ for salvation and then follows Christ in discipleship. Submission to Christ's lordship and a commitment to discipleship should follow a genuine conversion experience. The jailer cried out, "Sirs, what must I do to be saved?" Dr. G. Campbell Morgan wrote:

> The answer came quick and sharp, and vibrant with music that the listening man knew not of: "Believe on the one Lord Christ." Then he got this man, with all his house, and he taught

them, he told them the story, and revealed its meaning, and made its application.⁹

Acts 16:32-33 And they spake unto him the word of the Lord, and to all that were in his house. And he took them the same hour of the night, and washed their stripes; and was baptized, he and all his, straightway.

Paul and Silas led the jailer and his household to Christ. It was just afterward that we see the jailer demonstrate a changed character. Just a few hours earlier he had thrown Paul and Silas into the deepest, darkest hole in the prison. What was it that brought about this change?

I see the jailer in Philippi, washing their stripes, who but last night had plunged them into the inner prison, caring nothing for bleeding wounds, and who went to sleep till the earthquake woke him. It was not the earthquake that produced this result. It was that patient teaching, and the consequent belief into Jesus Christ, so that the very life of God possessed his soul, and he began the activities of God, the activities of eternal compassion.¹⁰

Ephesians 2:8-10 For by grace are ye saved through faith; and that not of yourselves: it is the gift of God: Not of works, lest any man should boast. For we are his workmanship, created in Christ Jesus unto good works, which God hath before ordained that we should walk in them.

Acts 16:32-33 provides an excellent illustration of the order of things set out in Ephesians 2:8-10. The jailer was born again by faith alone in the Lord Jesus Christ (2:8-9), and immediately after began the "good works" (2:10) that God had ordained for him as a believer.

ENDNOTES:

1. Kenneth Gentry, Jr., *Lord of the Saved*, p. 10.
2. Charles Bing, *Lordship Salvation: A Biblical Evaluation and Response*, pp. 6-7.
3. Ibid., p. 105.
4. Charles Ryrie, *So Great Salvation*, p. 106.
5. Charles Bing, *Lordship Salvation: A Biblical Evaluation and Response*, p. 106.
6. Everett Harrison, "Must Christ be Lord to Be Savior—No," *Eternity*, 10 September 1959.
7. Warren Wiersbe, *The Bible Exposition Commentary*, Vol. I, Matthew-Galatians, p. 468.
8. Robert Lightner: *Sin, the Savior, and Salvation*, p. 206.
9. G. Campbell Morgan, *The Acts of the Apostles*, p. 394.
10. Ibid., p. 394.

IS IT THE CHRISTIANS DUTY TO FIGHT FOR THE FAITH?

Jude 3 Beloved, when I gave all diligence to write unto you of the common salvation, it was needful for me to write unto you, and exhort you that ye should earnestly contend for the faith which was once delivered unto the saints.

It has been reported that Charles Spurgeon used to say, "I will sit at my gate, and sing my own tune." In other words, Spurgeon was saying that he had too much to do to get involved with every issue. He was speaking of nonessential issues.

On two occasions in South Africa a fellow Baptist missionary asked me to ignore the doctrinal differences on the gospel that I and other preachers had with another missionary, Pastor Doug Van Meter, and his associate pastor, Steve Miller. While they taught in our Bible college Van Meter and Miller introduced Lordship Salvation to the student body. The college president and I were not at first aware of this because while Lordship was being taught the president was away on furlough and I had not yet arrived in the country. Once we discovered what had been done we began to deal with the problem. Even after resigning from the college faculty Van Meter and Miller pursued our students and graduates to convert them to their Lordship position.

The first time the missionary approached me was at a pastor's fellowship in October 1998. He asked me not to look too deeply into the doctrinal differences and to remain quiet about Pastor Van Meter's position on the gospel. He asked me to keep silent for the sake of an appearance of unity among the American missionaries no matter what I believe about Lordship Salvation. He said, "It is not good for South African pastors to see American missionaries fighting over doctrinal issues."

The second time that missionary contacted me (March 1999) was by a telephone call. Again he asked me to look the other way, to ignore Pastor Van Meter's doctrine. My reply was, "what a man preaches in his own church to his own people is none of my concern. However, when a former member of our college faculty taught Lordship Salvation in our college and pursues our graduates that does concern me and requires my involvement." Then he said to me, "For you to question Pastor Van Meter's doctrine is to raise your hand against the Lord's anointed."

That missionary wanted me to ignore the biblical mandate in Jude 3 to "contend for the faith." He was asking me to ignore a major doctrinal difference for the sake of an appearance of unity. Ironically, at the close of that phone call, the missionary acknowledged to me that he also held to the Lordship interpretation of the gospel. That left little wonder as to why he twice vigorously encouraged me to ignore the Lordship teaching that Pastor Van Meter[1] was introducing to South African churches.

Another tactic some Lordship advocates in South Africa employed was to demonize those who disagreed with their Lordship position. What these men failed to disclose to third parties was that the alleged "fight" was over a doctrinal matter of fundamental importance. When the gospel is under siege, then it is not only right to fight; it is our duty to fight!

> Jude 3 Beloved, when I gave all diligence to write unto you of the common salvation, it was needful for me to write unto you, and exhort you that ye should earnestly contend for the faith which was once delivered unto the saints.

W. E. Vine defines "contend" from Jude 3 as follows:

> EPAGONIZOMAI (επαγωνιζομαι) signifies to contend about a thing, as a combatant, to contend earnestly. The word "earnestly" is added to convey the intensive force of the preposition.[2]

In an article in *FrontLine* magazine, Dr. Arno Q. Weniger, Sr., comments on Jude 3 as follows:

> Those verses contain the mandate! Those are the orders of the Captain of our salvation, and to my knowledge, they have never been withdrawn, rescinded, or countermanded. The job is not yet finished. Jude says it was "needful" in his day to "earnestly contend for the faith," but the apostasy has greatly deepened since then. Our days are more treacherous and deceitful than were Jude's.
>
> Take a second look at that phrase, "It was needful for me to write." Jude was not only prompted by a great need to write, but the phrase carried with it "an overpowering constraint." Kenneth Wuest translates it, "I had constraint laid upon me." By whom? The answer is the Holy Spirit. This business of contending is of the Spirit. It is His will that it be done! Don't think as some do, that this sort of a thrust is of the flesh. . . . So

don't downgrade this business of "contending." Don't think there is a higher road for one to take! Steep yourself in the Word, and after much prayer, as verse 20 indicates, go do it.[3]

Dr. Weniger gives an excellent example from the book of Nehemiah of how Christians are to be builders, but also ready for battle at a moments notice:

> Nehemiah 4:17-18 They which builded on the wall, and they that bare burdens, with those that laded, every one with one of his hands wrought in the work, and with the other hand held a weapon. For the builders, every one had his sword girded by his side, and so builded. And he that sounded the trumpet was by me.

Many years earlier the walls of Jerusalem had been leveled and many were lead away as captives by Nebuchadnezzer. The prophet Nehemiah was cup-bearer to the Persian king Artaxerses. When Nehemiah learned of the desperate situation and misery of his people back in Jerusalem he was deeply distressed. Nehemiah wept, mourned, fasted and prayed before the God of Heaven on behalf of the people.

> Nehemiah 1:4 And it came to pass, when I heard these words, that I sat down and wept, and mourned certain days, and fasted, and prayed before the God of heaven,

King Artaxerses allowed Nehemiah to return to Jerusalem to rebuild the wall. At Jerusalem Nehemiah found there were some men, enemies of Israel, who did not want the walls rebuilt. Nehemiah, therefore, divided the workforce in two. One half would continue with the construction, the other half would hold the weapons at the ready in case of attack. They were rebuilding the city, but also prepared to fend off any attack.

> Nehemiah 4:16-18 And it came to pass from that time forth, that the half of my servants wrought in the work, and the other half of them held both the spears, the shields, and the bows, and the habergeons; and the rulers were behind all the house of Judah. They which builded on the wall, and they that bare burdens, with those that laded, every one with one of his hands wrought in the work, and with the other hand held a weapon. For the builders, every one had his sword girded by his side, and so builded. And he that sounded the trumpet was by me.

Drawing a parallel from the passage, Dr. Weniger says:

> In one hand they held a sword, and in the other a trowel.... So on the one hand we are to build ourselves up in the most holy faith, and on the other hand, we are to contend most earnestly for it! Contending without one's own edification would be, in reality, engaging in a quarrel. Self-edification, without contending, would show a blatant indifference or disobedience to the Captain of our salvation. If we contend without building, or if we attempt to build without contending, we are out of balance in our ministry.[4]

Is Contending a Biblical Mandate?

Paul warned Timothy that he would be on battleground when it came to doctrine and he had a responsibility to "fight the good fight of faith." Timothy, a young pastor, was befriended and trained by Paul. Paul referred to Timothy as, "my own son in the faith," (1 Timothy 1:2). Paul refers to Timothy as a spiritual son because one of the results of Paul's ministry at Lystra was Timothy being saved. Paul took Timothy on his missionary journeys. At the time of Paul's writing this epistle Timothy was pastor of the church at Ephesus.

> 1 Timothy 1:18; 6:12 This charge I commit unto thee, son Timothy, according to the prophecies which went before on thee, that thou by them mightest war a good warfare. Fight the good fight of faith, lay hold on eternal life, whereunto thou art also called, and hast professed a good profession before many witnesses.

The Apostle Paul is clear on the duty of pastors, Christians in leadership positions, but his admonition applies to all believers.

> Titus 1:9 Holding fast the faithful word as he hath been taught, that he may be able by sound doctrine both to exhort and to convince the gainsayers.

Every Christian, not just the pastor, who has received the truth are to hold on to the truth, teach that truth and refute the teaching of all those who would undermine the truth. Paul then tells us what we are to do when we encounter a teacher of false doctrine: "Wherefore rebuke them sharply, that they may be sound in the faith" (Titus 1:13). With the church pastor in mind D. Edmond Hiebert wrote:

> The overseer must be known to "hold firmly to the trustworthy message," clinging to it despite the winds of false teaching and open opposition.... Doctrinal fidelity will give him a standing

> ability to perform a twofold task: First, he is to "encourage others by sound doctrine," appealing to them to adhere to and advance in their Christian faith. . . . Secondly, his work also demands that he "refute those who oppose" the true gospel and speak against it as the advocates of error. He must "refute" them by exposing their error and trying to convince them that they are wrong. Christian truth needs not only defense against attacks, but also clear exposition. Effective presentation of the truth is a powerful antidote to error.[5]

In Titus 1:9 the Bible says we must "exhort and convince" those who speak against the truth. In Titus 1:13 the Bible also says we are to "rebuke them sharply." If the advocate of Lordship Salvation cannot be convinced of his error, and he does not respond to a "rebuke," then his error must be exposed and its spread opposed. That is biblically "contending for the faith." Dr. Ernest Pickering wrote: "It is not a mark of graciousness to allow false teaching to be propagated."[6] The Bible teaches that we must refute and resist the doctrine of false teachers. It is a biblical command!

Is Contending Also for Today?

If a man invited to preach at your church brought a message in which he questioned the virgin birth of Christ, would you or your pastor remain silent? If that guest preacher taught any false doctrine, would it matter to you if he were South African, American, Chinese, or French? If that man teaches any false doctrine, would it matter if he were Catholic, Lutheran, Methodist, Baptist, or Charismatic?

Paul was a Jew. He ministered largely among Gentiles. From which ethnic group did he face the most opposition? The Jews, Judaizers, frequently challenged his apostolic authority. On one occasion, Paul (a Jew) corrected Peter (also a Jew):

> Galatians 2:11-14 But when Peter was come to Antioch, I withstood him to the face, because he was to be blamed. For before that certain came from James, he did eat with the Gentiles: but when they were come, he withdrew and separated himself, fearing them which were of the circumcision. And the other Jews dissembled likewise with him; insomuch that Barnabas also was carried away with their dissimulation. But when I saw that they walked not uprightly according to the truth of the gospel, I said unto Peter before them all, If thou, being a Jew, livest after the manner of Gentiles, and not as do the Jews, why compellest thou the Gentiles to live as do the Jews?

False teaching can and does come from within the body of Christ, His church. In the Book of Acts, Paul warns the elders of Ephesus that false teaching will come from both without and within the church:

> Acts 20:28-31 Take heed therefore unto yourselves, and to all the flock, over the which the Holy Ghost hath made you overseers, to feed the church of God, which he hath purchased with his own blood. For I know this, that after my departing shall grievous wolves enter in among you, not sparing the flock. Also of your own selves shall men arise, speaking perverse things, to draw away disciples after them. Therefore watch, and remember, that by the space of three years I ceased not to warn every one night and day with tears.

If a man comes into a Bible college and teaches Lordship Salvation, should the administration ignore this as though nothing eternal is at stake? Lordship Salvation is a very serious matter because it strikes at the heart of the gospel. To remain silent would be a betrayal of the students' trust and would in effect be an endorsement of the false teaching. When men speak at conferences and/or fellowships and teach Lordship Salvation as though it were the true gospel, should discerning pastors ignore that? Absolutely not! The Bible commands Christians and leaders in particular, to expose and reprove false teaching! It is right to sound the alarm and "contend for the faith." One of the greatest betrayals of Bible believing churches, organizations and unsuspecting Christians has been tolerance for and co-operation with:

- Liberals, skeptics and disobedient Christians who reject and/or undermine the fundamentals of our faith such as: the Virgin birth of Jesus Christ, His deity and the gospel.
- New and/or the so-called *"conservative"* evangelicals who compromise the biblical mandates on separation to fellowship with and work alongside unbelievers and/or disobedient brethren.

Is It Right to Judge?

A sermon excerpt by the late Pastor Franklin J. Huling
(Taken from the Sword of the Lord,
Vol. LXIV, No. 10, May 15, 1998)

The question is, "Is it right to judge?" That has puzzled many sincere Christians. A careful, open-minded study of the Bible makes it clear that concerning certain vital matters, it is not only right, but a positive duty to judge. Many do not know that the Bible commands us to judge.

The Lord Jesus commanded, "judge righteous judgment" (John 7:24). He told a man, "Thou hast rightly judged" (Luke 7:43). To others Jesus asked, "Why even of yourselves judge ye not what is right?" (Luke 12:57).

The Apostle Paul wrote, "I speak as to wise men; judge ye what I say" (1 Cor. 10:15). Again, Paul declared, "He that is spiritual judgeth all things" (1 Cor. 2:15). It is our positive duty to judge. Now there are several areas in which the Bible instructs us to judge. These areas include: immoral conduct of professing believers, disputes between Christians, judge ourselves, etc.

"Beware of false prophets" (Matthew 7:15) is the warning and command of our Lord Jesus Christ. But how could we "beware" and could we know they are "false prophets," if we do not judge? And what is the God-given standard by which we are to judge? "To the law and to the testimony: if they speak not according to this word, it is because there is no light in them" (Isa. 8:20). "Ye shall know them by their fruits" (Matt. 7:16), Christ said. "And in judging the fruits, we must judge by God's Word, not what appeals to human reasoning." Many things seem good to human judgment which are false to the Word of God.

The Apostle Paul admonished believers: "Now I beseech you, brethren, mark them which cause divisions and offenses contrary to the doctrine which ye have learned; and avoid them. For they that are such serve not our Lord Jesus Christ, but their own belly; and by good words and fair speeches deceive the hearts of the simple," (Romans 16:17-18).

This apostolic command could not be obeyed if it were not right to judge. God wants us to know His Word and then test all teachers and teaching by it. We are to "mark them" and "avoid them."

The Bible says, "Come out from among them, and be ye separate, saith the Lord" (2 Cor. 6:17). "From such turn away" (2 Tim. 3:5). "Withdraw yourselves" (2 Thess. 3:6). "And have no fellowship with the unfruitful works of darkness, but rather reprove them" (Eph. 5:11). "Abhor that which is evil; cleave to that which is good" (Rom. 12:9). "Prove all things; hold fast that which good" (1 Thess. 5:21).

It would be impossible to obey the above Bible injunctions unless it were right to judge!!!

Remember, nothing is "good" in God's sight that is not true to His Word.

The Apostle John wrote, "Beloved, believe not every spirit, but try [test, judge] the spirits whether they are of God: because many false prophets are gone out into the world" (1 John 4:1). Again John writes, "For many deceivers are entered into the world, who confess not that Jesus Christ is come in the flesh. This is a deceiver and an antichrist. . . . If there come any unto you, and bring not this doctrine, receive him not into [your] house, neither bid him God speed: For he that biddeth him God speed is partaker of his evil deeds." (2 John 7, 10-11). This Scripture commands us to judge between those who do and those who do not bring the true doctrine of Christ.

The New Testament Greek word that is most often translated "judge" or "judgment" is 'krino'. . . . On the one hand it means to distinguish, to decide, to determine, to conclude, to try, to think and call into question. That is what God wants His children to do as to whether preachers, teachers, priests, and their teachings are true or false to His Word.

Contending: What if I Do; What if I Don't?

Even on the foreign mission field when doctrine is wrong, nationality must not be an issue. On the mission field, it does not matter if the false teaching comes from an American missionary or a person native to that country. Christians of all nationalities are obligated to resist and "earnestly contend" against false doctrine no matter the source.

Fighting against false doctrine is good for nationals on the mission field to see. If one American missionary uncovered serious false teaching in another American missionary, should the situation be ignored and dismissed? Would it be better to play the ostrich and allow false doctrine to sweep away believers and churches? Resisting and fighting false doctrine will be unpopular, but clear distinctions on doctrinal lines will be drawn as a result. Contending should also cause believers to study out the issues to discern for themselves truth from error.

Judaizers infiltrated the first century churches, and Paul fought his own countrymen's false doctrine. Earlier from Galatians 2:11-14 we saw Paul had to publicly confront Peter at Antioch over an error. Paul withstood Peter when he was to be blamed. Both were apostles, both men of authority and co-laborers for Christ. Paul did not allow for personality, station or nationality to hinder him from contending when contending was the warranted course of action. Paul was not about to play politics when a doctrinal matter needed to be addressed.

There are always grave consequences from exposure to any false interpretation of the gospel, whether it is the sacramental system of the Roman Catholic Church (RCC) or Lordship Salvation. Most evangelicals agree that the Roman Catholic Church teaches a false gospel, a gospel based on human works through the sacramental system. I would not fellowship around or cooperate in any secular or religious effort with the priest of a Roman Catholic Church. Because the Bible says so I know that that kind of fellowship is unscriptural and dangerous. The Bible is very clear on separation from unbelievers.

> 2 Corinthians 6:14 Be ye not unequally yoked together with unbelievers: for what fellowship hath righteousness with unrighteousness? and what communion hath light with darkness?
>
> Ephesians 5:11 And have no fellowship with the unfruitful works of darkness, but rather reprove them.

The difference between a Christian and an unbeliever is the difference between night and day. Christians are not to be working in spiritual cooperation with unbelievers.

This doctrine of separation is not necessarily applied to Christians who may disagree with one another over a minor doctrine or practice. If one believes, however, that Lordship Salvation is a gospel of faith plus works, why then would he want to fellowship with or work in cooperation with another Christian who holds to that position? Could it be that it is easier to "contend" with the doctrine of the Roman Catholic priest than with that of the pastor from within your own sphere of influence? Since both systems are works-based interpretations of the gospel, why would one "contend" with and separate from the former, but not apply the biblical mandates to the latter? Could it be because there is no cost in lost friendships or misjudged motives to preach against the RCC's sacramental system and "mark" the priest as a teacher of a false gospel?

The Bible is clear on the matter of separating from a fellow Christian. Sometimes separating from a Christian brother is necessary. There may come a time when you must follow this difficult course of action. If you are compelled to break fellowship with another Christian because of his/her holding to the Lordship gospel let us hope it is with a heavy heart. Your motive ought to be fidelity to the Scriptures, and a desire for the brother to see his error and repent of it.

There will be a cost to "contend" with another otherwise Bible believing preacher in your own circles who holds to Lordship Salvation and biblically "mark" him because of his errant position. However, the Scriptural commands in Jude 3 to "earnestly contend for the faith," the commands from 2 Cor. 6:14-ff; 2 Jn. 6-11 to separate from unbelievers and 2 Thess. 3:6, 14-15 on disobedient brethren are not open to selective application. They are mandated courses of action found in the Word of God.

Many matters are not worth the energy to fight over. In matters of a non-major nature we must recognize the distinctives of individual soul liberty and the autonomy of the local church. Christian brothers can discuss and disagree on minor issues without condemning one another. Leave it to believers and local churches to arrive at their own positions on the non-essential issues.

Many Christian leaders would like for the Lordship matter to go away. You may have people dear to you on both sides of the issue, a predicament that creates an even more agonizing ordeal. The Lordship Salvation debate is a serious doctrinal matter. With God's help you must "earnestly contend for the faith" (Jude 3). You must stand guard for yourself, your family and your church against Lordship Salvation, and its advocates, just as aggressively as you would resist an attack on the inspiration of Scripture or the virgin birth of Christ. The duty of every Christian is to fight against any adversary of biblical truth. We must stand *in defense the gospel*; we must unashamedly proclaim the gospel and resist any assault upon it.

Christian leaders are generally willing to expose doctrinal error in denominational or fellowship circles outside their own, but there is a tendency to recoil when error is pointed out within one's own sphere of fellowship. As shown earlier the Apostle Paul warned the Ephesian elders that, "…of your own selves shall men arise, speaking perverse things" (Acts 20:30). It is not in keeping with the plain warning of the Apostle Paul to think that doctrinal deviation will not arise from within one's own camp. We must not think that doctrinal deviation will not rear its head close to home.

The doctrine of Lordship Salvation has caused divisions among members of the body of Christ. I am not insensitive to the situation of any one of you with a dear friend who you have come to find has adopted the Lordship interpretation of the gospel. But just where does your first loyalty lie? Don't you have a scriptural responsibility to consider serious allegations of doctrinal deviation, especially when bells of alarm are being rung from such a broad spectrum of evangelical Christianity?

Lordship Salvation is an assault on the gospel. Believers can be grateful for many pastors and Christians who, regardless of the personal cost, have held the high ground and put up a biblical and militant defense to retain the purity of the gospel, which was "once delivered unto the saints." Do not surrender the high ground of fidelity to the Scriptures. It is the Christian's duty to "contend for the faith." Preachers, you may not win a popularity contest by contending, but you will have been faithful to God and His call upon your life to feed and defend His sheep.

Recommended Reading

Moritz, Fred J. *Contending For The Faith.* Greenville, SC.: Bob Jones University Press, 2000.

Pickering, Ernest D. *Biblical Separation: The Struggle for a Pure Church.* Schaumburg, Ill.: Regular Baptist Press, 1979.

Pickering, Ernest D. *The Tragedy of Compromise: The Origin and Impact of the New Evangelicalism.* Greenville, SC.: Bob Jones University Press, 1994.

ENDNOTES:

1. Pastor Doug Van Meter has since adopted and is preaching Preterism, which is the belief that most or all end time Bible prophecy refer to events that have already happened in the first century church.
2. W. E. Vine, *Vine's Expository Dictionary of Old and New Testament Words,* p. 233.
3. Arno Q. Weniger, Sr., "The History and Future of the FBF," *FrontLine*: May-June 1998, pp. 11-12.
4. Ibid., p. 12, (emphasis mine).
5. D. Edmond Hiebert, "Titus," *The Expositor's Bible Commentary,* Vol. II, p. 431.
6. Ernest Pickering, *The Tragedy of Compromise,* p. 45.

A HEART TO HEART WITH PASTORS AND CHRISTIAN LEADERS

Why Learn About Lordship?

In 1997, while serving as a missionary in South Africa, I was speaking to a fellow American missionary. This missionary did not know what the contention between area missionaries over Lordship Salvation was all about. He was not happy that men were divided over the issue and said that he did not even know what the Lordship gospel was. I explained to him that Lordship Salvation is a serious deviation from the gospel, a serious doctrinal issue, other American missionaries were introducing it to South African national pastors, and I encouraged him to study the matter out for himself.

His closest ministerial friend in South Africa had been identified as the leading advocate of Lordship Salvation among American born Baptist preachers in the Johannesburg area. Therefore, he decided to begin reading on the subject. This missionary began by reading John MacArthur's book *The Gospel According to Jesus*. After reading a very little of that book, he sent me an e-mail. He said that what he was reading was, in his opinion, a contradiction of earlier works written by John MacArthur, which he had read. He expressed concern about what he was reading in *The Gospel According to Jesus.* We met at a pastor's fellowship a short time later, and there he told me that he stopped reading MacArthur's book, and he was not interested in reading anything more on Lordship Salvation, pro or con.

What happened in this case was that this man had just begun to identify problems with Lordship Salvation, which, in his case, meant that he might have to confront the fact that his friend in the ministry had adopted, and was propagating a works based interpretation of the gospel. Rather than coming to a conclusion and personal conviction through personal study, he opted to steer clear of the Lordship issue altogether. John MacArthur wrote about an experience similar to mine, "One very well known Christian leader told me that he had purposely avoided reading any books on the matter; he didn't want to be forced to take sides."[1]

It is a sad day when a well-meaning pastor or Christian leader, for the sake of maintaining a friendship or a fellowship, will avoid studying an issue because it may lead him to question a friend's doctrine. Preachers and Christian leaders, you are not doing your duty before God if your desire is to avoid a potential controversy. You have a scriptural responsibility to know what the Bible teaches! You need to study the Lordship issue to the point where you can state with conviction that either: 1) Lordship Salvation is simply a different way of saying the same thing, 2) Lordship Salvation is an acceptable difference of opinion on the gospel, or 3) Lordship Salvation is a faith plus works message, which should be exposed and its advocates admonished.

What account will you give before God if you have been avoiding a doctrinal controversy because of a personal friendship? What are the consequences if you allow a man into your pulpit who then introduces false teaching to your church membership? Where does your first loyalty lie—to the Word of God and your flock or to a personal friend?

Believers in our churches need to be informed of and warned about false doctrine. Through the electronic media and the Internet in particular they are increasingly being exposed to any number of egregious doctrinal errors. If you are a pastor you realize you can't be there to point out every error to people from your church when they are confronted with them. A pastor must teach in such a way that he edifies believers, but also exposes false doctrine and warns his people of the danger lest they succumb to error and are lead astray. If the ministry of warning is not in practice the church is at risk. The God ordained duty of every pastor is to both feed and defend the flock of God. The personal example and final charge of Paul to the Ephesian elders rings as loud and clear today as it did to the first century church.

> Acts 20:27-28 For I have not shunned to declare unto you all the counsel of God. Take heed therefore unto yourselves, and to all the flock, over the which the Holy Ghost hath made you overseers, to feed the church of God, which he hath purchased with his own blood.

How can the minister protect his people if he cannot recognize false doctrine himself? Granted, preachers cannot set out to learn and understand every false doctrine and cultic teaching in today's confused world. However, men who are part of the evangelical community have promoted Lordship Salvation for decades, and it has made inroads into churches, fellowships and Bible colleges. How can you protect those whom God has given you the oversight of if you cannot recognize the danger at your doorstep? Heaven help the church whose pastor allows a man into his pulpit who preaches a Lordship message, and the host pastor does not even recognize it. The damage is done, but if the pastor does not recognize what has been done, how can he set out to repair the damage, protect and recover his people from error?

I know a pastor who spent over three years picking up the pieces left by a former pastor and Lordship advocate. This new pastor labored to restore to his congregation the assurance of their salvation. These people, under the ministry of the previous pastor, were fed a steady diet of Lordship Salvation. Thankfully, the new pastor understood the Lordship issue and he began rectifying the situation through sound preaching and personal counseling.

The word *doctrine* appears forty-four times in the New Testament, sixteen times in the Pastoral Epistles (First & Second Timothy and Titus) alone. In the original text of the Pastoral Epistles, there are thirty-two references to "doctrine," "teach," "teacher," "teaches," and "teaching." First and Second Timothy and Titus are called Pastoral Epistles because they were written to pastors and outlined for them their pastoral duties. Since the Pastoral Epistles are primarily directed to ministers of the Word of God, ministers had better take heed to doctrine and teaching. Large portions of these epistles are dedicated to instructing Timothy and Titus to defend sound doctrine and resist false teaching. In First Timothy, Paul tells Timothy to stay at Ephesus and command certain men not to teach false doctrine.

> 1 Timothy 1:3 As I besought thee to abide still at Ephesus, when I went into Macedonia, that thou mightest charge some that they teach no other doctrine.

The Word of God warns that false teaching can come into the church through unbelievers or believers. Paul warned the Ephesian elders to "watch" (γρηγορεω, *gregoreo*) and be vigilant. The metaphor is to give strict attention, to be cautious, to be on guard. For the sake of their flocks, the pastors must be ever watchful! The Apostle Paul warned the men in his day; the written Word of God warns preachers today.

> Acts 20:29-31 For I know this, that after my departing shall grievous wolves enter in among you, not sparing the flock. Also of your own selves shall men arise, speaking perverse things, to draw away disciples after them. Therefore watch, and remember, that by the space of three years I ceased not to warn every one night and day with tears.

We must take the threat of false teaching seriously. You have a responsibility to determine for yourself whether Lordship Salvation is the gospel or if it is a false, non-saving message that frustrates grace (Gal. 2:21). If you believe Lordship is the gospel, then come out openly for it. If it is a departure from the biblical plan of salvation, then do not hesitate to come out openly against it. You, however, cannot make that determination unless you study the issue for yourself. Do not allow personal friendships to guide or alter your pursuit and study of the Word of God. The gospel is too important to this lost and dying world for you to stand idly by while men undermine and corrupt the "simplicity that is in Christ" (2 Corinthians 11:3).

How Do I Respond to Lordship?

In Romans 16:17-20, Paul delineates the Christian's responsibility toward the teachers of doctrinal error. Beginning in verse 17 and continuing through verse 20, Paul admonishes believers about their duty to God and the church as well as their response toward those who teach false doctrine and thereby cause divisions:

> Now I beseech you, brethren, mark them which cause divisions and offences contrary to the doctrine which ye have learned; and avoid them. For they that are such serve not our Lord Jesus Christ, but their own belly; and by good words and fair speeches deceive the hearts of the simple. For your obedience is come abroad unto all men. I am glad therefore on your behalf: but yet I would have you wise unto that which is good, and simple concerning evil. And the God of peace shall bruise Satan under your feet shortly. The grace of our Lord Jesus Christ be with you. Amen.

In Romans 16:17, the Bible instructs believers to "mark" false teachers; that is, to keep their eyes open, to scrutinize, to look at, to observe, and to stay fixed so that they can guard against the introduction of false doctrine. Pastors must keep a sharp eye out for false teaching. They stand as sentries protecting their flocks. In Paul's day, the Judaizers and Gnostics were making their influence felt in the new church, both in doctrine and practice. In our day, many more are working to infiltrate the church of God with false teaching.

Because of the danger from false teaching, Paul uses the word "beseech" (παρακαλεω, *parakaleo*). *Parakaleo* means "to admonish, exhort, to beg." Consequently, the instruction to mark false teachers is an urgent matter.

To *mark* means to identify. It is the translation of σκοπεω (*skopeo*). Thayer defines the term as follows:

> ... *to look at, observe, contemplate. To mark* ... to fix one's eyes upon, direct one's attention to, any one: Ro. xvi.17 ... σκοπειν is more pointed than βλεπειν; often i.q. *to scrutinize, observe.* When the physical sense recedes, i.e. *to fix one's (mind's) eye on, direct one's attention to,* a thing in order to get it, or owing to interest in it, or a duty towards it.[2]

Skopeo in this verse is a present infinitive functioning as the object of the present tense admonition *to beseech*. (Technically, *you* and *mark* are both objects of *beseech*. In Greek syntax, this construction is known as the double accusative of the person and thing.) An expanded literal translation could read, "Now brethren, I am admonishing and begging you to continually scrutinize the ones causing divisions and offences." That is, we are to take note of, and point out for others, those referred to in Romans 16:17-20 as the ones who "cause divisions and offences contrary to the doctrine which ye have learned."

Those who teach contrary doctrine cause divisions and they are to be marked. It is biblical to personally identify the teachers of a false gospel and point them out so that others may avoid them. I refer especially to those who are the prime instigators of positions that are a contradiction of and antithetical to the Scriptures. "We are to 'avoid' those who teach and practice things contrary to apostolic doctrine (Rom. 16:17)."[3] Paul uses the word *cause* (ποιεω, *poieo*), meaning produce, construct, form, or fashion in reference to those who are the authors of division through their false teaching. Ironically if you identify a brother who is promoting an aberrant interpretation of the gospel and biblically mark him, he will likely accuse you of being divisive. You must remember, however, that it is that man's contrary teaching, which is the actual cause of division among believers.

> It is often said that the divided condition of Christendom is an evil, and so it is. But the evil consists in the existence of the errors which cause divisions and not at all in the recognition of those errors when once they exist.[4]

Those who teach the Lordship gospel cause "offences" (σκανδαλον, *skandalon*). We get our English word *scandal* from this Greek word. "Offences" means a trap, snare, or any impediment placed in the way and causing one to stumble or fall. Lordship Salvation is a stumbling block for the lost and a potential impediment to spiritual growth for those who are saved. Lordship Salvation frustrates grace (Gal. 2:21) and can cause genuine believers to struggle with the assurance of their salvation. To be in fidelity with God's Word, to protect the saints, you must "mark" the men whose doctrine causes "offences."

Paul admonishes believers to "avoid" εκκλινω, (*ekklino*) those whom we have marked. The form of this verb would indicate that it is a present imperative, which simply indicates that this avoidance is neither a suggestion nor advice, but, in fact, a command. We are commanded by God to continually avoid the person who has been marked! Avoiding a man is synonymous with separating from him. This is a mandate from the Lord and we are obligated to obey Him. Thayer's lexicon lists several possible translations for the word, but indicates that in this text, it is best translated "to shun." We are to shun those who create scandal through their false teaching.

In Philippians 3:17 the word "mark" appears, but in an entirely different context.

> Philippians 3:17 Brethren, be followers together of me, and mark them which walk so as ye have us for an example.

In the Philippians passage Paul instructs believers to be "followers" of those who set the proper example. Paul instructs the believers to "mark" those who by their life demonstrate what biblical Christianity is and then to imitate those persons. In this usage of the word "mark," believers are to scrutinize spiritual men and women and imitate them. This is the positive side of marking for the purpose of identifying and imitating the pattern of godly men and women. Paul could set the kind of example to imitate, not many can today. In Philippians 3:17 Paul refers to more than just himself. From other passages we might conclude that Paul had in mind Timothy and Epaphroditus who also set that pattern to be imitated.

In Romans 16:17, however, the usage of "mark" indicates that believers are to scrutinize doctrine and "avoid" those who are found to be teaching contrary doctrine. Therefore, there is a positive and negative side when we are commanded to "mark." The positive side is for identifying and imitating the pattern of godly Christians. The negative side is for avoiding those who cause divisions and offences through the teaching of contrary doctrine.

As we have seen in earlier chapters Lordship advocates use orthodox terms to teach as truth that which is antithetical to Scripture. Although in other areas of doctrine those who hold to the Lordship gospel may be balanced and orthodox, but error is error, and Lordship Salvation is "contrary to the doctrine" of the gospel. The primary question becomes: What is our biblical obligation, in fidelity to God's Word, toward any teacher of false doctrine? The Scriptures instruct and mandate how we are to respond to those who teach contrary doctrine: "admonish him as a brother" (2 Thess. 3:15) and if he rejects our admonition, refuses to repent of his error, then we must "reject" (Titus 3:10) *mark* and *avoid* him.

Many pastors are teetering on the brink of the "agree to disagree" philosophy when it comes to the tough choices regarding those who teach Lordship Salvation. Difficult as it may be to "mark" and "avoid" because of a personal friendship or because of the personal cost involved failure to do so when it is clearly called for will result in grave consequences. In other words, ignoring those who teach false doctrine opens the door for divisions to be created in the church, maybe even in your church. Such divisions damage the natural unity of the church.

> Doctrinal differences necessitate division. However, it is not those who separate who cause the division, but those whose doctrine or behavior necessitates the separation (2/00 FrontLine). The Fundamentalist (who, by definition, practices Biblical separation) does not cause division between believers. Divisions are caused by the brother who does not hold to sound doctrine (e.g., separation), and the Lord requires separation from that errant brother (2/00 Foundation). The Fundamentalist thus is forced to choose between the fellowship of light (obey God, I John 1:7) and the fellowship of darkness (disobey God, Eph. 5:11). It is not unloving for the Fundamentalist to choose light over darkness, God over a disobedient brother. The disobedient brother by not practicing separation (abiding in light) is the one who is unloving (I John 2:10) and the one who causes division. If he loved his Fundamentalist brother he would abide in the light.[5]

Many a Christian has made a shipwreck of his walk with God for not having turned aside from false teachers. Once you make friendship and personality the test of orthodoxy and fellowship, you have set foot on the slippery slope of ecumenical compromise. Growing numbers of Christians are willing to minimize the importance of and fidelity to doctrine for the sake of unity. When a man betrays the Scriptures for the sake of friendship and unity, he is no friend of the Bible or believers. Separating from and marking false teachers sets a proper example of true Bible Christianity for believers who have been raised in an atmosphere that is not easily discriminated from the type of compromise found in political circles.

I would like to offer this expanded translation of Romans 16:17: "Now brethren, I strongly urge you to look at, to fix your eyes upon those who produce and author divisions and stumbling blocks contrary to the doctrine which you have learned; and I command you to continually shun, avoid, turn aside, and deviate from them."

In Romans 16:17 we are commanded to "mark" and "avoid" those who have adopted a theology and/or taken on practices that are "contrary to the doctrine which ye have learned." To separate from another Christian brother is probably the most unpleasant thing a pastor or any Christian ever has to do. Separation will cost you friends; you may be misjudged and possibly labeled as being divisive. But if you are going to be loyal first to Jesus Christ and the Word of God, you must practice biblical separation from men who take a position that is a deviation from a major doctrine of the Bible. Lordship Salvation is one of those deviations. If we are going to live for and please God, we must obey Him.

> 2 Corinthians 6:17 Wherefore come out from among them, and be ye separate, saith the Lord, and touch not the unclean thing; and I will receive you.

The word *separate* in 2 Corinthians 6:17 is αφοριζω (*aphorizo*). It means "to mark off from others by boundaries, to limit, to separate." In the negative sense, to separate is to depart from and exclude. In the positive sense, it is to appoint or set apart for some purpose. In the negative, a man is avoided and separated from to set him apart so that others will also avoid him. In the positive sense it is an act of dedication to God. We set ourselves apart from the man so that we will not be turned aside or stumble over the false teaching.

As we noted above, false teachers come from within the church as well as from without. Does the Bible ever call for separation from professing believers?

> 2 Thess. 3:6, 14-15 Now we command you, brethren, in the name of our Lord Jesus Christ, that ye withdraw yourselves from every brother that walketh disorderly, and not after the tradition which he received of us. . . . And if any man obey not our word by this epistle, note that man, and have no company with him, that he may be ashamed. Yet count him not as an enemy, but admonish him as a brother.

You will see in verse 14 that Paul says to "note that man." To "note" σημειοω, *semeioo*) that man is to mark, to distinguish by marking, to mark or note for one's self. The verse goes on to say, "have no company with him." Dr. Fred Moritz writes,

> An objective study of the New Testament leads first to the conclusion that the New Testament teaches that there are times when local churches and believers must reluctantly take the action of separating themselves from other believers. The purpose of such separation is purity. The local church is to take the extreme action of separation from a disobedient brother when necessary in order to preserve its purity of life and testimony. The second conclusion is that the New Testament also sets clear standards for that separation when it must be made. Those standards include the following . . . *The heretical brother*—Heresy, or deviant doctrine, that is promoted out of self-willed divisiveness (Titus 3:10).[6]

> 2 Thessalonians 3:4-6 And we have confidence in the Lord touching you, that ye both do and will do the things which we command you. And the Lord direct your hearts into the love of God, and into the patient waiting for Christ. Now we command you, brethren, in the name of

our Lord Jesus Christ, that ye withdraw yourselves from every brother that walketh disorderly, and not after the tradition which he received of us.

Looking at 2 Thessalonians 3:4 we see that Paul was confident that the believers of the Thessalonian church would do that which they were commanded of him. In verse six Paul makes plain that it is the command of the Lord Jesus Christ to "withdraw yourselves from every brother that walketh disorderly," and Paul fully expected them to obey this command. Commenting on 2 Thessalonians 3:6, Dr. Leon Morris writes,

> He commands, he does not simply advise. Moreover, he speaks "in the name of our Lord Jesus Christ." This is at once a reminder of the very real authority that Paul exercised, and of the seriousness of any refusal to obey. Paul was not giving some private ideas of his own when he spoke "in the name." The substance of his command is that they "withdraw" from the erring. In view of verse 15. . . it stands for the withholding of intimate fellowship. The verb has the idea of retreating within oneself (cf. its use of furling sails). Such a line of conduct is meant as would impress on the offenders that they had opened up a gap between themselves and the rest.[7]

2 Thessalonians 3:14-15 And if any man obey not our word by this epistle, note that man, and have no company with him, that he may be ashamed. Yet count him not as an enemy, but admonish him as a brother.

In 2 Thessalonians 3:14-15 Paul not only reiterates the command found in verse six, but he also gives practical instruction on how the command is to be obeyed.

Do not have fellowship with those who will not listen to the Word of God. Paul is claiming for his epistle that it is the Word of God and to be heeded as a command of God. Have your fellowship with those who are in obedience to the Word of God and who are living according to its standards.[8]

Paul is telling the church members what action they should take, not asking for an opportunity of taking action himself. "Note that man" means more than simply "notice" him. It means "mark him out,". . . . The treatment of such a person is withdrawal of fellowship. The treatment is primarily intended to bring him back to his rightful position. At the same time it is punishment.

It is noteworthy that Paul puts the injunction not to treat him as an enemy before that to admonish him. He is eager to protect the brother's standing, and to see to it that what is done to him is from the best of motives, and that it secures the desired result.[9]

In 2 Thess. 3:6-15 God tells us to avoid those who do not walk in an orderly way by "working not at all." If we are to avoid people who simply do not work we certainly ought to "withdraw" from those who are far more dangerous to the cause of Christ through corruption of His gospel.

If you know a brother whom you suspect holds to Lordship Salvation, give him the benefit of the doubt, but do make every effort to get a clarification from him personally. If you ultimately learn that he holds to Lordship Salvation, that he will not receive your instruction, rejects your admonitions and will not repent of his error, determined to propagate his errors then do what is right.

> 2 Timothy 2:25 In meekness instructing those that oppose themselves; if God peradventure will give them repentance to the acknowledging of the truth.
>
> Titus 1:9 Holding fast the faithful word as he hath been taught, that he may be able by sound doctrine both to exhort and to convince the gainsayers.

Men are becoming increasingly reluctant to address the issue of whether the Bible mandates separation from "every brother that walketh disorderly" (2 Thess. 3:6). All too often the guiding factor seems to be "what are the ramifications of dealing with the issue," rather than "what is the Scriptural thing to do?" You ought to make a sincere and genuine effort to recover a brother from doctrinal error. If your effort fails, your only recourse is to withdraw from him.

One of the recurring themes of the Bible is that God blesses obedience to Him and His Word, but He judges disobedience.

> Deuteronomy 11:26-28 Behold, I set before you this day a blessing and a curse; A blessing, if ye obey the commandments of the LORD your God, which I command you this day: And a curse, if ye will not obey the commandments of the LORD your God.
>
> 1 Samuel 12:14-15 If ye will fear the LORD, and serve him, and obey his voice, and not rebel against the commandment of the LORD, then shall both ye and also the king that reigneth over you continue following the LORD your God: But if ye will not obey the voice of the LORD, but rebel against the commandment of the

LORD, then shall the hand of the LORD be against you, as it was against your fathers.

Isaiah 1:19-20 If ye be willing and obedient, ye shall eat the good of the land: But if ye refuse and rebel, ye shall be devoured with the sword: for the mouth of the LORD hath spoken it.

Following Christ in this regard is central to the concept of being a good disciple. As already discussed, Christ taught that there is sometimes a high human cost to discipleship. Dr. Ernest Pickering in his classic *Biblical Separation* wrote:

> When our brethren do things that are wrong—caused by an incomplete knowledge of or deliberate disobedience to some teaching of Scripture—we should not merely continue fellowship with them as those who have done nothing wrong, but we should warn them, remonstrate with them and seek to recover them to a Biblical position. . . . If one should ask, Does 2 Thessalonians 3 teach secondary separation?—then the response would have to be given, It depends on what you mean by secondary separation. . . . It is the principle of refusing to condone, honor or utilize persons who continually and knowingly are following a course of action which is harmful to other believers and to the welfare of the churches.[10]

What About Spurgeon's Stand for Doctrinal Purity?

In his day, Charles H. Spurgeon valiantly fought against false teaching and the mood for compromise in order to maintain unity. Many believe that this struggle contributed to his death at a relatively young age. Although the majority of Spurgeon's Baptist contemporaries agreed with his doctrinal stand,

> They preferred unity above the maintenance of doctrinal purity. He attacked the position by saying, "first pure, then peaceable; if only one is attainable, choose the former. Fellowship with known and vital error is participation in sin. . . . To pursue union at the price of truth is treason to the Lord Jesus."[11]

Following are selected excerpts from an article written by Charles Haddon Spurgeon in 1888. Spurgeon wrote this article to explain why he had separated from the London Baptist Association. From his article, we learn that we must be willing to separate from those institutions and persons who have strayed from the major tenets of our faith, especially the gospel.

The Drift of the Times

Sound the Alarm!
Separation Not Alone Our Privilege But Our Duty

As soon as I saw, or thought I saw, that error had become firmly established, I did not deliberate but quitted the body at once. Since then my counsel has been, "Come ye out from among them." If I have rejoiced in the loyalty to Christ's truth which has been shown in other courses of action, yet I have felt that no protest could be equal to that of distinct separation from known evil.

The Brethren in the Middle

The brethren in the middle are the source of this clinging together of discordant elements. These who are for peace at any price, who persuade themselves that there is very little wrong, who care chiefly to maintain existing institutions, these are the good people who induce the weary combatants to repeat the futile attempt at a coalition which, in the nature of things, must break down. If both sides could be unfaithful to conscience, or if the glorious gospel could be thrust altogether out of the question, there might be a league of amity established; but as neither of these things can be, there would seem to be no reason for persevering in the attempt to maintain a confederacy for which there is no justification in fact and from which there can be no worthy result, seeing it does not embody a living truth. A desire for unity is commendable. Blessed are they who can promote it and preserve it! But there are other matters to be considered as well as unity, and sometimes these may even demand the first place.

Separation A Duty

Numbers of good brethren in different ways remain in fellowship with those who are undermining the Gospel; and they talk of their conduct as though it were a loving course of action which the Lord will approve of in the day of His appearing. We cannot understand them. The bounden duty of a true believer towards men who profess to be Christians and yet . . . reject the fundamentals of the Gospel is to come out from among them. . . . Complicity with error will take from the best of men the power to enter any successful protest against it. If any body of believers had errorists among them but were resolute to deal with them in the name of the Lord, all might come right; but confederacies founded upon the principle that all may enter, whatever views they hold, are based upon disloyalty to the truth of God. If truth is optional, error is justifiable.

The Army of Intermediates Should Cease Being Politic

There are now two parties in the religious world, and a great mixed multitude who from various causes decline to be ranked with either of them. In this army of intermediates are many who have no right to be there; but we spare them. The day will come, however, when they will have to reckon with their consciences. When the light is taken out of its place, they may too mourn that they were not willing to trim the lamp nor even to notice that the flame grew dim.

Our present sorrowful protest is not a matter of this man or that, this error or that, but of principle. There is either something essential to a true faith—some truth which is to be believed—or else everything is left to each man's taste. We believe in the first of these opinions, and hence cannot dream of religious associations with those who might on the second theory be acceptable. Those who are of our mind should, at all costs, act upon it.

Separation, The Only Complete Protest

At any rate, cost what it may, to separate ourselves from those who separate themselves from the truth of God is not alone our liberty but our duty. I have raised my protest in the only complete way by coming forth, and I shall be content to abide alone until the day when the Lord shall judge the secrets of all hearts; but it will not seem to me a strange thing if others are found faithful and if others judge that for them also there is no path but that which is painfully apart from the beaten track.[12]

Spurgeon's sermon above is a penetrating reminder that there are doctrinal truths worth contending (Jude 3) over, and if need be making the difficult decision to "mark," "avoid" and "withdraw" from brethren (Romans 16:17; 2 Thess. 3:4-6; 14-15). The Lordship Salvation interpretation of the gospel is a departure from truth that meets the criteria for the biblical mandates to "contend" and/or "withdraw." To reiterate from Spurgeon, "Fellowship with known and vital error is **participation in sin** . . . . To pursue union at the price of truth **is treason to the Lord Jesus.**"

Should Doctrinal Deviations be Dismissed?

When a man's doctrine is brought into question based on public statements he has made, is it unreasonable to ask that man to clarify his doctrine in clear, unvarnished terms? Is it unreasonable to search the Scriptures to determine the soundness of a man's theological position? We live in a day of confusion and deception over several vital doctrines. The gospel is under assault today just as it has been in every generation since the first century. It is, therefore, crucial that men of God, called by God to the ministry, declare God's Word and resist assaults on the truth of God's Word. Lordship Salvation cannot be ignored. Even for those who have personal friendships at stake, fidelity to the Word of God must take precedence.

It is unwise and dangerous to dismiss doctrinal deviation simply because its source is a previously trusted friend, fellowship, or institution. Fidelity to biblical truth is the greatest expression of love. The Psalmist wrote,

> Psalm 119:63 I am a companion of all them that fear thee, and of them that keep thy precepts.

ENDNOTES:

1. John MacArthur, *Faith Works:The Gospel According to the Apostles*, p. 22.
2. Joseph Thayer, *Greek-English Lexicon of the New Testament*, p. 579.
3. Ernest Pickering, *Biblical Separation: The Struggle for a Pure Church*, p. 146.
4. J. Gresham Machen, *Christianity and Liberalism*, p. 50.
5. Calvary Contender, March 1, 2000.
6. Fred Moritz, *Be Ye Holy: The Call to Christian Separation*, pp. 82-83.
7. Leon Morris, *The New International Commentary on the New Testament: The First and Second Epistles to the Thessalonians*, p. 251.
8. John F. Walvoord, *The Thessalonian Epistles*, p. 156.
9. *The New International Commentary on the New Testament: The First and Second Epistles to the Thessalonians*, p. 258-259.
10. Ernest Pickering, *Biblical Separation: The Struggle for a Pure Church*, pp. 221-222.
11. E. Wayne Thompson, *This Day in Baptist History*, p. 529.
12. *Sword of the Lord*, September 9, 1994.

A FINAL WORD

It was disconcerting to me and my missionary co-worker that the Lordship advocates working as missionaries from the States whom we had to biblically "contend" with in South Africa steadfastly refused to discuss the Lordship gospel on a doctrinal level. Instead they tried to turn the doctrinal difference into a personality clash. For instance they would say, "Only a few angry Fundamentalists are attacking Lordship Salvation because they are jealous of John MacArthur's popularity and his ministry's success." These men were attempting to divert attention away from their Lordship position, and a frank discussion of the doctrine, by creating a personality conflict where there was none.

It would seem reasonable to me that men who claim the Bible as their sole authority should meet together and discuss their doctrinal positions, which we had pressed for all along. This at least allows for a better mutual understanding, if not reconciliation. The Bible teaches that doctrine is the basis for all unity and practice. How then can men call for unity while simultaneously being unwilling to openly discuss their doctrinal positions?

Well before John MacArthur's book *The Gospel According to Jesus* was released, and since then as well, many Bible believing preachers, colleges, seminaries, and associations have come out against Lordship Salvation.

Lordship Salvation had already been rejected long before John MacArthur was associated with it. Men such as John Stott, J. I. Packer, Walter J. Chantry, and Martyn Lloyd Jones are among the most noteworthy advocates of the Lordship gospel prior to MacArthur's book being published. Lordship Salvation has not been rejected because of any one personality associated with the position. The rejection of Lordship Salvation is due to it being a deviation from the historic gospel found in the Scriptures.

The Lordship position has, since 1988, been widely associated with John MacArthur because he has embraced it as a distinctive teaching of his ministry and in several of his books, which I have cited above. While the Lordship Salvation position was not new in 1988, its promotion by such a prominent evangelical as John MacArthur provided for the position a new credibility and unprecedented influence across a broad spectrum of evangelical Christianity. It must be stressed again, however, that those who reject Lordship Salvation, reject it solely because of its doctrinal deviation from God's Word, not because of any personal animosity toward or professional jealousy over any teacher of Lordship Salvation.

The Disconnect

In the preceding pages I have shown that many respected pastors and commentators reject Lordship Salvation as a works based gospel. I have demonstrated from the Bible that Lordship Salvation is not an accurate representation of the gospel of Jesus Christ. Those who hold to and expound Lordship Salvation steadfastly deny there is any meritorious work in submission. Remember, John MacArthur accurately represents what the Lordship gospel is. He has written more on the position than any other Lordship advocate. His position is that of the Lordship advocates in general, whether or not they want to be identified with his ministry or other doctrinal positions. John MacArthur stated:

> Surrender to Jesus as Lord is no more a meritorious human work than believing he is Savior. Neither act is a good deed done to earn favor with God. Both are the sovereign work of God in the heart of everyone who believes.[1]

How does the Lordship advocate disconnect works from the call for lost men to make an upfront commitment to cross bearing and following in discipleship to become a Christian? Dr. MacArthur's Calvinistic presuppositions are evident in the quote above. He says believing and surrender are works God must perform in the heart of man. MacArthur's statement above is flawed at the outset. Earlier we noted that faith is the issue for salvation, not surrender. It is antithetical to the Scriptures to define the condition for salvation in terms of "surrender." Furthermore, we have already discussed Calvinism's regeneration before faith view in the order of salvation. (See Appendix 'B' for an extended discussion of Calvinism's regeneration before faith teaching.)

For most Lordship advocates faith, repentance, believing and surrender are all God's work and therefore cannot be ascribed to man performing a personal work to "earn favor with God." Since God did the work, man could not have made any contribution. Lordship advocates believe lost men cannot in any way participate in the salvation experience, therefore, whatever the experience is, real or promised, it cannot be "a meritorious human work." This is how Lordship advocates disconnect works from their position.

If someone were to believe making a pledge to a charitable organization or performing good deeds to meet the needs of the homeless would earn them favor with God, Dr.

MacArthur and Lordship advocates would rightly say these acts would not lead to salvation.

> That is the kind of response the Lord Jesus called for: wholehearted commitment. A desire for him at any cost. Unconditional surrender. A full exchange of self for the Savior. It is the only response that will open the gates of the kingdom. Seen through the eyes of this world, it is as high a price as anyone can pay. But from a kingdom perspective, it is really no cost at all.[2]

When we come to this quote, however, we again have the dilemma. Dr. MacArthur has already stated that believing and surrender are the work of God, but here he is demanding a high price from the sinner for entry into the kingdom of God. One is left to ponder: Is it man that must pay the high price of "unconditional surrender" for salvation, or is it the "sovereign work of God" performed on man's behalf? How can unsaved man be expected to pay the high price, or even know what that price is, if as many Lordship advocates believe lost men cannot respond to the gospel in the first place?

For salvation, John MacArthur's Lordship system requires an upfront commitment to "unconditional surrender," or as is often stated, "submission to the Lordship of Christ." Earlier we learned that this is "Bilateral Contract Salvation...*a promise for a promise.* The lost sinner '***promises***' future obedience in exchange for God's '***promise***' of eternal life." Demanding the high price of discipleship in "exchange" for salvation creates a precondition to merit the free gift of God. Lordship's call on the lost for a promise to perform any "meritorious human work" to become a Christian is not the gospel according to Jesus!

Dr. MacArthur has referred to salvation not only as having a "cost," but also as an "exchange." Once you enter the word "exchange" into the discussion you have two parties entering into an agreement, and each brings something to the table. On one hand the Lordship advocate says lost men cannot participate in the salvation process. Yet he requires from the sinner a commitment to self denial, cross bearing and following for the reception of eternal life. Only through a misunderstanding of Scripture based on human reasoning can these polar opposites be reconciled.

Disconnect from your mind that any offer of surrender, even the desire to pay the high price of discipleship, will open the gates of Heaven. If man comes to the Savior seeking salvation and forgiveness of sin, he better come to Him with empty hands and an open heart, because that is all he has. The lost man has nothing to offer in word, deed or action (past, present or future) that will satisfy and appease a holy God. He has nothing to offer in "exchange" for salvation. If there was a price to pay for salvation it would be infinite and man cannot afford it. The lost man is hopeless, helpless, and Hell-bound! When through the ministry of the Holy Spirit and God's Word he sees himself in that condition and recognizes Jesus Christ as his only hope for salvation he is ready to be born again. Once that man repents and places his faith in the Person and finished work of the Lord Jesus Christ he is regenerated, converted, justified, and born into the family of God.

Powerful & Penetrating Summary

Numerous on-line reviews and/or discussion threads opened immediately following publication of the original edition of this book. At one particular *pseudo*-fundamentalist blog a full review was published. A lengthy discussion thread ensued. One man submitted a number of helpful comments in that thread. Elements of his commentary were among the most penetrating observations of Lordship theology I have read in recent years. With his permission I have cited below a brief compilation of his various comments.

> When one gets faith wrong and makes it a work or quality of the soul, they then must have faith as a gift of God. In order for that to happen they then need regeneration to precede faith. **With that then they load all sorts of expectations upon the soul desiring to come to Christ.** This is probably why MacArthur indicates one cannot be saved without "unconditional surrender…full exchange of self for the Saviour." **His subsequent books do not clarify or moderate these kinds of statements, but only reinforce them.**
>
> This is wrong and an unbiblical definition of faith and what one must do to be saved. It demands certain qualities be present in the soul. That is clearly works! It is very disheartening to see people that would endorse MacArthur's position. They should point out its errors. **These are not merely over statements as in question and answer sessions.** MacArthur has made his position very clear. It is not classic Calvinism, but Puritan. He has been accused by others of bordering on a Roman Catholicism works salvation… . Of course, from MacArthur's viewpoint, all these qualities are part of faith so he repeatedly states that "salvation is by faith alone."
>
> The biblical gospel is not a Lordship gospel or a non-lordship gospel. It is a simple gospel of faith in Christ and it has a simple definition of faith. Faith involves the intellect, sensibilities, and the will, but is a simple receiving of truth by reliance upon it. **No full surrender, no leaving all, no turning from sin.** All that follows is the very first aspects of sanctification. It is not part of the Gospel. We show our faith by our works but we have our faith when simply trusting in Christ.

I believe I am representing Lordship Salvation correctly in stating that no one can properly "desire" to give up sin prior to being saved. **Desiring to give it up should not be an issue included in the gospel message.** A desire to do good is a quality of the soul. A "desire" to do good is works. Faith, rather than being a quality of the soul, is simply receiving something. It is relying on another. It expresses no desires for the soul. It seeks to receive the qualities and work of another as sufficient to save the soul. Also, the "unconditional surrender" and "full submission" quotes from MacArthur indicate more than just desire, but full awareness and full submission to Christ. If some Lordship Salvation advocates wish to distance themselves from MacArthur and revise the issues they are free to do so.

The concept of "Lordship Salvation" should not even be in the Christian vocabulary. There is simply salvation in Christ alone by faith alone. That salvation brings "union with Christ" and that results in justification (by identity with His death, burial, and resurrection), regeneration with the indwelling Spirit and new nature formed, and all the other blessings of salvation such as continuing regeneration work in sanctification and adoption. But in order to have union with Christ we must respond to the convicting work of the Spirit (which is not regeneration) and by God's enabling grace have faith in Christ. That faith emanates from us to God. It is our faith and not God's.

There is no justification and regeneration without union with Christ. Jesus Christ is Lord of all and Lord of all believers. **He becomes our Lord or Master at the time of union with Him.** It is not a requirement to understand this or acknowledge it at the time of faith anymore than it is a requirement that we know anything about justification and regeneration. It would be good for the soul to explain as much as possible to the hearer, but many are saved knowing very little. And even with explanation a lost man cannot comprehend it.

Errors in Offsetting Pairs

The Grace Evangelical Society's *Crossless* gospel and Lordship Salvation are two sides of the same counterfeit coin. From their respective ends of the soteriology pendulum swing, both deny the complete perfection and sufficiency of Christ's work on the cross, demonstrated by His resurrection. The *Crossless* gospel excludes the Person of Christ, His finished work on the cross and bodily resurrection from the necessary content of saving faith. Lordship Salvation undermines the sufficiency of His cross and resurrection by front-loading faith in Christ's atoning work with a commitment to what is expected of a disciple.

These doctrinal errors seem to always come in offsetting pairs. It is one of the Devil's devices, which has the effect of throwing God's children off balance in their understanding of the one true gospel of Jesus Christ. Of the two, however, Lordship Salvation is the more dangerous, as it is more subtle, not as easily recognized and more widespread.

Blogging in Defense of the Gospel

Shortly after the 2006 release of the original edition of *In Defense of the Gospel* I opened a blog site. I opened my blog because my book generated a great deal of debate and discussion. I felt a blog was needed for me to be able to deal in a timely manner with certain aspects of the debate. Furthermore, I wanted to provide an Internet home for those who reject Lordship Salvation and would appreciate ready access to articles, answers and discussion of the Lordship controversy. There are dozens of articles, many with discussion threads, at my blog on the doctrine of Lordship Salvation, the Grace Evangelical Society's *Crossless* gospel and various related subjects. You may visit and interact directly with me at- www.indefenseofthegospel.blogspot.com

What If You Have Been Wrong?

You may be an individual who has already adopted the Lordship position. You may be on the fence about the Lordship position. It is possible that after having read this book you may feel that you made a mistake, or are about to make a mistake in regard to the Lordship Salvation interpretation of the gospel.

It is my hope and prayer that if you are having reservations about Lordship Salvation, if you are having doubts about what you have been exposed to, you will take it before the Lord and search the Scriptures once again. Can an evangelistic appeal that requires submission and a commitment to perform the "good works" (Eph. 2:10) expected of a mature born again believer be the gospel of salvation by grace through faith? Is the saving grace of God contingent upon, as John MacArthur suggests, an "exchange of self for the Savior?" Does the Lord call on the lost for a "wholehearted commitment" to obedient Christian living before He grants the gift of eternal life?

Admitting you were wrong on a particular doctrine is one of the hardest things for a believer to do. It takes a high measure of belt-tightening and swallowing of pride to make an admission like that, but it is a sign of great character. It shows a teachable, humble spirit, and demonstrates your loyalty to Scripture. Christians who genuinely love and care for you will rally to your side and appreciate your candor and humility.

What is My Hope for You?

My hope for any reader, regardless of fellowship or affiliation, is multi-fold:

- That you clearly understand and are equipped to recognize Lordship Salvation.
- That you see the Lordship debate as a fundamental doctrinal issue of vital importance.
- That you see there is a substantive difference between Lordship Salvation and the historic gospel handed down throughout church history.
- That you consider Lordship's faulty building blocks, such as presenting passages meant for discipleship as though they are evangelistic appeals to the lost.
- That you understand the harmful ramifications that Lordship teaching and preaching brings to a ministry, to evangelism, and to individual Christians.
- That you prayerfully consider what response God requires from you on this issue.

I am hopeful this book will serve to alert and awaken Christians:

- To recognize Lordship Salvation as a false, non-saving works based interpretation of the gospel that frustrates grace (Gal. 2:21).
- To avoid being influenced by those who propagate it.
- To instruct fellow believers in their spheres of influence so they will forewarned against being lead toward embracing Lordship theology.
- To biblically respond to this works-oriented teaching by marking and avoiding those who hold to Lordship Salvation, especially the prime instigators of it.

At the start of this book I noted that the Lordship debate revolves around the **requirements for**, not what should be the **results of** salvation. Lordship Salvation places demands on the sinner for salvation that the Bible does not. A new life through submission to the lordship of Christ should come as a natural result of salvation, but the Scriptures never identify submission as a requirement for salvation, justification.

Is God satisfied with the finished work of Jesus Christ? Is God satisfied with His Son's propitiation for the sins of the whole world? Is God satisfied with Christ's atoning work? Since we are assured from the Scriptures that God is fully satisfied, why is John MacArthur's Lordship "salvation [only] for those who are willing to forsake everything?" Why must the lost come to Christ for salvation with a "wholehearted commitment" to bear the cross, "full-scale self-denial," and "even [the] willingness to die for His sake if necessary?"[3] Since Jesus paid it all why does Lordship Salvation condition eternal life on faith plus commitment of life and the lifelong performance of that commitment?

What I have written is *In Defense of the Gospel*! I am unashamedly against the interpretation of the gospel commonly known as "Lordship Salvation." There are many areas where one must balance soul liberty and Christian charity and agree to respect different views. The gospel, however, is not an area in which we can agree to disagree. The doctrine of Lordship Salvation and the efforts of Lordship advocates must be vigorously debated, and biblically resisted. May God protect unsuspecting believers and the lost from the egregious errors of Lordship Salvation.

ENDNOTES:

1. John MacArthur, *The Gospel According to Jesus: What is Authentic Faith*, p. 232.
2. Ibid., p. 150.
3. John MacArthur, *The Gospel According to Jesus: What is Authentic Faith*, p. 224.

APPENDIX A
WHAT ABOUT CALVINISM?

by
Lou Martuneac

It is beyond the scope and purpose of this appendix to fully explore the history and theology of John Calvin (1509-1564) and the development of Calvinistic theology. Scholars and theologians both for and against Calvinism have for centuries articulated and debated this issue. My notes do not add anything new to the debate over Calvinism, and they will not end the debate. This debate has been going on for centuries and in my opinion will never be settled among men this side of Heaven. I reject the erroneous suggestion coming from some Calvinists that one must be purely Arminian or Calvinist. Stated plainly: I do not identify with the theology of John Calvin or Jacobus Arminius (1560-1609). My desire is to simply stand where the Bible stands, whether or not that identifies me with a particular system of theology.

Divine Sovereignty and Human Freedom

Several times in this book I speak of keeping a balance in your theology, or keeping a balance between two points of doctrine. In the matter of God's sovereignty and man's free will and/or his responsibility to say that there is a balance at the center would not be appropriate. Both divine sovereignty and human responsibility are truths found in the Word of God. They are not competing truths, they are truths! They are truths that cannot be reconciled. The free will of man does no violence to God's sovereignty! In short, freedom of will is no threat to, nor is it a denial of the sovereignty of God. In my opinion God's sovereignty is actually magnified when we allow for the free will of man and His sovereignty to co-exist. His sovereignty is not diminished and is done no damage by or through the will of man.

Our finite minds cannot comprehend every truth found in the Word of God. Once you try to reconcile these doctrines you are going to veer toward a theological ditch and quite possibly fall into a trap of doctrinal error. Only in the mind of our infinite God can the twin truths of Divine Sovereignty and Human Freedom be reconciled.

Charles Spurgeon spoke on the matter of trying to reconcile difficult doctrines:

> Brethren, be willing to see both sides of the shield of truth. Rise above the babyhood which cannot believe two doctrines until it sees the connecting link. Have you not two eyes, man? Must you needs put one of them out in order to see clearly?
> Faith & Regeneration

The Five Points of Calvinism

Calvinism is a system of theology founded by John Calvin. Some commentators contend that in some points of doctrine the Calvinism held to by many today is somewhat of a shift from Calvin's own position. In any event Calvinism is best known for its emphasis on five distinct doctrines. These are technically known as the "Five Points of Calvinism." The whole of Calvinism rests on these five points and they are inseparably linked. The five points are commonly recognized and defined from the acronym **T-U-L-I-P**. Taking each in turn the letters of the acronym stand for: Total Inability, Unconditional Election, Limited Atonement, Irresistible Grace and Perseverance of the Saints. There is no way to adequately define these five points in just a few pages. So that you have a basic understanding of the five points I am providing the following definitions and a biblical answer for each.

Total Inability

Man is altogether depraved, he does not seek God, and he has no natural ability to respond to a holy God. All of mankind is dead in his sins. Without the supernatural help of Almighty God, mankind is doomed and totally without hope of redemption. The Bible does teach the total depravity of man.

> Jeremiah 17:9 The heart is deceitful above all things, and desperately wicked: who can know it?
>
> Romans 3:10-12 As it is written, There is none righteous, no, not one: There is none that understandeth, there is none that seeketh after God. They are all gone out of the way, they are together become unprofitable; there is none that doeth good, no, not one.

In Ephesians 2:1-4, the Bible clearly teaches that the lost man is dead in his sins.

> Ephesians 2:1 And you hath he quickened, who were dead in trespasses and sins.

Calvinism takes the depravity of man and shifts to a position of total inability. Total inability teaches that man is unable to participate, respond to or cooperate with God in the salvation process. Total inability sees lost man as absolutely unable to hear or respond to spiritual things, including the gospel. Calvinism entirely rules out the free will of man to respond to the gospel and choose to believe on the Lord Jesus Christ.

The Calvinist believes man is so "dead in trespasses and sins" that he must first be regenerated: That is to say, born again, made alive by the Spirit of God, and given the new nature prior to and apart from personal repentance toward God and faith in Jesus Christ (Acts 20:21). Even faith, according to Calvinism, is a gift that was given to him after regeneration.

Calvinism views the convincing and convicting work of the Spirit (John 16:7-11) as part of the inward call of the Spirit through the Word preached. Calvinism's total inability, however, negates the universal convicting and convincing work of the Holy Spirit. In the Bible God invites (Isaiah 1:18), and Christ draws all men (John 12:32), but no man has the innate ability to respond without the working of the Holy Spirit (John 16:7-11) to convince him of "sin, righteousness, and judgment."

> Isaiah 1:18 Come now, let us reason together, says the LORD: though your sins are like scarlet, they shall be as white as snow; though they are red like crimson, they shall become like wool.

> John 12:32 And I, if I be lifted up from the earth, will draw all men unto me.
>
> John 16:7-11 Nevertheless I tell you the truth; It is expedient for you that I go away: for if I go not away, the Comforter will not come unto you; but if I depart, I will send him unto you. And when he is come, he will reprove the world of sin, and of righteousness, and of judgment: Of sin, because they believe not on me; Of righteousness, because I go to my Father, and ye see me no more; Of judgment, because the prince of this world is judged.

Ephesians 2:1 is very clear, but in John 16:7-11 Jesus identifies the Holy Spirit as the One Who works in the hearts of all men. The Holy Spirit of God uses the Living Word of God to do His convicting work, pointing lost men to the Son of God. Man is born again from above as a result of the gospel being made real to his heart by the Spirit of God. If man chooses to respond in repentance toward God and faith in Christ through that work of God's Spirit, he is regenerated and born again.

Unconditional Election

In eternity past God chose certain individuals from all of mankind for salvation. His election of these was not determined by or conditioned upon any virtuous quality in man that God in His omniscience and foreknowledge saw from eternity past. Calvinism believes God's election was not based on whom He saw would respond to the gospel in faith and repentance. God's choice of certain individuals unto salvation rested solely in His own sovereign will.

For the Calvinist God has elected only a select group of the world's population for Heaven, while all the rest enter this world headed to an eternal existence in Hell. Some Calvinists have told me they believe God takes an "active" role in bringing the elect to salvation, but as for the rest, He is completely "passive" toward, and essentially abandons them on the road to Hell. Another man told me he believes God graciously, and according to His own good pleasure, chose some men for salvation while; passing over the rest. We, therefore, have two groups: one chosen by God for Heaven, the other group, in spite of a universal and sincere offer of the gospel, is headed for Hell.

> 2 Corinthians 5:18-19 And all things are of God, who hath reconciled us to himself by Jesus Christ, and hath given to us the ministry of reconciliation; To wit, that God was in Christ, reconciling the world unto himself, not imputing their trespasses unto them; and hath committed unto us the word of reconciliation.

The ministry of reconciliation is for every soul in the entire world. No unsaved person is outside the scope and reach of reconciliation. All may come (Matt. 11:28), all may drink the living water freely (John 4:10-14) and no man need perish (2 Peter 3:9). Reconciliation is freely offered, effectual, effective, and available to all of the world's population without exception.

In my opinion unconditional election is arrived at partially through an out of balance view of predestination. Most Calvinists will insist that God predestined the elect for salvation. Some go further holding to a double-predestination. That is God predestined the elect for Heaven and all the rest He predestined to Hell. Nowhere in the Bible does predestination mean God has predestined a select group to Heaven, and all the rest are consigned to live out their lives headed for Hell. The word "predestination" appears only four times in the Bible: Romans 8:28-29 and Ephesians 1:5, 11. When it does appear it always has to do with the future of born again believers.

> Romans 8:28-29 For whom he did foreknow, he also did predestinate to be conformed to the image of his Son, that he might be the firstborn among many brethren. Moreover whom he did predestinate, them he also called: and whom he called, them he also justified: and whom he justified, them he also glorified.
>
> Ephesians 1:5 Having predestinated us unto the adoption of children by Jesus Christ to himself, according to the good pleasure of his will.
>
> Ephesians 1:11 In whom also we have obtained an inheritance, being predestinated according to the purpose of him who worketh all things after the counsel of his own will.

When the term "predestinate" or "predestinated" appears in Scripture it never refers to that moment in time when a lost man receives Jesus Christ as Savior and is born into the family of God. Predestination is for those whom God did foreknow would be saved. Growing into Christ likeness and final glorification ultimately is the object of predestination.

The Bible repeatedly invites sinners to come to Christ. Unconditional election is inconsistent with numerous open invitations in the Bible for all sinners to come to Christ and be saved.

> Matthew 11:28 Come unto Me, all ye that labor and are heavy laden, and I will give you rest.
>
> Romans 10:13 For whosoever shall call upon the name of the Lord shall be saved.

All are welcome! "Whosoever," means whosoever! God does not unconditionally choose some for salvation and forsake the rest of mankind to an eternal existence in the Lake of Fire. The lost man who hears the saving message of the gospel, comes to realize his lost condition and need of salvation, but will not come to Christ, refuses to respond because he does not want to come to Christ. Men go to Hell because when they have the opportunity to respond to the gospel they choose to reject the gift of eternal life.

The convicting and convincing work of the Holy Spirit (John 16:7-11) comes upon a lost man and he may refuse to repent and by faith trust Christ for salvation. That man has chosen Hell for himself rather than the free gift of God, which is eternal life through Jesus Christ. This fault is his own because he could have come, but chose to reject the open invitation.

> John 3:36 He that believeth on the Son hath everlasting life: and he that believeth not the Son shall not see life; but the wrath of God abideth on him.
>
> John 5:40 Ye will not come to Me that ye might have life.

Limited Atonement

A Limited Atonement or Particular Redemption is the most controversial of the five points. Many in the Reformed camp back away from this point of Calvinism. Many five-point Calvinists consider those who do not fully embrace a limited atonement as falling short of being a true Calvinist.

The five point Calvinist believes Christ died only for the elect; the shed blood of Christ and His atoning work on the cross was intended only for the select group chosen for salvation. This means Christ's substitutionary death paid the penalty of sin only for certain sinners, and not for the sins of all mankind past, present and future.

You may hear expressions such as, "Christ's atonement was sufficient for all, but efficient only for genuine believers." More than any of the other five points this one is inconsistent with Scriptures that plainly contradict a limited atonement. The power and reach of the sacrificial death of Jesus Christ simply knows no limits.

> John 3:16 For God so loved the world, that He gave His only begotten Son, that whosoever believeth in Him should not perish, but have everlasting life.
>
> 1 John 2:2 And He is the propitiation for our sins: and not for ours only, but also for the sins of the whole world.

In the following verse (Isaiah 53:6) you read the word. "all." It appears twice: once at the beginning and once at the end of the verse. The first appearance speaks to the fact of universal sin. All mankind is lost and in sin. The second appearance speaks to the fact of the sins of the whole world were laid on Christ. Jesus Christ bore and died for the sins of the whole world. His atoning death was not a limited act. His salvation is available to all, but only imparted to those who receive Him by faith.

> Isaiah 53:6 All we like sheep have gone astray; we have turned every one to his own way; and the LORD hath laid on him the iniquity of us all.

Irresistible Grace

Calvinism teaches that the Holy Spirit extends a special inward calling, but only to those elected to salvation. Through this calling the sinner is irresistibly drawn to Christ and the Spirit causes the sinner to cooperate. The lost man may have no desire for Christ, no interest in the claims of the gospel, but he has no choice in the matter. Because he has been unconditionally elected for salvation the Spirit puts the choice in his mind, removes any barrier or hindrance and compels him to respond to the gospel invitation. This irresistible grace cannot be rejected and does not depend on man's cooperation.

The ability of individuals to reject Christ's offer of salvation answers Calvinism's irresistible grace. The Bible teaches that man can be reproved over and over, and resist the working of the Holy Spirit in his heart. What was your experience? Did you accept Jesus Christ the first time you heard the gospel? Or was it like so many others: several exposures to the gospel over a period of years until you finally realized you were lost, without hope, and that you needed and desired to be saved. Many believers would tell you they were not converted the first time they heard the gospel or read a gospel tract. In fact, very few people are saved at the time they are first exposed to the gospel. There are undoubtedly cases such as that, but those cases are very few. Normally a man will hear the gospel several times, initially reject the free "gift" before finally accepting Christ.

The Holy Spirit does strive, but a time comes when He may strive no more.

Genesis 6:3 My Spirit shall not always strive with man.

Proverbs 1:24-26 Because I have called, and ye refused; I have stretched out my hand, and no man regarded; But ye have set at nought all my counsel, and would none of my reproof: I also will laugh at your calamity; I will mock when your fear cometh.

This certainly does not sound like irresistible grace. It is plain: God calls and men refuse. People do resist the call of God and thereby resist and reject His grace.

Proverbs 29:1 He, that being often reproved hardeneth his neck, shall suddenly be destroyed, and that without remedy.

Notice the word *often* in Proverbs 29:1. God is not in the business of making one invitation, giving only one opportunity to be saved. A man can "harden his neck" even after many reproofs by God.

John 5:40 Ye *will not* come to Me, that ye might have life.

The verse teaches that men can and do reject Christ.

> Acts 7:51-52 Ye stiffnecked and uncircumcised in heart and ears, **ye do always resist the Holy Ghost**: as your fathers [did], so [do] ye. Which of the prophets have not your fathers persecuted? and they have slain them which shewed before of the coming of the Just One; of whom ye have been now the betrayers and murderers.

The above passage is from the preaching of Stephen to the Jewish religious leaders just before they had him stoned. Note that verse fifty-one plainly says that these men "resisted" the Holy Ghost. They had surely seen and heard Jesus Christ Himself preaching, and came away resisting the Holy Spirit. Verse fifty-two shows that even their fathers, the Jews, had resisted the Holy Ghost from Abraham down to the time of Christ.

> Matthew 23:37 O Jerusalem, Jerusalem, [thou] that killest the prophets, and stonest them which are sent unto thee, how often would I have gathered thy children together, even as a hen gathereth her chickens under [her] wings, and ye would not!

God's grace was rejected. It was not irresistible. One preacher said, "If grace is irresistible it is not grace at all."

Perseverance of the Saints

This final point of Calvinism presents somewhat of a problem in providing a clear definition. There are two views on Perseverance of the Saints. The traditional position is found in Reformed confessions of faith. The non-traditional view is typically found in some Baptist and Evangelical circles. The common denominator is that the elect are eternally secure and will persevere in the faith. The way Perseverance commonly addresses those who fall away is to conclude they were never saved in the first place or will return eventually. In its most extreme form Perseverance is articulated as the only way to ensure "final salvation," i.e., glorification.

> There is no doubt that Jesus saw a measure of real, lived-out obedience to the will of God as necessary for final salvation.[1]

> Endurance in faith is a condition for future salvation. Only those who endure in faith will be saved for eternity.[2]

> The kingdom is not for people who want Jesus without any change in their living. It is only for those who seek it with all their hearts; those who agonize to enter. Many who approach the gate turn away upon finding out the cost. Lest someone object that this is a salvation of human effort, remember it is only the enablement of divine grace that empowers a person to pass through the gate....While justification and sanctification are distinct theological concepts, both are essential elements of salvation. God will not declare a person righteous without also making him righteous.[3]

In regard to eternal security the Bible is clear. Security has nothing to do with persevering; it is about the preserving power of God. In regard to those who have been genuinely born again the Bible says,

> John 10:28-29 And I give unto them eternal life; and they shall never perish, neither shall any man pluck them out of my hand. My Father, which gave them me, is greater than all; and no man is able to pluck them out of my Father's hand.

Ephesians 1:13 In whom ye also trusted, after that ye heard the word of truth, the gospel of your salvation: in whom also after that ye believed, ye were sealed with that Holy Spirit of promise.

2 Timothy 1:12 For the which cause I also suffer these things: nevertheless I am not ashamed: for I know whom I have believed, and am persuaded that he is able to keep that which I have committed unto him against that day.

1 Peter 1:3-9 Blessed be the God and Father of our Lord Jesus Christ, which according to his abundant mercy hath begotten us again unto a lively hope by the resurrection of Jesus Christ from the dead, To an inheritance incorruptible, and undefiled, and that fadeth not away, reserved in heaven for you, Who are kept by the power of God through faith unto salvation ready to be revealed in the last time. Wherein ye greatly rejoice, though now for a season, if need be, ye are in heaviness through manifold temptations: That the trial of your faith, being much more precious than of gold that perisheth, though it be tried with fire, might be found unto praise and honour and glory at the appearing of Jesus Christ: Whom having not seen, ye love; in whom, though now ye see him not, yet believing, ye rejoice with joy unspeakable and full of glory: Receiving the end of your faith, even the salvation of your souls.

A saved man's eternal security, his assurance and position in Christ are not dependent on how he performs as a Christian. He is saved and secure because of what Jesus Christ has done for him. Calvinists I interact with do not believe one may lose his salvation. Calvinists do, however, believe if the convert does not evidence a consistent pattern of demonstrable submission to the lordship of Christ, he may have never been saved in the first place.

<u>What Is Hyper-Calvinism?</u>

I am uncomfortable with, and reject all five points of Calvinism. There are Calvinists who are uncomfortable with the extremes of the so-called hyper-Calvinism, but what is hyper-Calvinism? I have found that people vary in their definition of what constitutes a hyper-Calvinist. Some believe, for example, that if a man holds to the Limited Atonement position (Christ's blood was shed only for the elect) he is a hyper-Calvinist. Although I believe that Calvinism's limited atonement is out of balance with and contradicts the Scriptures, I do not agree that holding to that position necessarily makes one a hyper-Calvinist.

So how do I specifically define hyper-Calvinism? For me there is one historically definitive mark of hyper-Calvinism. This identifying mark of a hyper-Calvinist is when he refuses to preach the gospel to every sinner, when he has little concern for missions and evangelism, when he refuses to offer an open and universal invitation to every sinner. In his book *Spurgeon v. Hyper-Calvinism: The Battle for Gospel Preaching* Iain H. Murray accurately defines this form of hyper-Calvinism,

> Hyper-Calvinism views gospel preaching solely as a means for the ingathering of God's elect. It argues that such words as, "Trust in Christ and you will be saved," should only be addressed to elect sinners for it is their salvation alone which the preacher should have in view. . . . Gospel preaching for Hyper-Calvinists means a declaration of the facts of the gospel but nothing should be said by way of encouraging individuals to believe that the promises of Christ are made to them particu-

larly until there is evidence that the Spirit of God has begun a saving work in their hearts, convicting them and making them 'sensible' of their need. . . . A universal proclamation of good news, with a warrant for every creature, lay at the heart of his (Spurgeon's) understanding of Scripture.

Another area of concern that flows from Calvinistic theology, which I mentioned above, is: regeneration must precede faith. Earlier I mentioned Calvinism takes the total depravity of man (Jeremiah 17:9), but push it to the position of total inability. The Bible says that man is dead in his sins (Eph. 2:1). The problem begins where the Calvinist believes lost men cannot understand or respond to the gospel unless he has first been regenerated, that is: born again by the regenerating power of the Holy Spirit. The Calvinist maintains that only after a lost man has been regenerated can he express faith in Jesus Christ and call upon the name of the Lord. I address this issue here and elsewhere because it appears to be the position of most pro-lordship advocates, and is a presupposition that leads to Lordship's theology.

In my opinion, if a man teaches regeneration must precede faith, he has the *ordo salutis* (order of salvation) out-of-order. Faith, not regeneration is the trigger for the events that occur simultaneously at the moment of salvation. Those simultaneous events are: faith, repentance, regeneration, conversion, justification and adoption.

Through interaction with Reformed theologians I have found that regeneration before faith, while in my opinion is error in its own right, leads to even greater error. What is the "greater error?" Some of the men I have interacted with in online discussions take the regeneration before faith position to such an extreme they insist God regenerates some infants in the womb, who years later will express faith in Christ. The infant regeneration position is just about as far to the left as one can go in Reformed circles. Men I have interacted with, who hold to infant regeneration, have cited the following passages in support.

> Jeremiah 1:5 Before I formed thee in the belly I knew thee; and before thou camest forth out of the womb I sanctified thee, and I ordained thee a prophet unto the nations.
>
> Luke 1:15 For he shall be great in the sight of the Lord, and shall drink neither wine nor strong drink; and he shall be filled with the Holy Ghost, even from his mother's womb.

Doctrinal buildings should not be set up with these ambiguous passages. What happened to Jeremiah and John the Baptist was a totally unique, one of a kind experience. Taking an infant regeneration position places regeneration in a chronological order that can be far removed from personal faith in Jesus Christ. The events in the *ordo salutis* become chronological far beyond the "casual" or "logical" order as expressed by some Calvinists. Years ago some Puritan types were preaching regeneration as an infant and then acceptance of the gospel well down the road of life. Consequently, one ends up with regenerate unbelievers, which is a true heresy.

Is regeneration before faith a mark of hyper-Calvinism? Admittedly, regeneration before faith does not necessarily fit the classic definition of hyper-Calvinism. As some men slide deeper into extremes, such as infant regeneration, we may one day have to reopen a discussion over the potential inclusion of additional defining characteristics of hyper-Calvinism.

Whenever possible, I choose to exercise Christian charity and allow for a believer to exercise his own conscience, and I allow for the autonomy of local churches. Once, however, a man's Calvinism leads him to withhold an open proclamation of the gospel, with an invitation to every sinner, I would no longer in good conscience be willing to fellowship with him, and would not hesitate to identify him as a man to be scrutinized and avoided.

> Romans 16:17-18 Now I beseech you, brethren, mark them which cause divisions and offences contrary to the doctrine which ye have learned; and avoid them. For they that are such serve not our Lord Jesus Christ, but their own belly; and by good words and fair speeches deceive the hearts of the simple.

If I may recommend an excellent book, which I quoted from above, it would be *Spurgeon v. Hyper-Calvinism: The Battle for Gospel Preaching* by Iain H. Murray. There is no doubt that Charles Haddon Spurgeon (1834-1892) was an ardent Calvinist, while at the same time an eminent winner of souls. Spurgeon preached the "whosoever shall call" gospel and passionately invited all sinners to respond the gospel and receive Christ. Many of his early years in ministry were, in part, embroiled in a theological battle against the hyper-Calvinists of England. Spurgeon vigorously resisted the extremes and proliferation of hyper-Calvinism in his day. Many are familiar with Spurgeon's resistance to modernism and ultimate separation from the Baptist Union of England. That controversy may have led to his early demise. However, the former battle against the advocates of hyper-Calvinism was for Charles Spurgeon just as important and intense with very much at stake

ENDNOTES:

1. John Piper, *What Jesus Demands From the World*, p. 160.
2. R. C. Sproul, *Grace Unknown*, p. 198.
3. John MacArthur, *The Gospel According to Jesus*, pp. 183, 187.

APPENDIX B
DOES REGENERATION PRECEDE FAITH?

by
Pastor George Zeller

Regeneration is the sovereign act of God whereby He imparts His very life and His very nature to the believing sinner (John 1:12-13; Titus 3:5). Man's first birth is natural; his second birth is spiritual and supernatural. His first birth makes him a member of a fallen race; his second birth makes him a member of a redeemed race. His first birth gives him a depraved nature (Eph. 2:3); his second birth makes him a partaker of the divine nature (2 Peter 1:4). The moment a person is born again he receives a new life (John 6:47; 1 John 5:12) and a new position as a child of God (John 1:12; 1 John 3:1-2). In short, he is a new creature in Christ (2 Cor. 5:17).

Today there are those of a Reformed persuasion who teach that regeneration precedes faith. They would say that a person must be born again before he believes. They would say that a person must have God's LIFE before he can believe in Christ.

Why do such men teach this? The doctrine of man's total depravity has been carried to the extreme by some Calvinists resulting in a wrong understanding of man's inability. They believe that the sinner is dead in sin and totally unable to respond to the gospel. They believe he first must be regenerated and only then will he be able to believe the gospel.

The Philippian jailer once asked, "What must I do to be saved?" (Acts 16:30). If Paul had been an extreme Calvinist he might have said, "You can do nothing to be saved, absolutely nothing. You are dead in sin and totally unable to exercise saving faith. You are totally unable to respond to God until you are regenerated!" How different was the answer Paul gave: "Believe on the Lord Jesus Christ and thou shalt be saved" (Acts 16:31).

We agree that no one can believe on Christ apart from God's great and gracious working in the heart which involves both enabling and enlightenment (John 6:44,65; Matthew 11:27; 16:16-17; Acts 16:14). It is interesting that God sometimes commands a person to do what in himself he is totally unable to do. One example involves the man with the withered hand (Mark 3:1-5). Christ gave him the command, "Stretch forth thine hand!" How could he do this if he suffered from paralysis? Christ commanded, the man obeyed and God enabled! Christ enabled him to do the impossible! So also the sinner is commanded to believe on Christ. If the sinner fails to obey this command then he is guilty of disobeying the gospel (2 Thess. 1:8). He will never be able to use this excuse: "Lord, the reason I did not believe on Christ was because I was totally depraved and unable to believe." No, the reason men do not come to Christ is because they refuse to do so: "And ye will not come to Me, that ye might have life" (John 5:40).

Does regeneration precede faith? Actually they both take place in the same moment of time. The moment a person believes on the Lord Jesus Christ he is regenerated (born again). The moment he receives Christ by faith he also receives God's gift of eternal life. It all happens in an instant of time. Yet logically as we think about this great transaction, we must put an order to it. Does the Bible indicate that a person must be regenerated so that he can believe or does the Bible teach that a person must believe in order to be regenerated? Do we need life in order to believe or do we need to believe in order to have life?

The Bible clearly teaches this: believe and thou shalt live! "Verily, verily, I say unto you, He that believeth on Me hath everlasting life" (John 6:47). "That whosoever believeth in Him should not perish, but have eternal life" (John 3:15). The extreme Calvinist says, "live and thou shalt believe!"

Please notice that John 1:12 does not say this: "But as many as have been regenerated, to them gave He the power to believe on His Name, even to those who have become the children of God." Notice also that John 20:31 says, "believing ye might have life." It does not say, "having life ye might believe." In his helpless and hopeless condition the sinner is told to LOOK to the Lord Jesus Christ AND LIVE (John 3:14-16; Numbers 21). [We sing the hymn, "Look and Live." The extreme Calvinist should rename the hymn: "Live and Look."]

The extreme Calvinist teaches that a person must have life in order to believe. The Lord Jesus taught that a person must believe (come to Christ) in order to have life (John 5:40). Why do people not believe on Christ? Is it because they have not been regenerated or because they refuse to come to Christ by faith (John 5:40; 2 Thess. 2:10,12)?

If regeneration precedes faith, then this would make faith unnecessary since the person would already be saved. If a person is regenerated, then he is born of God and a member of God's family. If you are a member of God's family then you are already saved so what need is there for faith?

Charles Spurgeon, a strong Calvinist himself, recognized the folly of saying that the sinner must be regenerated before he can believe:

> If I am to preach the faith in Christ to a man who is regenerated, then the man, being regenerated, is saved already, and it is an unnecessary and ridiculous thing for me to preach Christ to him, and bid him to believe in order to be saved when he is saved already, being regenerate. Am I only to preach faith to those who have it? Absurd, indeed! Is not this waiting till the man is cured and then bringing him the medicine? This is preaching Christ to the righteous and not to sinners.

For a moment, let's assume that what the extreme Calvinists are saying is true. If regeneration precedes faith, then what must a sinner do to be regenerated? The extreme Calvinists have never satisfactorily answered this. Shedd's answer is typical. Because the sinner cannot believe, he is instructed to perform the following duties: (1) Read and hear the divine Word. (2) Give serious application of the mind to the truth. (3) Pray for the gift of the Holy Spirit for conviction and regeneration. Roy Aldrich's response to this is penetrating:

> A doctrine of total depravity that excludes the possibility of faith must also exclude the possibilities of hearing the Word, giving serious application to divine truth and praying for the Holy Spirit for conviction and regeneration. The extreme Calvinist deals with a rather lively spiritual corpse after all.

The problem with this position is that it perverts the gospel. The sinner is told that the condition of salvation is prayer instead of faith. How contrary to Acts 16:31 where the sinner is not told to pray for conviction and regeneration. The sinner is simply told to believe on the Lord Jesus Christ.

Reprinted by permission

APPENDIX C
SUMMARY OF LORDSHIP SALVATION FROM A SINGLE PAGE

by
Lou Martuneac

In each of the three editions of Dr. John MacArthur's *The Gospel According to Jesus* there is a single page that summarizes the Lordship Salvation interpretation of the gospel. The page I refer to appears in the original and revised versions, pp. 218 and 252 respectively. In the *20th Anniversary* edition, you will turn to page 250 and read, "One of the most comprehensive invitations to salvation in all the epistles comes in James 4:7-10... The invitation in 4:7-10 is directed at those who are not saved..."

This is the passage in James that Dr. MacArthur refers to as an "invitation to salvation."

> James 4:7-10 Submit yourselves therefore to God. Resist the devil, and he will flee from you. Draw nigh to God, and he will draw nigh to you. Cleanse your hands, ye sinners; and purify your hearts, ye double-minded. Be afflicted, and mourn, and weep: let your

laughter be turned to mourning, and you joy to heaviness. Humble yourselves in the sight of the Lord, and he shall lift you up.

At this point I want to remind my readers that the crux of the Lordship Salvation controversy is over the requirement for salvation, NOT what should be the results of salvation. In this section on the James passage Dr. MacArthur is making his application to, "those who are not saved."

Is the epistle of James, "directed at those who are not saved?" The epistle begins, "James, a servant of God and of the Lord Jesus Christ, to the twelve tribes which are scattered abroad, greeting. **My brethren**, count it all joy...," (James 1:1-2). "Brethren" appears approximately 190 times in the New Testament, and when does appear it is used almost exclusively in reference to born again Christians. James was writing to "brethren," Jewish Christians.

Does MacArthur view the carnality that James addresses as though it proves these "brethren," were never saved in the first place? He obviously views them as, "sinners... unregenerate...in desperate need of God's (saving) grace." MacArthur's answer to the problem is that they need to be born again. He goes on to delineate what he believes are the ten "imperatives" for the reception of eternal life. The saving message to "sinners," the "unregenerate," according to MacArthur is,

> "...submit yourself to God (salvation); resist the devil (transferring allegiance); draw near to God (intimacy of relationship); cleanse your hands (repentance); purify your hearts (confession); be miserable, mourn, weep and let your laughter and joy be turned to gloom (sorrow). The final imperative summarizes the mentality of those who are converted: 'Humble yourselves in the presence of the Lord'."

If MacArthur's statement was shared as instruction to Christians on how they should live wisely as born again disciples of Jesus Christ that would be a fair interpretation of the passage. He is, however, stating what he believes are the necessary conditions of saving faith that results in a lost man becoming a Christian.

On this single page (250) of *The Gospel According to Jesus* is the Lordship's classic error of failing to properly distinguish between the doctrines of salvation and discipleship. Lordship Salvation frontloads faith with commitments to the "good works" (Eph. 2:10) one would expect of a mature born again disciple of Christ.

Do we find salvation by the grace of God through faith in Christ (Eph. 2:8-9) anywhere in James 4:7-10? No, we do not, because James is addressing "brethren" some of whom behaved as "carnal" Christians.

This example from *The Gospel According to Jesus* exemplifies and affirms the error of Lordship Salvation. The crux of the Lordship controversy is contained in the three paragraphs of that single page. That page is all one needs to know to realize Lordship Salvation has changed the terms of the gospel into a non-saving, man-centered message that frustrates the grace.

> Galatians 2:21 I do not frustrate the grace of God: for if righteousness come by the law, then Christ is dead in vain.

APPENDIX D
THE RELATIONSHIP BETWEEN GOD'S GRACE AND LORDSHIP LEGALISM

by
Pastor George Zeller

This brings us to a teaching of our day, common in Reformed circles, popularly known as LORDSHIP SALVATION.

Essentially Lordship salvation teaches that simple faith in Jesus Christ is not enough for salvation. Something else is needed. A solid commitment to Christ as Lord is needed. A person needs to surrender to the Lordship of Christ. A willingness to obey Christ's commands is necessary. Also the sinner must fulfill the demands of discipleship or be willing to fulfill them. This includes loving Christ supremely, forsaking possessions, etc. (see Luke 14:25-33).

What do Lordship teachers do with Acts 16:30-31? ["And brought them out, and said, Sirs, what must I do to be saved? And they said, Believe on the Lord Jesus Christ, and thou shalt be saved, and thy house."] This verse teaches that the sinner must do the believing and that God must do the saving. It teaches that faith and faith alone is necessary for salvation.

It does not say, "Believe and surrender to Christ's Lordship and fulfill the terms of discipleship and thou shalt be saved." It simply says, "Believe on the Lord Jesus Christ." What does it mean to believe? The hymn-writer has explained it in very simple terms, "Tis so sweet to trust in Jesus, just to take Him at His Word, just to rest upon His promise, just to know THUS SAITH THE LORD!"

Those who teach Lordship salvation are forced to redefine saving faith. It means more than just simple, childlike faith in Jesus Christ. They might say something like this: "We believe in Acts 16:31 just as much as you do, but you need to understand what the word 'believe' really means. 'Believe' means more than just believe. Saving faith involves much more." What does it mean to believe on the Lord Jesus Christ? Lordship salvation teachers would say that it involves the following: It means surrendering to His Lordship. It means turning from sin. It means submitting to His authority and to His Word. It means obeying His commands, or at least having a willingness to obey. It means fully accepting all the terms of discipleship.

Consider this last statement. Does saving faith really involve accepting all the terms of discipleship? Does saving faith really include such requirements as loving Christ supremely, forsaking all that one has, denying self, etc. (Luke 14:25-33, etc.)? A saved person should do all of these things, but he does not do these things in order to be saved. He is saved because he throws himself upon the mercy of a loving Saviour who died for him. One reason why he needs to be saved is because he does not love Christ supremely. He is guilty of breaking the greatest commandment! It is not our COMMITMENT that saves us, it is our CHRIST who saves us! It is not our SURRENDER that saves us, it is our SAVIOUR who does! It is not what I do for God; it's what God has done for me.

Avoid the dangerous error of taking what should be the RESULT of salvation and making it the REQUIREMENT of salvation: It is because I am saved that I surrender to His Lordship (Rom. 12:1-2). It is because I am saved that I turn from sin and begin to learn what it means to live unto righteousness (1 Pet. 2:24). It is because I am saved that I follow Him in willing obedience (1 John 2:3-5). It is because I am saved that I agree to the terms of discipleship and begin to learn all that discipleship involves (Luke chapter 14).

It is because I am saved that I submit to His authority over every area of my life (Rom. 6:13). I do these things because I am saved by the grace of God, not in order to be saved. Do not turn the results into requirements! Don't turn the grace of God into legalism [adding unbiblical requirements to the gospel message].

Don't confuse saving faith with that which saving faith ought to produce. Don't confuse repentance with the fruits of repentance. Behavior and fruit are the evidences of saving faith but they are not the essence of saving faith. Don't confuse the fruit with the root. Before you can "come after" Christ in discipleship (Luke 9:23; Matt. 11:29-30), you must "come unto" Christ for salvation (Matthew 11:28). Discipleship is not a requirement for salvation; discipleship is the obligation of every saved person.

Salvation involves Christ loving me (Rom. 5:8; Gal. 2:20); discipleship involves me loving Christ (Matthew 10:37). Because we are justified freely by His grace we measure up to the full demands of God's righteousness in Christ (2 Cor. 5:21). Because we are frail we often fail to measure up to the full demands of discipleship (Luke 14:25-33). The requirements of discipleship are many; the requirement for salvation is simple faith and trust in the Saviour.

APPENDIX E
THE "NO LORDSHIP"
COUNTER-CLAIM

An excerpt from *The Gospel of the Christ: A Biblical Response to the Crossless Gospel Regarding the Contents of Saving Faith* (Thomas L. Stegall, pp. 125-127.)

In spite of past precedent and practice, those aligned with the Grace Evangelical Society and its view of the gospel may still claim that it is unfair to label their teaching as "crossless." They may point out the fact that they each individually hold to faith in Christ's cross-work and that they often do include the preaching of the cross in their evangelism. They may even claim that they do require belief in Christ's cross-work in one respect, namely for sanctification and spiritual growth in the Christian life. So in light of these facts how can their view justly and rightly be called "crossless"? They may even try to draw a parallel to the way their view is being labeled "crossless" and the way Lordship Salvationists refer to the Free Grace position as the "no-lordship" view.[41] G.E.S. proponents may object that since Free Grace people do believe in the Lordship of Christ, it is unfair and inaccurate to refer to our view as the "no-lordship" view; and in just the same way, since they do believe in the cross-work of Christ and have a place for it, it is unfair and inaccurate to refer to their view as "crossless." So, is applying the phrase "crossless gospel" to the G.E.S. doctrine on the contents of saving faith really no different than the phrase "no-lordship" being applied unfairly to the Free Grace position?

There is at least one significant reason why this is not an equal or valid comparison. When Lordship Salvation proponents refer to the Free Grace position as the "no-lordship" view, they are specifically referring to the subject of eternal salvation, not sanctification in the Christian life per se. They are referring to our view as the "no-lordship salvation" view. As this applies to the Free Grace movement historically, "no-lordship salvation" would not be an accurate or appropriate designation since Free Grace advocates have traditionally viewed belief in the Lord Jesus Christ as a requirement for eternal salvation or justification, just as Acts 16:30-31 and Romans 10:9-10 teach. While Lordship Salvationists have traditionally understood believing in Christ as "Lord" to include the inherent component of *submission of one's life* in service to Christ, Free Grace proponents have traditionally understood belief in Christ as "Lord" to mean belief in His deity due to His divine attribute and position of sovereignty.[45] In this respect, to claim that Free Grace people promote a "no-lordship salvation" is an inaccurate and misleading description of our position, since we have historically required belief in Jesus as "Lord" in the deistic sense specifically for justification and eternal salvation and not only for sanctification in the Christian life. However, the same can no longer be said of the Free Grace movement as a whole due to the advent of the new G.E.S. view of the gospel that doesn't even require belief in Christ's cross-work or His deity for eternal life.[46] For this reason, the charge of a "no-lordship" salvation has tragically become true and fitting right now for the G.E.S. faction of the Free Grace movement.

In light of these considerations, it would be neither inappropriate, nor contrary to historical precedent, to use the designation "crossless gospel" for the current theological controversy in the Free Grace camp. Yet, if we choose to do so, we must also be ready and willing to qualify what exactly we mean by the phrase. No label is perfect or immune from misinterpretation; and "crossless gospel" is no exception. Undoubtedly some evangelicals who are uninformed of the current controversy will interpret the phrase to mean that some Free Grace people are no longer even preaching the cross. Though the cross has been a glaring omission or de-emphasis in the evangelism of some Free Grace leaders in recent years, this is not the primary implication of the phrase "crossless gospel."

Our use of the phrase is simply in keeping with the way in which 99% of evangelical and fundamental Christendom understands the term "gospel." There is a consensus among evangelicals, whether Lordship or Free Grace, that the gospel is the message which people must believe in order to become a Christian and belong to Jesus Christ. Beyond that, opinions on the gospel diverge drastically. But it is highly doubtful that the rest of the evangelical world will pick up the nuance that certain crossless teachers are now putting on the term "gospel." Probably less than 1% of evangelicals interpret the word "gospel" in the manner that these crossless proponents are now using it, as being a Christian-life message that is only necessary to believe for sanctification and spiritual growth rather than for regeneration.

For these reasons, the phrase "crossless gospel" is still appropriate, even though some may dislike it or even despise it. Other Free Grace people who are opposed to the new crossless saving message have recently proposed and begun using other labels, such as the "G.E.S. gospel," the "promise-only gospel," and the "crossless faith" view. These are also accurate and appropriate designations that may eventually become the standard phraseology. If that happens, I personally would have no objections to changing my own terminology since the doctrinal position defended in this book is in no way dependent upon the use of a particular phrase. "Crossless gospel" is largely a convention used throughout this book and throughout the current controversy to abbreviate the new doctrinal error of our day. It is much easier to say "crossless gospel" than "the crossless content of saving faith." The latter expression is not nearly as recognizable to the average Christian and often requires further explanation. But regardless of what labels are used, it is virtually guaranteed that those on the so-called "Refined" side will not accept any label or descriptive phrase that we on the so-called "Traditional" side come up with unless it portrays their doctrine favorably, which is something we simply cannot do because we regard the crossless gospel to be utterly contrary to the Word of God.

ENDNOTES:

44. Bob Wilkin, "We Believe Jesus is Lord," *Grace in Focus* 23 (March/April 2008): 1-2.
45. Charles C. Bing, *Lordship Salvation: A Biblical Evaluation and Response*, GraceLife edition (Burleson, TX: GraceLife Ministries, 1992), 104; Thomas R. Edgar, "What Is the Gospel?" in Basic Theology: Applied, ed. Wesley and Elaine Willis & John and Janet Master (Wheaton, IL: Victor Books, 195), 158; J. B. Hixson, "Getting the Gospel Wrong: Case Studies in American Evangelical Soteriological Method in the Postmodern Era" (Ph.D. dissertation, Baptist Bible Seminary, 2007), 77-78; Robert P. Lightner, *Sin, the Savior, and Salvation: The Theology of Everlasting Life* (Nashville: Thomas Nelson, 1991), 204; Lou Martuneac, *In Defense of the Gospel: Biblical Answers to Lordship Salvation* (n.p.: Xulon Press, 2006), 170-75; Charles C. Ryrie, *So Great Salvation: What It Means to Believe in Jesus Christ* (Wheaton, IL: Victor Books, 1989), 69-70.
46. Hodges, "How to Lead People to Christ, Part 1," Lopez, *Romans Unlocked*, 216; Niemela, "Objects of Faith in John: A Matter of Person AND Content"; Wilkin, *Confident in Christ*, 10.

APPENDIX F

A REVIEW OF WALTER J. CHANTRY'S *TODAY'S GOSPEL: AUTHENTIC OR SYNTHETIC?*

by
Dr. Stewart Custer

A Baptist pastor has indicted the entire practice of modern conservative evangelism. Walter J. Chantry, in *Today's Gospel: Authentic or Synthetic?* (London: Banner of Truth Trust. 1970. 93 pp)., charges that the doctrine and practices of the "evangelical wing of the Protestant church" are unbiblical and dangerous (p. 121). He urges that churches "rethink the way of salvation" (p. 16). He maintains that the sole biblical standard for personal evangelism is the Lord's interview with the rich young ruler in Mark 10:17-27 (p. 16).

If modern personal work does not follow the exact pattern our Lord used, it is not the genuine gospel (p. 17). Therefore, Mr. Chantry argues, the personal worker must preach the character of God ("There is none good but one, that is, God"). To tell a lost person, "God loves you and has a plan for your life," is "terribly misinforming"(p. 29). The personal worker must also preach the law of God (pp.

35f).. Just to quote Romans 3:23 ("For all have sinned," etc). is not sufficient (p. 38). "You must dwell on the subject at length. Exposit the Ten Commandments until men are slain thereby" (p. 43).

The personal worker must also preach repentance (pp. 47f). Mr. Chantry rejects the idea of urging the sinner to "accept Jesus as your personal Saviour." These words are "wholly inadequate to instruct a sinner in the way to eternal life" (p. 48). "Scripture always joins repentance and remission of sins" (p. 50). (As a matter of fact, of course, it does not; see Acts 10:43; Rom. 3:25; Heb. 9:22). Mr. Chantry charges that "evangelicals have invented the idea of 'carnal Christians'" (p. 54). He admits that Paul used the term but thinks that Paul was referring to "babes in Christ . . . who had an area of carnal behaviour" (p. 54). When you consider that Paul was concerned over factions in the church (I Cor. 1); an open case of immorality (I Cor. 5); abuses concerning food (I Cor. 8), the Lord's supper (I Cor. 11), and spiritual gifts (I Cor. 12-14); and doctrinal heresy concerning the resurrection (I Cor. 15), Chantry's position strains the Scripture severely. Mr. Chantry thinks that a good sermon ends not with a call to decision, but rather with the convicted sinners sent home to think it all over (p. 66). He derides the idea that evangelism is as simple as A, B, C: "Just accept, believe, and confess. A three-sentence prayer and you will be safe for eternity" (p. 80). He attacks the idea of "simplicity and brevity in evangelism" (p. 80). He calls upon evangelicals to "rise above deadening evangelical tradition" (p. 92).

It is plain that Mr. Chantry has removed himself from the evangelical tradition. He is not an evangelical; he is a dangerous outsider. His implication that all evangelicals are encouraging an "easy-believism" is a misrepresentation. The vast majority of evangelicals are deeply disturbed by "easy-believism." Most born again personal workers are careful to show the sinner that Christ is not a fire-insurance policy, after accepting which the sinner may go off and live like the devil. Most personal workers explain to their converts the importance of the Christian life and the necessity of prayer, Bible study, and Christian fellowship. The idea that all evangelical personal workers are using unbiblical methods to gain statistics is simply false. Most personal workers have a definite series of Scripture passages which they discuss with the lost person. The personal worker knows that these verses are effective for the lost, because in most cases he himself was converted by those same verses.

The basic fallacy of Mr. Chantry's position is his assumption that all personal work must follow the pattern of our Lord's words to the rich young ruler (Mark 10:17-27). The young ruler had an idol in his life: his great possessions. Whenever a personal worker detects such an idol in the life of the one he is witnessing to, he certainly ought to use the law to reveal the presence of such an idol. But the Lord used a different method in talking to Nicodemus (John 3) and to the woman at the well (John 4). Philip did not follow the same pattern when he talked with the Ethiopian eunuch (Acts 8).

One of the clearest descriptions of a soulwinner's words that resulted in conversion is Peter's testimony to Cornelius (Acts 10:38-43). Peter mentioned a number of important subjects: (1) Jesus of Nazareth went about doing good and healing. (2) He was crucified. (3) God raised Him up on the third day. (4) The apostles were witnesses of His resurrection. (5) This Jesus is the Judge at the last day. (6) Everyone who believes in Him will receive forgiveness of sins. It is significant that there was no discussion of the law of God and the word repentance was not used. Before Peter had finished all that he had intended to say, the Holy Spirit fell on all those who were listening (v. 44). All the rest of the theological verbiage which Peter had in mind was thus demonstrated to be unnecessary. His audience believed; the Holy Spirit regenerated them. The idea that hours of theological discussion is necessary for salvation is unscriptural. If it were true, many more theologians would be converted than the laity. It is clear, however, that very few contemporary theologians are converted men.

If a Christian, approaching the scene of an automobile accident, sees a poor dying man stretched out alongside the road, he should not drive on, saying to himself, "I do not have the time adequately to present the gospel." He should get off his theological high horse, take his Bible in hand, and tell that poor lost soul how to find eternal life in Christ. If he cannot do it in the two minutes before the ambulance arrives, he is incompetent as a soulwinner. If he has more time, he should use it; but if he does not, he should use what time he has to tell the victim of the good news which is the power of God unto salvation (Rom. 1:16).

Originally published in *Biblical Viewpoint* 7 (1973): 155-57. (c) 1973 Bob Jones University. Reproduced by permission. All rights reserved.

APPENDIX G

"UNLESS THE LORD JESUS IS LORD OF ALL HE IS NOT LORD AT ALL."

by
Lou Martuneac

Many Lordship advocates are fond of saying, "Unless the Lord Jesus is Lord of all, He is not Lord at all." Most of them use this phrase and do not know who coined it and in what context it was stated. In my possession is a sermon preached by J. Hudson Taylor during his missionary work in China. The sermon appears in a little known book by Hudson Taylor titled, *Days of Blessing*. The sermon is from John's gospel, chapter 6. It is in this sermon that the above quotation appears.

Hudson Taylor was not preaching the Lordship conditions of submission and commitment to be saved, but is rather encouraging believers to learn to depend completely on God through total surrender of self and possessions. Lordship advocates hear this phrase, "Unless the LORD JESUS is LORD OF ALL He is not LORD AT ALL," and erroneously apply this to an evangelistic appeal. J. Hudson Taylor coined that saying and he never meant it to be a reference to the reception of salvation experience.

If the Lordship advocate were to read Hudson Taylor's sermon in its entirety, he would quickly see that Taylor was not preaching a gospel message. Hence this quotation from Taylor cannot be used to support the Lordship Salvation position. Taylor preached a sermon that applies to the born-again believer. He preached on the subject of abiding in Christ and living in dependence upon Him for power and service. For example Taylor said,

> But you say, "I have been feeding for years: yet the abiding is broken; how is this?" It may be that the eyes of your understanding need enlightening: you are not apprehending, and consequently not appropriating by faith, the fruits of abiding. For myself, I can say that for sixteen or seventeen years after my conversion I had no idea of what abiding in Christ was. . . . And so I learned what abiding in Christ is, and the importance of feeding on Him.[1]

Taylor is sharing a personal testimony of his post-conversion experience. Later Taylor continues:

> We cannot bear fruit if we are not abiding: fruit is the evidence of abiding. Now the fruits of abiding must be claimed by faith. What are they? Answers to prayer, abundant fruitfulness, and a Christ-like walk. "He that abideth in Me and I in him, the same beareth much fruit;" and fruit shall remain or abide.[2]

The child of God can only accomplish fruit bearing. No man "abideth" in Christ unless he is one in Christ through salvation. Jesus said, "Abide in me, and I in you. As the branch cannot bear fruit of itself, except it abide in the vine; no more can ye, except ye abide in me" (John 15:4). Just as the Lord was addressing His disciples, in the excerpt above there can be no question that Taylor was addressing the believer. Taylor was not telling the unsaved to pray and expect their prayers to be answered, to bear spiritual fruit, and to be "Christ- like?" Hudson Taylor was not making or leading up to a gospel appeal.

Following is the excerpt in which the phrase above appears, and in its context:

> Let me refer, in conclusion, to two points which are essential to our success- 1. All the loaves and fishes must be given to the Lord Jesus. Unless there is absolute consecration of all we have, and all we are, the multitude will not be fed. If the Lord is to create and multiply, it might seem to make no difference whether there is one loaf or a dozen; nevertheless, if the disciples had said, "we must keep half of them for ourselves," what a blessing they would have lost! In my own early life, as many of you know, I nearly lost a great blessing by wanting to keep back a paltry half-a-crown. The last penny we have must be put into the Lord's hands. If we keep back one penny what does it show? An independent proprietorship. *Unless the* LORD JESUS *is* LORD OF ALL *He is not* LORD AT ALL. If I can keep back a single thing from Him, I make myself an independent proprietor. If there is anything I hold back, I dethrone Him; and hence I lose the blessing.[3]

At best, Lordship advocates are misrepresenting Taylor's statement because they never knew it was coined by Taylor and in what context he said it. One could argue Lordship advocates misuse Taylor's words to reinforce their interpretation of the gospel. Hudson's own account of his salvation experience leaves no doubt that he would oppose the Lordship interpretation of the gospel.

> And now let me tell you how God answered the prayers of my mother and of my beloved sister . . . for my conversion. On a day I can never forget . . . I had a holiday, and in the afternoon looked through my father's library to find some book with

which to while away the unoccupied hours. Nothing attracting me, I turned over a basket of pamphlets and selected from amongst them a Gospel tract that looked interesting, saying to myself: "There will be a story at the commencement and a sermon or moral at the close. I will take the former and leave the latter for those who like it."

I sat down to read the book in an utterly unconcerned state of mind, believing indeed at the time that if there were any salvation it was not for me, and with a distinct intention to put away the tract as soon as it should seem prosy. . . .[4]

At this juncture Hudson Taylor speaks of his mother's intercessory prayer for his conversion. Then he continues with his personal testimony:

I in the meantime had been led in the way I have mentioned to take up this little tract, and while reading it was struck with the phrase: "The finished work of Christ."

"Why does the author use this expression?" I questioned. "Why not say the atoning or propitiary work of Christ?" Immediately the words "It is finished" suggested themselves to my mind. "What was finished?"

And I at once replied, "A full and perfect atonement and satisfaction for sin. The debt was paid for our sins, and not for ours only, but also for the sins of the whole world."

Then came the further thought, "If the whole work was finished and the whole debt paid, what is there left for me to do?"

And with this dawned the joyful conviction, as light was flashed into my soul by the Holy Spirit, that there was nothing in the world to be done but to fall down on one's knees and accepting this Saviour and His salvation praise Him for evermore."[5]

One can plainly see that Hudson Taylor's own conversion did not include commitment of his life to the lordship of Christ. There is no "exchange" of submission for salvation. In his own words there was nothing "left for me to do."

ENDNOTES:

1. Hudson Taylor, *Days of Blessing*, p. 25.
2. Ibid., p. 26.
3. Ibid., p. 26, (capitals and emphasis his).
4. Ibid., p. 26.
5. Hudson Taylor: *The Growth of a Soul*, Vol. 1, pp. 66-67.

APPENDIX H

DOES "FINAL SALVATION" SERVE AS A COVER FOR WORKS-SALVATION?

by
Pastor Tom Stegall

At my blog, *In Defense of the Gospel*, I posted a series (Oct/Nov 2009) that in part addressed Lordship Salvationists use of the term, "final salvation." In *What Jesus Demands From the World*, (p. 160) Dr. John Piper wrote,

> "There is no doubt that Jesus saw a measure of real, lived-out obedience to the will of God as *necessary for final salvation*." (emphasis added)

That statement by Piper raised a great deal of discussion and generated several more articles in the series. One installment from the series was, *Is the Term "Final Salvation" Necessarily Wrong?* In the scores of articles at my blog each is accompanied by a discussion thread. Occasionally a thread comment is posted that in my opinion merits repeating as a main page article. With that I offer for your consideration an edited version of a thread comment, turned article, turned appendix entry to this book.

I am so grateful that this topic of *"final salvation"* is being addressed. This is a critical subject. So often this phrase serves as a cover for Works-salvation. Bible-believing Christians need to be far more discerning these days than we have been. It is truly disturbing to read the statements of so-called "evangelical, fundamental" or "Protestant" leaders these days that sound perilously close to Romanism.

A great question was raised, *"Isn't this usage of 'final salvation' by Lordship Salvationists just the 'escape clause for closet Catholicism'?!"* I would say, technically *"No,"* but practically *"Yes!"* As one who was saved out of Catholicism and who was definitely trusting in his own works and righteousness before being born again by God's grace, I will tell you it sure hits me as diluted Catholicism when I read the Lordship Salvation statements of leaders like John Piper and John MacArthur.

Here is an interesting spiritual exercise. See if you can identify whether the following quotes come from a Calvinist author, Arminian, or Roman Catholic:

1) "Endurance in faith is a condition for future salvation. Only those who endure in faith will be saved for eternity."

Calvinist, Arminian or Roman Catholic?

2) "The Scriptures repeatedly exhort us to persevere, to 'hang in there.' It is only the one who endures to the end who will be saved."

Calvinist, Arminian or Roman Catholic?

3) "There is no cleansing from sin, and no salvation, without a continual walking in God's light."

Calvinist, Arminian or Roman Catholic?

4) "We cannot 'earn' our salvation though good works, but our faith in Christ puts us in a special grace-filled relationship with God so that our obedience and love, combined with our faith, will be rewarded with eternal life."

Calvinist, Arminian or Roman Catholic?

5) "The kingdom is not for people who want Jesus without any change in their living. It is only for those who seek it with all their hearts, those who agonize to enter. Many who approach the gate turn away upon finding out the cost. Lest someone object that this is a salvation of human effort, remember it is only the enablement of divine grace that empowers a person to pass through the gate." . . . "While justification and sanctification are distinct theological concepts, both are essential elements of salvation. God will not declare a person righteous without also making him righteous."

Calvinist, Arminian or Roman Catholic?

And Now for the Answers:

1) [Calvinist] R.C. Sproul, *Grace Unknown*, 198.

2) [Roman Catholic] Joseph Kindel, *What Must I Do to be Saved?*, 79.

3) [Arminian] Guy Duty, *If Ye Continue*, 141.

4) [Roman Catholic] Tract, *Pillar of Fire*, Pillar of Truth, p.23

5) [Calvinist] John MacArthur, *The Gospel According to Jesus*, pp. 183, 187.

By showing this, I don't mean to deny that legitimate differences exist between Protestants (Arminian or Calvinist) and Roman Catholics, especially over the role of the sacraments in salvation, but I think any honest reading of these quotes also shows that their respective doctrines of salvation ultimately end up in the same place: you better have works that go with your enduring faith if you want to arrive at "*final salvation.*"

The modern state of affairs among Evangelicals (such as Piper & MacArthur), some Fundamentalists and Roman Catholics is so abysmal and confusing these days regarding salvation, perhaps a new theological term ought to be coined to lump them all together: **Roman Calminians**!

SELECTED BIBLIOGRAPHY

Belcher, Richard P. *A Layman's Guide to the Lordship Salvation Controversy.* Southbridge, Miss: Crowne Publications, Inc., 1990.

Bing, Charles C. *Lordship Salvation: A Biblical Evaluation and Response.* Burleson: GraceLife edition, 1992.

Bruce, F. F. *The New International Commentary on the New Testament: The Book of Acts.* Grand Rapids, Mich.: William B. Eerdmans Publishing Company., 1960.

_____. *Romans.* Grand Rapids, Mich.: William B. Eerdmans Publishing Company, 1983.

Chantry, Walter J. *Today's Gospel: Authentic or Synthetic.* Carlisle, PA.: The Banner of Truth Trust, 1997.

Gentry, Kenneth L. *Lord of the Saved: Getting to the Heart of the Lordship Debate.* Phillipsburg, N.J.: Presbyterian and Reformed Publishing Company, 1992.

Harrison, Everett F. "Romans." *The Expositor's Bible Commentary*, Frank E. Gaebelien, ed. Vol. 10, 1-172. Grand Rapids, Mich.: Zondervan Publishing House, 1976.

Hiebert, D. Edmond. "Titus." *The Expositor's Bible Commentary*, Frank E. Gaebelien, ed. Vol. 2. Grand Rapids, Mich.: Zondervan Publishing House, 1976.

Hodge, Charles. *A Commentary On First & Second Corinthians.* Carlisle: The Banner of Truth Trust, 1974.

Holy Bible. KJV. All Scripture citations are taken from the KJV, except where quotations include citations from other versions.

Ironside, H. A. *Lectures on Romans*. New York: Loizeaux Brothers, 1946.

_____. *First Corinthians*. Neptune: Loizeaux Brothers, 1979.

Lightner. Robert P. *Sin, the Savior, and Salvation: The Theology of Everlasting Life*. Grand Rapids, Mich.: Kregel Publications, 1991.

Mare, W. Harold. "1 Corinthians." *The Expositor's Bible Commentary*, Frank E. Gaebelien, ed. Vol. 10, 173-297. Grand Rapids, Mich.: Zondervan Publishing House, 1976.

MacArthur, John F. *The Gospel According to Jesus*. Grand Rapids, Mich.: Zondervan Publishing House, 1988.

_____. *The Gospel According to Jesus: Revised & Expanded Edition* Grand Rapids, Mich.: Zondervan Publishing House, 1994.

_____. *Faith Works: The Gospel According to the Apostles*. Nashville, TN.: Thomas Nelson Publishers, 1993.

_____. *The Gospel According to Jesus: What is Authentic Faith?* Grand Rapids, Mich.: Zondervan Publsihing House, 2008.

_____. *Hard to Believe: The High Cost and Infinite Value of Following Jesus*. Nashville, TN.: Thomas Nelson Publishers, 2003.

McGee, J. Vernon. *Thru the Bible with J. Vernon McGee*, Vols. I-V. Pasadena, Calif.: Thru the Bible Radio, 1983.

Machen, J. Gresham. *What Is Faith?* Grand Rapids, Mich.: William B. Eerdmans Publishing Co., 1925.

Morgan, G. Campbell. *The Acts of The Apostles*. New York: Fleming H. Revell Company, 1924.

_____. *The Corinthian Letters of Paul*. Old Tappan: Fleming H. Revell Company, 1946.
Moritz, Fred. *Be Ye Holy: The Call to Christian Separation*. Greenville, S.C.: Bob Jones University Press, 1994.
Moule, H. C. G. *Romans*. Minneapolis: Klock & Klock Christian Publishers, 1982 (reprint).
Mueller, Marc. *Lordship Salvation Syllabus*. Panorama City, CA: Grace Community Church, 1981, 1985.
Mullenix, Joel. *What Is The Gospel?* Sermon, November 2, 1997.
Murray, Iain H. *Spurgeon v. Hyper-Calvinism: The Battle for Gospel Preaching*. Carlisle, Pa.: Banner of Truth Trust, 1995.
Packer, J. I. *Evangelism and the Sovereignty of God*. Downers Grove, Ill.: InterVarsity Press, 1961.
Pickering, Ernest D. *Biblical Separation: The Struggle for a Pure Church*. Schaumburg, Ill.: Regular Baptist Press, 1979.
_____. *The Tragedy of Compromise: The Origin and Impact of the New Evangelicalism*. Greenville, S.C.: Bob Jones University Press, 1994.
Plummer, William S. *Commentary on Romans*. Grand Rapids, Mich.: Kregel Publications, 1971.
Robertson, Archibald T. *Word Pictures in the New Testament*. Vols. I-VI. New York: Harper & Bros., 1930.
Ryrie, Charles C. *Balancing the Christian Life*. Chicago: Moody Press, 1969.
_____. *So Great Salvation*. Wheaton, Ill.: Victor Books, 1989.
Spurgeon, Charles H. *The Treasury of the New Testament*. Vols. I-IV. London: Marshall, Morgan & Scott, Limited, n.d.
Stott, John R. W. *Basic Christianity*, 2d ed. Grand Rapids, Mich.: Wm. B. Eerdmans Publishing Co., 1971.
Strong, A. H. *Systematic Theology*. Old Tappan: Fleming H. Revell Company, 1979.

Talbert, Layton. "Salvation: Divine Determination or Human Responsibility?" *Preach the Word* (April-June 1998) 5, 22-26.

Tenney, Merrill C. "The Gospel of John." *The Expositor's Bible Commentary*, Frank E. Gaebelien, ed. Vol. 9. Grand Rapids, Mich.: Zondervan Publishing House, 1976.

Thayer, Joseph Henry. *Greek-English Lexicon of the New Testament*. Grand Rapids, Mich.: Baker Book House, 1977.

Thiessen, Henry C. *Introductory Lectures in Systematic Theology*. Grand Rapids, Mich.: Wm. B. Eerdmans, 1949.

Van Gelderen, John. *Engine Truths*. Ann Arbor, Mich.: Preach the Word Ministries, Inc., 1999.

Vine, W. E. *Vine's Expository Dictionary of Old and New Testament Words*. Tarrytown: Fleming H. Revell Co., 1981.

Weniger, Arno Q., Sr. "The History and Future of the FBF." *FrontLine* (May-June 1998): 11-12.

Wiersbe, Warren W. *The Bible Exposition Commentary*: Vols. I-II. Wheaton, Ill.: Victor Books, 1989.

Zodhiates, Spiros. *The Hebrew-Greek Key Study Bible*. World Bible Publishers, 1984.

CPSIA information can be obtained at www.ICGtesting.com
Printed in the USA
LVOW13s2321260314

379056LV00001B/68/P